To Sam Golden
on the occasion of a happy
visit to Detroit
January 17, 1973
Donald D. Eddy

A BIBLIOGRAPHY OF JOHN BROWN

John Brown
Charcoal and chalk sketch by Peter Kahn,
after the oil portrait in the vicarage in Wigton,
Cumberland
Size of sketch: 24″ × 18″

A Bibliography of
JOHN BROWN

by
Donald D. Eddy

Published by
THE BIBLIOGRAPHICAL SOCIETY OF AMERICA
NEW YORK
1971

PUBLICATION OF THE
LATHROP COLGATE HARPER, LITT.D.,
TRUST FUND

Library of Congress Catalog Card Number 72-185918

Dedicated to
Donald F. Bond
Scholar, Teacher, Friend

Acknowledgments

Any scholar in writing a book becomes indebted to many people, but this is especially true of the compiler of a bibliography. I wish to thank the staffs of the following libraries for their unfailing courtesy and assistance during my visits within the past five years: American Philosophical Society; Bodleian Library; Boston Athenaeum; Boston Public Library; British Museum; Bryn Mawr College; Cambridge University Library; University of Chicago; Columbia University; Library of Congress; Cornell University; Folger Library; Free Library of Philadelphia; General Theological Seminary, New York; The Grolier Club; Harvard University; Haverford College; Historical Society of Pennsylvania; University of Illinois; Indiana University; Lambeth Palace Library; Library Company of Philadelphia; Newberry Library; New-York Historical Society; New York Public Library; University of Pennsylvania; Pierpont Morgan Library; Sion College Library; University of Toronto; Union Theological Seminary, New York; Wellesley College; and Yale University.

Dozens of other libraries have been extremely helpful in sending books on interlibrary loan, in answering numerous questions, and in promptly filling many requests for Xerox prints. For such assistance I am especially indebted to the staffs of the Henry E. Huntington Library, the National Library of Ireland, the National Library of Scotland, Princeton University, and the University of Texas.

John Brown has become a well-known name to many staff members of Cornell University's Olin Library. I wish to express my gratitude to Miss Barbara Brown, Mrs. Mary Burlitch, Miss Marcia Jebb, Mrs. Virginia Reid, and Mrs. Caroline Spicer of the Reference Department, and Mrs. Jane Woolston of the Department of Rare Books.

I have received notable assistance from many antiquarian

booksellers, whose help has far transcended any monetary considerations. I thank especially Robert J. Barry, Jr., Martin G. Hamlyn, Ralph T. Howey, Richard Macnutt, Bryan Maggs, Arnold Muirhead, Michael Papantonio, Justin Schiller, and Stephen Weissman.

I thank the Grolier Club of New York for granting me permission to quote from the manuscript printing ledgers of William Bowyer. I am equally grateful to the Bodleian Library, Oxford, for permission to quote from William Bowyer's paper stock ledger (MS. DON b.4), the manuscript accounts of William Bowyer and James Emonson (MS. Eng. misc. c.141), and various letters written by or to John Brown (MS. Eng. misc. c.390; MS. Toynbee d.19). For permission to use photographs of printed material in their collections as illustrations in this book, I thank the Henry E. Huntington Library and Art Gallery, the National Library of Scotland, New York Public Library, the University of Pennsylvania Library, and Pennsylvania State University Library.

I gratefully acknowledge receipt of four Humanities Faculty Research Grants from Cornell University which made possible much of my work on John Brown.

For many acts of kindness and assistance, I thank Miss Fiona Macmillan, Guildhall Library; Professor Denis Donoghue, University College, Dublin; Dr. J. D. Fleeman and Dr. D. F. Foxon, Oxford University; J. H. Loudon, National Library of Scotland; Mrs. Ann Cullen, Newcastle upon Tyne; the Reverend George Winder, Vicar of Wigton; Dr. Katherine A. Rankin; Miss Marjorie G. Wynne and Herman W. Liebert, Beinecke Library, Yale University; Professors Scott B. Elledge, George H. Healey, and Peter Kahn, Cornell University; and Professor Joseph B. Dallett, Carleton University. As always, I am grateful to my wife for her encouragement and support.

D.D.E.

Cornell University
July 26, 1971

Contents

Illustrations

Note: It has long been questioned whether the oil painting in the vicarage in Wigton is a portrait of John Brown or a portrait by him of his father. William Hutchinson certainly believed that the portrait was of John Brown. In his *History of the County of Cumberland* . . . (Carlisle, 1794) he says: ". . . if that portrait of himself, which is now in the vicarage house of Wigton, was also painted by him, as some have thought it was, it clearly evinces the hand of a master. The features are exact, dark and saturnine; but the eyes are animated with much penetration and fire" (II, 472). However, see T. W. Carrick's *History of Wigton* . . . (Carlisle, 1949), p. 29.

Unfortunately the painting did not photograph satisfactorily enough for reproduction.

Introduction

This bibliography describes all first editions of works written by John Brown, including those published posthumously. Except for four short poems, all of the items were first published separately. With three exceptions—one item by Brown, two of Browniana—all separately published eighteenth-century printings of later editions and translations are also described. (For the principles of inclusion of Browniana, see the introduction to that section.) The order of works is chronological according to the date of publication of the first edition. For each work the editions are listed in this order: London editions, Dublin editions, English language editions published elsewhere (e.g., Belfast, Edinburgh, Boston, Philadelphia, or New York), translations. Each book is described according to standard bibliographical principles. For dates of publication and a chronological list of all items in this bibliography, see Appendix I.

Omissions and the Degressive Principle

The one work by John Brown for which I do not list all eighteenth-century editions is *Barbarossa*. For that play—which has appeared in more separate editions than any other work of Brown's—I list all editions published through 1770, the date of the fifth London edition. Later editions usually print the mutilated text of a shortened acting version, so beyond 1770 I describe only those editions which proved to be quite scarce, or bibliographically interesting, or historically significant (e.g., the first two American editions); but I omit the common and uninteresting editions such as those printed for John Bell, whether issued separately or included in the numerous issues of *Bell's British Theatre*.

There are two items of Browniana for which I do not list all separately published eighteenth-century editions—Lyttelton's

Dialogues of the Dead and Joseph Priestley's responses to John Brown's proposed code of education.

Initially I described all eighteenth-century editions of Lyttelton's *Dialogues of the Dead,* often bibliographically complex and fascinating; but the numerous editions overly extended the Browniana section and their inclusion could not be justified by relevance to Brown. I decided to describe only those editions published in 1760, the year of Brown's reply to Lyttelton.

Joseph Priestley is an author who often reworked the same material and ideas, presenting the results under a variety of titles. He objected to John Brown's *Thoughts on Civil Liberty,* especially to the section on education, and he presented his objections in several different forms. His first version was presented in 1765 in *An Essay on a Course of Liberal Education* (see below, no. 141); a revised and greatly expanded version was published in 1768 in *An Essay on the First Principles of Government* (no. 142); and an enlarged edition of that work was published in 1771 (no. 143). Subsequent printings of both titles are listed in the notes, with appropriate references to Ronald E. Crook's *Bibliography of Joseph Priestley* (London, 1966). It did not seem significant to give full descriptions of later editions and translations or to trace further permutations of the material under different titles.

Thus, the normal bibliographical degressive principle is operative only with the Priestley items. Certain editions of *Barbarossa* and Lyttelton's *Dialogues* are omitted entirely, but those editions which are included are described fully.

Although three are used as illustrations, playbills are not described in this bibliography. They are an interesting subspecies of Browniana, but they do not meet my criteria for inclusion in that section. Other omissions, such as Shaftesbury's *Characteristicks,* are discussed in the introduction to Browniana.

This is a bibliography of printed material, so manuscripts are not listed. This principle of exclusion does not create much loss; there are no known literary manuscripts in Brown's hand, and there are scribal fair-copy manuscripts of only two published works, *Barbarossa* and *Athelstan* (now in the Huntington Library). The library of St. John's College, Cambridge contains a scribal copy of Brown's brief note entitled "The Jesuits"; it was first printed in the *Biographia Britannica* (London, 1780 [II, 674]).

Brown's letters present a slightly different problem. The letters of Brown to Robert Dodsley (contained in Bodleian MS. Toynbee d.19) are quoted extensively in the notes to items nos. 1–6, below, for two reasons: first, they are unpublished, and this printing makes them publicly available; second, they pertain directly to the printing of Brown's works and so are appropriate to a bibliography. Other long and fascinating letters—such as the ten letters to David Garrick in the Forster Collection of the Victoria and Albert Museum, or the letter to Catherine the Great in the library of St. John's College, Cambridge—are not used in any notes, for two reasons: first, they have been published; second, they are primarily biographical in content and so are not appropriate to a bibliography (but they will be included and discussed in my biography of Brown).

It may be noted, however, that the letters to Garrick discuss two works by Brown which if completed at least were never performed or published: an oratorio or opera entitled "Armida," and a thoroughly revised version of Ben Jonson's *Bartholomew Fair*. Apparently the manuscripts of both works have disappeared.

Another major manuscript is that of Brown's "Principles of Christian Legislation," which in 1764 was advertised as, "With all convenient Speed will be published," but it never was and presumably has now vanished. In his will Brown directed his executors to revise, correct, and publish this manuscript. They decided not to do so, and that decision was the basis of some dispute; see, for example, the *Gentleman's Magazine*, LXI (Sept., 1791), 790; (Nov., 1791), 995–996; LXII (Jan., 1792), 9–12.

Additions to the Canon

The term "canon" is used loosely; for with the exception of the lists in the *DNB*, the *CBEL*, and Sir Sydney Roberts' short bibliography in the "Uncollected Authors" series in the *Book Collector* (IX [1960], 180–187; X [1961], 198), there has not been a serious attempt to establish the canon of John Brown's writings since Andrew Kippis' life of Brown in the *Biographia Britannica* in 1780.

To those lists this bibliography adds dozens of new items—new titles, new editions, and new translations, plus the items of Browniana. I believe the new items are adequately explained and documented, yet perhaps two deserve special mention:

1. John Brown's letters to Robert Dodsley (in Bodleian MS. Toynbee d.19) have not been published previously nor—so far as I have been able to ascertain—have they received any scholarly notice. These letters show that John Brown translated two Latin poems which were printed in Dodsley's *Museum* as "The Puppet-Show" and "Scating"; see below, nos. 4 and 5, note 3.

2. Throughout the 1750's David Garrick, as manager of Drury Lane Theatre, frequently used a journalistic technique for advertising his new plays. Short pamphlets, usually anonymous, giving the "story" of the new play, and occasionally illustrated with engravings of popular actors and actresses in their new roles, were published one to four weeks before the date of the first performance. In the case of Brown's first play, the *Account of Barbarossa* (see below, no. 18) was published December 9, 1754, and the play had its initial performance at Drury Lane on December 17, the play itself not being published until December 23.

So far as I have been able to determine, there is no external evidence indicating that John Brown is the author of the *Account*; I find the internal evidence convincing but inconclusive.

First, the *Account* is no casual summary of the story of the play; it is a careful blending of paraphrases and quotations from the actual source of the play, *A Compleat History of the*

Piratical States of Barbary . . . (London, 1750). It seems unlikely that the author of the *Account* would have known the precise source of the unpublished play unless he had consulted John Brown in some detail, or unless he were John Brown. The source is not evident from the text of the play; and even if a Grub Street hack hired to write the *Account* had been given a complete manuscript of the play, he could have done little more than summarize.

More important is the fact that the author of the *Account* is quite coy about concealing the name of the author of the play—indeed, that element of secrecy is one of the enticements used to lure the reader of the pamphlet. In the first paragraph the author mentions "the Curiosity of the Publick" and says that "as several Gentlemen of Eminence in the Republick of Letters have been mention'd as the Author, it may, perhaps, be agreeable to the Town, to have the following short Account . . ." (pp. 5–6). The pamphlet concludes by saying, "But, by the Policy of the Managers, the Conduct of this Tragedy is as much a Secret, as either the Name of the Author, or the subsequent Part of the History itself" (p. 19).

Brown kept secret his authorship of the play until after it had proved successful on the stage, but the success did not alter the opinion of his friends. For example, on January 31, 1755, William Warburton wrote to Richard Hurd: "Browne has told me the *grand secret*; and I wish it had been a secret still to me . . . I am grieved that either these *unrewarding times*, or his *love of poetry*, or his *love of money*, should have made him overlook the duty of a Clergyman in these times, and the dignity of a Clergyman in all times, to make connexions with Players. Mr. Allen is grieved. You are sufficiently grieved, as I saw by your postscript in a letter to him . . ." (*Letters from a Late Eminent Prelate*. Second Edition. [London, 1809], page 182). Furthermore, Brown had learned early in November, 1754, that he was to be awarded the degree of Doctor of Divinity from Cambridge, which was awarded—so far as one can determine—in January, 1755. It was an awkward time for Brown to have his first play produced.

Yet Brown was a vain man who was proud of his play. The necessity for secrecy must have irked him extremely, and hence the arch references to the unknown author of *Barbarossa* in the *Account*. I find it difficult to believe that anyone but Brown could have written the *Account*. I wish it were not so, for it adds nothing to Brown's reputation to be credited with a piece which, at best, can be considered only competent journalism. Presumably Brown found it irresistible to spend an evening compiling a piece which might attract people to the play but almost surely would provoke readers of the pamphlet to inquire about the identity of the author of *Barbarossa*. That would be reward enough, even for a man of Brown's vanity.

Deletions from the Canon

1. In the *First-Line Index of English Poetry 1500–1800 in Manuscripts of the Bodleian Library Oxford* (Oxford, 1969), Miss Margaret Crum attributes an eight-line manuscript poem to John Brown (see entry Y-22; MS. Rawl. poet. 207, p. 177). The manuscript is inscribed "By the auth[r] of an Essay on Satire / To the auth[r] of the 2 Essays on Man, on his being anonymous."

The handwriting is not Brown's, but the copy could have been made by anyone. However, Brown's poem *An Essay on Satire* was not published until 1745; and it is difficult to imagine anyone's writing then who would refer to the *two* parts of the *Essay on Man*, let alone mentioning their being anonymous.

Walter Harte (1709–1774) seems a more likely candidate for authorship. His poem *An Essay on Satire* was published in 1730. The first two parts of Pope's *Essay on Man* were published anonymously in February and March, 1733, and Pope took great care to conceal his authorship. Harte was a friend of Pope's and presumably was aware of the ruse. If therefore he wrote the poem in April or early May, 1733, he would naturally refer only to the two parts of the *Essay on Man* and might well jest about the anonymity of their author.

Miss Crum agrees with this reasoning and informs me that

she has corrected the Bodleian's interleaved copy of the *First-Line Index.*

2. The catalogue of the Bibliothèque Nationale lists, under John Brown, three copies of: "Considérations sur les rapports qui lient les hommes en société, ou des Élémens de l'organisation sociale, traduit de l'anglais, du D. Brown, sur la troisième édition, avec un discours préliminaire et des notes, par . . . D. F. Donnant . . .—*Paris, Obré,* an VIII." The attribution of this work to John Brown is continued in other reference books, such as the *Dictionnaire de Biographie Française* . . . Paris, 1967 (XI, 527). Furthermore, Charles Alfred Rochedieu in his *Bibliography of French Translations of English Works 1700–1800* (Chicago, 1948), p. 36, says that the work is a translation of Brown's *The Mutual Connexion between Religious Truth and Civil Freedom* (see below, item no. 6 of this bibliography).

The book was not written by John Brown but by William Laurence Brown, 1755–1830 (see the *DNB*). It is entitled *An Essay on the Natural Equality of Men* . . . and was first published in Edinburgh in 1793. The book proved popular and went through numerous editions, including the third (London, 1799), which was the basis of the translation into French by Denis-François Donnant. I compared the English and French versions, and Donnant's is a careful translation, chapter by chapter, of the entire book. (The chapter headings are all translated quite literally; one wonders why Donnant created a new general title for the book.)

I believe the first person to associate correctly Donnant's translation and W. L. Brown's *Essay* was Hermann M. Flasdieck in his *John Brown (1715–1766) und seine Dissertation on Poetry and Music* . . . Halle (Saale): Max Niemeyer, 1924, page 61, note 5.

3. Charles Avison (d. 1770) was the author of *An Essay on Musical Expression,* first published in London by Charles Davis in 1752. A second edition, revised and greatly expanded, was published by Davis the following year. A third edition was published in London by Lockyer Davis in 1775, the same

year that a German translation was published in Leipzig.

Some libraries list this work as having been written by John Brown, basing their attribution upon a statement made by Andrew Kippis in his life of Brown in the second edition of the *Biographia Britannica*: "Besides what our Author published in his own name, in 1751, he had the principal hand in the composition of another book, which came out in that year, and was well received; Mr. Charles Avison's Essay on musical Expression" (London, 1780 [II, 655]). However, when the third volume of the *Biographia Britannica* was published in 1784, Kippis included an extensive note on Brown in the "Corrigenda and Addenda to the Second Volume," part of which reads as follows:

> In p. 655, agreeably to what was generally regarded as an undoubted fact, we asserted, that Dr. Brown had the principal hand in Mr. Charles Avison's Essay on Musical Expression. But we are now informed, from the united testimonies of Robert Page, Esq; of Newcastle-upon-Tyne, of a worthy and learned Clergyman in that neighbourhood, and of another of the same description at Carlisle, that this was not the case. Mr. Avison did, indeed, send his manuscript to Dr. Brown, who made some corrections in the style, and recommended some alteration in the order and disposition of the parts, but could in no sense be considered as the writer of the work. There are few authors who do not subject their compositions to the criticism of their friends, before they suffer them to appear in public. This was all that was done by Mr. Avison, with regard to his Essay on Musical Expression.

Clearly this work must not be attributed to John Brown.

4. Ralph Straus, in his *Robert Dodsley* (London, 1910), pp. 85–86, suggests that Brown may have written some of the "Historical Memoirs" printed at the end of each issue of Dodsley's periodical *The Museum*. However, Brown did not

contribute to that section of the *Museum*; see below, item no. 5, note 4 for a presentation of the evidence.

5. There are two additional ghosts which probably should be laid to rest here; for although neither one has been formally attributed to Brown, both caused a good deal of confusion in the eighteenth century—and some in the twentieth.

(a) In the spring of 1756 the dispute in England concerning the Jesuit author Archibald Bower was reaching its height and prolonged pamphlet warfare was to begin in June. Early in April, David Garrick and John Brown had a long interview with Bower; and soon it became public knowledge that this interview had taken place, although its results were unknown. In its issue of April 6–8, 1756, the *Evening Advertiser* printed a lengthy defense of Archibald Bower, written presumably by an Anglican clergyman, and signed J. B. Many people assumed this letter was written by John Brown. For example, in a letter dated April 13, Sir Henry Bedingfield (at that time the main antagonist of Bower) stated to Thomas Birch (another staunch opponent of Bower) that he assumed that John Brown was the author of the printed letter. Birch sent a copy of the newspaper to Prior Park, where William Warburton and John Brown were visiting with Ralph Allen. On April 15 Brown wrote to Birch, assuring him that he had not written the letter nor had he seen or heard of it until the newspaper arrived. In the *Evening Advertiser* of May 18–20, 1756, Sir Henry Bedingfield asserts in an advertisement that Archibald Bower was responsible for the statements in the printed letter signed J. B. A few days later Bower responded to Bedingfield in the same newspaper, saying in part, "As for the paper signed J. B. in the Evening Advertiser of the 8th of April, I knew nothing of it till I read it in that paper."

So the matter stands. The authorship of the J. B. letter remains undetermined—although presumably written by Bower or one of his friends—but Brown is exonerated. (For the manuscripts and the printed materials just mentioned, see British Museum Add. MSS. 4234.)

(b) In *James Boswell: The Earlier Years 1740–1769*, Frederick

A. Pottle says that "In an amusing passage in his journal Boswell tells how he once found Thomas Percy, the distinguished editor of *Reliques of Ancient English Poetry*, trying by the most approved research techniques to locate for General Paoli an unpublished defence of the Corsicans by Dr. John ('Estimate') Brown, a defence which Boswell himself had invented and had long since forgotten about" (New York, 1966), page 307. What started Percy on the search for the imaginary manuscript was a news item written by Boswell and printed in the *London Chronicle* of October 9–11, 1766, page 360—less than two weeks after John Brown had been buried. It was often reprinted in other English and continental newspapers. For Boswell's full account of the hoax, see *Boswell for the Defence 1769–1774*, ed. William K. Wimsatt, Jr. and Frederick A. Pottle (New York, 1959), pages 64–65.

Paper

In an admirable article entitled "The Bibliographical Description of Paper," G. Thomas Tanselle asserts that "There can by this time be no doubt that a bibliographer's routine examination of a book is deficient if it does not include an analysis of paper as well as of type-impressions," while also stating that there are many reasons for the neglect of paper, including "the simple one of ignorance: bibliographers have not known what to say about paper" (*SB*, XXIV [1971], 30, 29).

While not choosing to indict oneself for not abiding by Mr. Tanselle's strict standards, yet one may question the desirability or significance of describing the paper in each of the normally produced trade books listed in this bibliography. Although John Brown was a vain man, few of his works display any vanity in typography or paper—there are no large paper copies, no engraved title-pages, no frontispieces, portraits, or illustrations.

There is an exception. In the printing of *Honour*, his first poem, John Brown had three copies impressed on fine paper. However, since none of these copies has been identified with certainty, one can only speculate about the nature of the fine paper used (see below, no. 1, "Paper").

William Bowyer's Paper Stock Ledger (Bodleian MS. DON b.4) frequently gives the names of the dealers who supplied paper for the print shop. In the early 1750's, for instance, several of Brown's works were printed on paper supplied by Bloss, while later Johnson provided the paper for *An Additional Dialogue of the Dead*, the *Cure of Saul*, and the *Dissertation*. But Bowyer's business relationships with his suppliers, however interesting, are only tangentially related to John Brown; besides, such business matters will be discussed by K. I. D. Maslen in his forthcoming edition of Bowyer's ledgers.

Of more direct relevance are the attacks on John Brown for the extravagant use of paper in his works. In discussing the *Estimate*, for instance, James Ralph charges Brown with the "Sin of Venality" for the *Estimate*'s "scanty Page and overgrown Margin" (*The Case of Authors*, pp. 17–18; see nos. 114–115, below). In fact, this charge is the sole burden of the *Letter to the Reverend Dr. Br—n* (see no. 127, below). At a time when authors customarily sold their works to publishers largely on the basis of the number of printed sheets involved, a work with comparatively little printed matter and large margins was considered an imposition on the public. But it is difficult to understand why Ralph, in a work presenting "the case of *authors*," should attack Brown rather than admire him for having made a profitable deal with Lockyer Davis. The publisher, not the author, determined the number of sheets, the manner of printing, and the price of the finished book.

A matter directly related to paper is format, and in the late 1740's three of Brown's works were printed as small quartos on sheets of Foolscap or Large Foolscap. The use of large folios for short poems generally died with Pope and Swift; and although the shift to quartos accelerated in the late forties, the size of quartos for poetry had not yet become standardized. Both the second edition of the *Essay on Satire*, 1749 (see no. 3) and the first edition of *On Liberty*, 1749 (see no. 7) are printed as small quartos (approximately $8\frac{1}{2}'' \times$

6½″) which would look unusual to the London reading public even a few years later. Brown's sermons published by Dodsley in 1747 (see no. 6) are also printed in that size.

In the descriptions in this bibliography, measurements are given only of uncut copies. The maximum height and width of a leaf is measured to the nearest sixteenth of an inch.

Copies, and their Scarcity

Copies are listed in alphabetical order according to the names of the libraries. Those copies which I have examined personally are marked with an asterisk. In most instances, those copies which I have not seen I have verified by writing to the libraries concerned and asking questions about the copies—e.g., the locations of half-titles, the misnumbering of pages, or the presence of variant press figures.

After listing the copies, one hesitates to indulge in the "numbers game," especially when one is fully aware of the imprecise reality behind the façade of accuracy presented by numbers. There are several reasons why the lists of copies are necessarily incomplete: There are libraries whose holdings I have not checked; libraries have made purchases since I visited them; the books were there when I was but were uncatalogued; the books were catalogued under authors or other main entries unknown to me; and so on. Also, previously unknown editions continue to turn up: since the completed typescript of this book was sent to the printer, with all items consecutively numbered 1–151, four items have been added (nos. 50A, 97A, 118A, and 136A). There is every reason to believe that single copies of previously unknown editions will continue to appear, although it is certainly disconcerting to have them do so!

Nothing said above is meant to imply that my search for John Brown material was hasty or perfunctory; quite the contrary. In the past six years I visited many of the major libraries in England, Canada, and the United States; I received Xerox prints of the holdings of dozens of other libraries; I examined the pertinent printed catalogues and bibliographies; and I regularly visited and corresponded with many antiquarian booksellers. I used the National Union Catalogue at the Library of Congress, and then wrote to each library listed for verification. (In my experience the accuracy of NUC listings was low: it ranged from a maximum of fifty per cent all the way to zero in a few instances. *Caveat lector!*)

So, after a protracted search with an unknown degree of error inherent in the results, it may still prove valuable to analyze the lists of copies in this bibliography. Of a total of 155 items, 83 could be located in only five or fewer copies: for five items (nos. 65, 66, 71, 97A, and 127) no copies were located; for 17 items, one copy; for 21 items, two copies; for ten items, three copies; for 14 items, four copies; and for 16 items, five copies.

Of the major collections, the British Museum has 94 of the 155 items; D. D. Eddy has 69; the Bodleian has 69; Yale has 58; Harvard has 57; Cornell has 47; and Cambridge University Library has 39. Thus, the British Museum has fewer than two-thirds of the items, and Yale and Harvard each have just over one-third. Furthermore, copies are widely distributed: 27 of the 155 items are not to be found in any of the five largest collections listed above. (One of the pleasant aspects of my search was the discovery of truly rare items in unexpected places.)

One must not hastily conclude that John Brown material is scarcer than similar items printed in the same period. Brown was a popular writer; and the printing ledgers indicate that many of his works were printed in editions larger than normal, so one would expect that a correspondingly larger number survived.

Two recent studies confirm the scarcity of mid-eighteenth-century imprints. In 1968 the Oxford Bibliographical Society published *A Ledger of Charles Ackers*, edited by D. F. McKenzie and J. C. Ross. Appendix I lists 441 items printed by Ackers, mostly during the period 1732–1748. Of these items, an extensive search was unable to locate any copies of 137. Nor do the missing items always represent small printings of ephemera. For instance, during this period Ackers printed 275,000 copies of Thomas Dyche's *Guide to the English Tongue*, of which a world-wide search has uncovered a total of five copies.

Further evidence of scarcity may be found in a study of that unusually popular piece of moral didacticism, Robert Dodsley's *Oeconomy of Human Life* (see my check list in the *Cornell Library Journal*, no. 7 [Winter, 1969], 49–88). I located 142 editions of the *Oeconomy*, in English and in translation, printed from 1750 through 1800. Once again, the holdings were well distributed among various libraries. Seventeen libraries had one or more eighteenth-century editions not recorded elsewhere: the British Museum had 36, Yale had nine, Cornell had six, and so on.

All available evidence confirms the impression that a high percentage of the surviving copies of works printed in this period are quite scarce and are widely distributed. Furthermore, since there is a lack of bibliographical control over this material, no student of the period can presently conduct an investigation with any confidence that he has available to him, in *any* library, either the quantity or quality of material necessary for his researches.

Where all is needed, every bit helps; and studies such as this volume contribute their widow's mite. Vastly more helpful will be David Foxon's bibliography of all separately printed English verse, 1701–1750, now being printed at Cambridge University Press. But the problem is so large that ultimately the only solution is an Eighteenth-Century Short-Title Catalogue. Work has started; and at this time five universities in central New York State (SUNY-Binghamton, SUNY-Buffalo, Cornell, Rochester, and Syracuse) are engaged in a pilot project for the National Eighteenth-Century Short-Title Catalogue Committee. Cards have been culled from all libraries in these universities, and I am now engaged in editing more than 20,000 entries. It will be a beginning.

Printing and the Book Trade

Many generalizations have been made about printing and publishing practices in mid-eighteenth-century England; and as interest in the subject increases, it is works such as this bibliography which will provide the specific information necessary for testing and re-evaluating the generalizations.

For example, how common was the practice of reissuing a book with a new title-page (including reissues of old sheets and new impressions from standing type)? There are a number of examples: The fourth edition of the *Essays on the Characteristics* (no. 13) is a reissue of the third. (In this instance the decision may be attributed to John Brown rather than to Charles Davis. As soon as Brown learned, early in November, 1754, that he was to be awarded the degree of Doctor of Divinity from Cambridge, he immediately had Davis order new title-pages for the remaining copies of the third edition of the *Essays*. Brown was awarded the degree in January; and on January 31, 1755, the "fourth edition" of the *Essays* by "John Brown D.D." was published.) The second edition of *An Additional Dialogue of the Dead* (no. 62) is a reissue of the first. The second, third, fourth, and fifth Newcastle editions of *On the Natural Duty of a Personal Service . . .* (nos. 64, 65, 66, and 67) are reissues of the first—and all five were published in one week. The second edition of the *Dissertation* (no. 77) is a reissue of the first. The second, third, and fourth editions of the *Letter to the Rev. Dr. Lowth* (nos. 95, 96, and 97) are reissues of the first—and all four were published in less than three weeks. The second edition of Ralph's *Case of Authors* (no. 115) is a reissue of the first. The third edition of the *Letters to the Estimator* (no. 122) is a reissue of the second. For Robert Lowth's *Letter*, the third edition (no. 146) is a reissue of the second, and the fourth edition, second issue (no. 148) is a reissue of the fourth edition, first issue.

Thus, 14 items (i.e., nine per cent) of the 155 in this bibliography are reissues. It seems significant that the most popular and frequently printed items, such as *Barbarossa* and the *Estimate*, were never merely reissued with new title-pages.

In discussing press figures, it is often assumed that if two editions of a work are printed by one printer within a short period of time, and if identical press figures are located in the same positions on the same pages, then those portions of the text are of the same impression. This common assumption is not necessarily valid. For example, in the first three editions of the *Essays on the Characteristics*, in every single instance of gatherings with identical press figures on the same pages, collation of the text showed that they were of completely different settings of type. (See the discussion of the printing of this book, below, pages 33–36.) Apparently as pressmen became increasingly accustomed to using figures in printing, they tended to put them in the same locations in the formes.

For each work having press figures, I have used the customary form of presentation: page number followed by figure. For the five London editions of the *Essays on the Characteristics* and the seven London editions of the *Estimate*, I have also listed the press figures in the tabular presentation suggested by G. Thomas Tanselle—a method extremely useful in comparing various editions of a work.

One of the values of this bibliography lies in its reliance upon the manuscript printing ledgers of William Strahan and, especially, William Bowyer. The ledgers are useful in many ways. One can speak of the popularity of a work when he knows the exact number of copies printed in each edition. Even though many works—and this is especially true of later editions—were not advertised in the newspapers, one can estimate with a high degree of accuracy the date of publication of such an edition by noting in the ledger the date on which the printer delivers the first large shipment of the book to the publisher. One can often determine which sections of a large or popular book were assigned to a given printer. And, with the aid of the ledgers, one can untangle many bibliographical complexities which otherwise might prove to be Gordian knots; for example, see the discussion of the various editions of Lowth's *Letter*, nos. 144–148, below.

In citing information from the ledgers, I use the system of numbering employed by the printers in their manuscript indexes to the ledgers. In Bowyer's ledgers the upper right hand corner of each recto is numbered, but the printers refer to the entire opening by that number. For example, 57^v and 58^r form one opening which is numbered 58 by the printers.

Determining the dates of publication of various works is always difficult, and it is unquestionably the most time-consuming element in the compilation of a bibliography. (I have spent many months working with newspapers and periodicals in the libraries of the British Museum, Yale, Cornell, etc.) But reading book reviews and newspaper advertisements is the best way for a bibliographer to learn of publications he has not yet seen in libraries, and of course the dates of publication are useful in many ways—for example, it is impossible to discuss any pamphlet warfare intelligently until the chronology of the pieces has been established. Where they could be ascertained, exact dates of publication are given for most of the London imprints; see each item of the bibliography and Appendix I.

Appendix II is an index of printers, publishers, and booksellers. There one may find many names, dates, and addresses not listed in the Plomer-Bushnell-Dix *Dictionary of Printers and Booksellers . . . from 1726 to 1775* (Oxford, 1932).

John Brown

There are many ways of studying John Brown: as a popular eighteenth-century author, some of whose works outsold comparable writings by Samuel Johnson; as a liberal Whig, whose views on religion, female education, slavery, civil liberty and other topics make him a more representative figure of the times than many members of Johnson's circle; as a poet, some of whose poems have been very highly praised by critics ranging from William Warburton to R. D. Havens; as an early "pre-Romantic," whose prose and poetry were instrumental in interesting the English in the Lake District; as the author of some successful pieces of political rhetoric, which were praised by many knowledgeable people, including Edmund Burke and Voltaire; as a man interested in the American colonies, and perhaps the earliest fund raiser for the University of Pennsylvania and Columbia University; as a leading proponent of utilitarianism, of whom John Stuart Mill said in 1838, "We never saw an abler defence of the doctrine of utility than in . . . Brown's 'Essays on the Characteristics'"; as an influential writer on education, whose works were the immediate cause of two of the earliest full-length books by Joseph Priestley; as a writer of oratorios, whose *Cure of Saul* was praised as superior to anything written by Handel; as a polemicist, frequently engaged in literary warfare; as a dramatist, closely associated with David Garrick; or as a fascinating personality.

Here is a fertile field for future critics and biographers; may this bibliography prove useful to them.

The Reverend John Brown

Chronology of Life, Education, and Positions

Born Rothbury, Northumberland	November 5, 1715
Lived in Wigton, Cumberland	1715–1732
At St. John's College, Cambridge	
Admitted as sizar	May 8, 1732
Matriculated in the university	December 18, 1732
B.A. degree, with distinction	1735/36
Returned to Wigton	1736
Nominated to minor canonry at the Cathedral Church, Carlisle	November, 1737
Ordained Deacon, by Sir George Fleming, Bishop of Carlisle	February 26, 1737/38
Took oaths as minor canon at the Cathedral Church, Carlisle	April 28, 1738
Nominated to Cathedral lectureship	June 23, 1739
Ordained Priest, by Sir George Fleming, Bishop of Carlisle	December 23, 1739
M.A. degree from St. John's College, Cambridge	1739
Vicar of Morland, Westmorland	1743–1756
Appointed Chaplain to the Bishop of Carlisle, by Dr. Richard Osbaldeston	1747(?)
Vicar of Lazonby, Cumberland	1752–63
D.D. degree from St. John's College, Cambridge	1755
Rector of Great Horkesley, Essex	1756–60
Resigned lectureship at the Cathedral Church, Carlisle	November 14, 1757
Resignation handed in formally to Dean and Chapter	November 23, 1757

Vicar of St. Nicholas, Newcastle-on-Tyne	1760–66
Appointed Archdeacon of Northumberland	1761
Died "at his apartments in Pallmall"	September 23, 1766
The remains of the Rev. Dr. Brown "were interred in the vault at St. James's church" London	October 1, 1766

THE WRITINGS OF JOHN BROWN

1.

HONOUR. / A / POEM. / Inscribed to the / Right Hon[ble] the Lord Viscount *LONSDALE.* / [rule] / [two quotations, from Virgil and Shakespeare] / [rule] / *LONDON:* / Printed for R. Dodsley at *Tully*'s-*Head* in *Pall-Mall*, and / sold by M. Cooper at the *Globe* in *Pater-Noster-Row.* 1743.

Half-title: [row of type ornaments] / HONOUR. / A / POEM. / [row of type ornaments] / (Price One Shilling.)

Collation: 4°: *A*⁴ B–C⁴

Contents: Page *1* half-title, *2* blank, *3* title, *4* blank, *5* 6–23 text of poem, *24* advertisement.

Press figures: none.

Number of copies printed: The number is not known, but probably it was small, because the edition was printed at Brown's expense. See Brown's letters to Robert Dodsley in the note, below.

Paper: Three copies of this poem were printed on fine paper (Brown's letter to Dodsley, Dec. 24, 1743; see below), but so far none have been identified with certainty. (Where is the copy Brown sent to "the Rev[d] D[r] Bolton, Dean of Carlisle"?) In all copies examined the watermark is a fleur-de-lis (Heawood 1706); some sheets of this paper have the initials IV as a countermark, some do not. However, if the Cornell copy is held tightly and measured, it is $\frac{1}{8}$" thick, excluding binding and endpapers; while the D. D. Eddy copy, for example, is only $\frac{1}{16}$" thick if measured the same way. Is, perhaps, the Cornell copy one of the three printed on fine paper?

Size of an uncut copy: $10\frac{5}{8}$" × $8\frac{7}{16}$" (Folger Library copy, in original blue wrapper, stitched; Harvard copy).

Date of publication: December 20, 1743 (*London Daily Post and General Advertiser*). Advertisements: "Next Tuesday will be publish'd . . ." (*General Evening Post*, Tues., Dec. 13–Thurs., Dec. 15, 1743); "This Day is publish'd . . ." (*London Daily Post and General Advertiser*, Tues., Dec. 20, 1743).

Copies: *Bodleian; *British Museum; Christ Church, Oxford; University of Cincinnati; *Cornell; *Folger Library; *Harvard (Horace Walpole's copy); Huntington Library; *Illinois (lacks half-title); Leeds University (Brotherton Collection); *Newberry Library; *University of Pennsylvania; Princeton; *Yale; *D. D. Eddy.

Subsequent printings:

1. This poem was reprinted in the eleven London editions of Dodsley's *Collection of Poems by Several Hands*: 1—1748; 2—1748; 3—1751; 4—1755; 5—1758; 6—1763; 7—1765; 8—1766; 9—1770; 10—1775; 11—1782. It was also reprinted in the Dublin (1751) edition of Dodsley's *Collection* (II, 76–88).

2. It was also reprinted in the first collected edition of Brown's poems: Robert Anderson, M.D. (ed.). *The Works of the British Poets. With Prefaces, Biographical and Critical.* 13 vols. London and Edinburgh, 1795. X, 884–887. An abridged version is printed in Thomas Park's *Supplement to the British Poets* (London, 1809), Vol. IX, pages 149–159.

Note:

The following letters—quoted, with permission, from Bodleian MS. Toynbee d.19—illustrate John Brown's initiation into the world of printers and booksellers. Presumably late in the summer of 1743 Brown submitted his manuscript of *Honour. A Poem* to Robert Dodsley, who must have replied in a politely evasive note.

> S[r]
>
> I wish you had told me directly whether you are willing to purchase the Copy of the Poem I sent you, upon any Terms, or not. If you are, I desire you will let me know what you can give: If you are not, pray inform me particularly upon what Terms you will print, and sell it, upon

the Author's Account. I beg you will be as particular as you can in your Answer, because I suppose the proper Time for publishing draws on. Your last Letter had almost miscarry'd for want of a necessary word in the Direction which you will see in my first Letter to you. I am S[r]

Your humble Servant
J. Brown

Carlisle Sept: 1743.

Dodsley replied giving the requested details, and Brown's answer seems surprisingly modern in its expression of concern about the high cost of printing.

S[r]

The Terms upon which you propose to print the Poem are reasonable enough: But I did not think the Expence of Print Paper Advertising &c: would have risen quite so high. Perhaps you think of printing it in Folio; but I would have it rather in Quarto; for as it will hardly exceed twenty Pages, a Folio of those Dimensions makes in my Eye an awkward disproportioned Figure. I suppose the Expence of printing it in Quarto must be rather less than in Folio. I should chuse to have it done pretty much in the Manner of D[r] Young's late Pieces. As to the Time of publishing it, I shall leave that to You, as you must know which is the properest better than I. If such a thing is practicable, (as I am told it is) I would have a printed Copy sent down by way of Proof, as I cannot expect that you in the hurry of Business should revise it with that Care, as an Author does his own Productions. Whenever you do this, pray divide the Copy into two Packets directed to me, and put them under Covers directed to the Right Rev[d] The Lord Bishop of Carlisle at Rose Castle near Carlisle Cumberland. I thank you for your Compliments, which I am afraid are higher than the thing deserves. I should think my self much obliged to you, if you could procure me any Emendations or various Readings from any person who has Abilities in this Way: I see you are M[r] Pope's Bookseller; but am afraid this is too great a Favour to be expected from Him. I desire the following Alterations may be made:

In the title Page for "the Lord Viscount Lonsdale," read "The right honourable the Lord Viscount Lonsdale."

Line 1st. for "See, the whole world" &c: read "Yes: All, my Lord, usurp fair Honour's Name."

Line 230th. for "Still sway'd by what is *decent* just & true" read "Still sway'd by what is fit and just and true."

These are all I can at present recollect. I am

S^{r}. Your humble Servant
J. Brown

Carlisle, Oct. 8th. 1743.

Honour. A Poem was published December 20, 1743, and Brown's next letter gives instructions for the distribution of copies.

S^{r}.

A Day or two after you receive this there will be thirty five Copies of my little Poem called for all stitched in Marble; two of them on fine Paper: Likewise one Copy of your Poem, wch. I desire may be covered the same Way. The remaining Copy on fine Paper I desire you will direct and get convey'd "To the Rev^{d}. D^{r}. Bolton Dean of Carlisle at Reading Berkshire, Carriage Paid. There must be five more cover'd with Marble Paper and sent as Presents from the Bishop of Carlisle as follows:

To M^{rs}. Fleming at M^{r}. Robinson's Watchmaker in the broad Way near Queen's Square Westminster, one.

To M^{rs}. Wilkinson at the Rev^{d}. M^{r}. Wilkinson's in the Savoy, two.

To M^{r}. Rook at the Roll's Chapel, two.

These five you will place to my Account, unless some other Person should pay you for them. Pray let me hear what Progress it is like to make as soon as you can judge of it. I am

S^{r}. Your humble Servant
J. Brown

Carlisle Dec: 24th. 1743.

2.

AN / ESSAY on SATIRE: / Occasion'd by the / DEATH of Mr. *POPE.* / [rule] / [quotation] / [rule] / [cut] / *LONDON:* / Printed for R. DODSLEY at Tully's Head in Pall-Mall. / [rule] / M.DCC.XLV. / [Price One Shilling.]

Collation: 4°: A–D^4

Contents: Page *i* title, *ii* blank, iii–iv Contents, *5* 6–32 text.

Press figures: none.

Size of an uncut copy: $10\frac{7}{8}'' \times 8\frac{1}{2}''$ (Harvard copy).

Date of publication: April 24, 1745 (*Daily Advertiser; General Advertiser*). "Printed for R. Dodsley and sold by M. Cooper."

Copies: National Library of Australia; *Bodleian G. Pamph. 1703 (2); *British Museum 12273.m.1.(19); University of Chicago; University of Cincinnati; *Cornell; Duke; *Harvard (Horace Walpole's copy); Hull University; Huntington Library; *Illinois; *Indiana; Leeds University (Brotherton Collection); *Newberry Library; Princeton; Texas (3 copies); *Yale; *D. D. Eddy.

Subsequent printings:

The text of this edition of the poem was reprinted in the first four editions of Dodsley's *Collection of Poems by Several Hands*: 1—1748; 2—1748; 3—1751; 4—1755. It was also reprinted in the first Dublin (1751) edition of Dodsley's *Collection* (II, 103–123).

Note:

Brown wrote this poem in the winter of 1744/45, and on February 18 he sent an early draft to Dodsley. This time, however, Brown asked Dodsley to purchase the copyright. The following letters—quoted, with permission, from Bodleian MS. Toynbee d.19—illustrate Brown's increasing confidence in dealing with his London publisher.

Carlisle. Feb: 18th 1744/45

Mr Dodsley

Along with this I have sent you An Essay on Satire in

two small Parcels. As to the Terms of printing—I am sorry to find, in these upon which my other little Poem was printed, that the Interests of the Author and Bookseller are so weakly connected. Upon this Account I do not chuse to have this Essay printed upon that Agreement: If you think, upon perusing this Copy, that you can purchase it with Convenience to yourself, I desire you will let me know as soon as possible, upon what Terms you are willing to purchase it. If not, pray acquaint me with your Resolution, and I shall either desire Mr Dixon to take the Copy, or shall call for it myself. I intended to have been in Town some time ago, but have been prevented by a very violent Storm of Snow: As soon as the Roads are passable without Difficulty, I hope I shall have the Pleasure of seeing you in Town. In the mean time I am

S^r^—Your most humble Servt

J: Brown

P.S. I believe I shall add some 30 or 40 Lines to the Essay.

Dodsley apparently purchased the copyright and published *An Essay on Satire* on April 24, 1745, but the poem did not sell very well. On October 17, 1745 Brown wrote to Dodsley about the possible publication of some prose essays, adding this paragraph:

> . . . I am really very sorry to hear of the Success of my other Essay. I am apt to think it was too late in the Season; tho' I think you might have published it three weeks sooner at least: But perhaps I speak with the Partiality of an Author. I wish I may ever have an Opportunity of reimbursing You, if I have, I shall not omit it.

3. *The Second Edition (1749)*

AN / ESSAY [red] / ON / SATIRE, / Occasioned by the Death of Mr. *POPE.* / Inscribed to / Mr. *WARBURTON.* [red] / [rule] / The SECOND EDITION; corrected and enlarged by the / AUTHOR, in the same Manner in which it is in- / serted in the new Edition of Mr. *Pope*'s Works, now / in the

Press. / [rule] / *By* JOHN BROWN, *M.A.* [red] / [rule] / [quotation] / [rule] / *LONDON:* [red] / Printed for R. DODSLEY at *Tully*'s-head *Pall-mall*; / and sold by M. COOPER in *Pater-noster-Row.* / [rule] / MDCCXLIX. [red] / [Price One Shilling.]

Collation: 4°: A–D⁴

Contents: Page *1* title, *2* blank, *3*–4 Advertisement, 5–6 Contents, *7* 8–29 text of poem, 30–32 note. Page 14 misnumbered 13, 15 misnumbered 14, 16 misnumbered 19 (in some copies; see note 1), and 27 misnumbered 72 (in some copies; see note 2).

Press figures: none.

Size of an uncut copy: 8½″ × 6⅞″ (Pennsylvania State University copy).

Date of publication: March 16 or 17, 1749 (*General Advertiser*). Advertisements: "Tomorrow will be published . . ." (*General Advertiser*, Wed., March 15, 1749); "This Day is published..." (*General Advertiser*, Fri., March 17, 1749). There is no advertisement in the issue of March 16.

Copies: *British Museum (2 copies); *Harvard; Pembroke College, Cambridge (inscribed to the Rev. Dr. Long, Master of Pembroke Hall, from the Author); *Pennsylvania State University; Rylands Library, Manchester; Victoria and Albert Museum (Dyce Collection).

Notes:

1. Page 16 exists in two states: in the first it is incorrectly numbered 19 (Pennsylvania State University; British Museum 11630.b.7.[12.]); in the second it is correctly numbered (British Museum 161.l.15; Harvard).

2. Page 27 exists in two states: in the first it is incorrectly numbered 72 (Pennsylvania State University and both British Museum copies); in the second it is correctly numbered (Harvard).

3. In the Pennsylvania State University copy, line 251 is

corrected in an eighteenth-century hand to read, "Ere Lewdness the stain'd Garb of Honour wore." Except for changes in accidentals, this is the reading found in the first edition of 1745 (line 237) and Warburton's edition of Pope, 1751 (III, xvi, line 251).

4. In this second edition, many lines are added, rearranged, or revised. Since this version of the poem was to be included in Warburton's edition of Pope's *Works*, Warburton is now specifically praised in passages which were addressed to the reader in the first edition. For example, lines 11–12 of the first edition read, "But thou whose eye, from passion's film refin'd, / Can see true greatness in an honest mind." In the second edition these lines read, "But You, O WARBURTON! whose Eye refin'd / Can see the Greatness of an honest Mind."

Subsequent printings:

1. This revised, second edition text was reprinted in the fifth through the eleventh editions of Dodsley's *Collection of Poems by Several Hands*: 5—1758; 6—1763; 7—1765; 8—1766; 9—1770; 10—1775; 11—1782.

2. This text, slightly expanded but without the long footnote on ridicule, was reprinted in William Warburton's edition of the *Works of Alexander Pope*, first published June 18, 1751 (*Daily Advertiser*). This version of Pope's *Works* was extremely popular, and twelve authorized editions were published in London alone before John Brown died in 1766: 1—1751; 2—1751; 3—1752; 4—1753; 5—1754; 6—1756; 7—1757; 8—1757; 9—1760; 10—1764; 11—1766; 12—1766. Of course, it was also reprinted in many later editions of the Warburton text—e.g., *The Works of the English Poets. With Prefaces, Biographical and Critical, by Samuel Johnson.* London, 1790. (XLVI, 1–21). (Copies: *British Museum.)

3. It was also reprinted in the first collected edition of Brown's poems: Robert Anderson, M.D. (ed.). *The Works of the British Poets. With Prefaces, Biographical and Critical.* 13 vols. London and Edinburgh, 1795. (X, 877–881.) It is also to be found in Samuel J. Pratt's *The Cabinet of Poetry*. London:

Printed for Richard Phillips, 1808. 6 vols. (V, 332–347). (Copies: *British Museum.)

Note:

Although the first edition of the *Essay on Satire* was published April 24, 1745, the poem apparently did not come to the attention of William Warburton until more than a year later, at which time he wrote to Robert Dodsley:

> I saw by accident on the road a Poem called "An Essay on Satire, occasioned by the Death of Mr. Pope;" and was surprized to see so excellent a piece of poetry, and, what was still more uncommon, so much good reasoning. I find it has been published some time. If it be not a secret, I should be glad to know the Author. If I have leisure, I shall give some account of it for the literary news of your *Museum*. It will be a better ornament to it than the dull book of Travels in the Second Number [dated April 12, 1746].
>
> I am,
>
> Your very humble servant,
>
> W. Warburton

(as quoted in Nichols' *Literary Anecdotes* [London, 1812], V, 587).

After receiving Dodsley's answer, the future Bishop of Gloucester wrote what is apparently his first letter to Brown on Christmas eve, 1746 (quoted, with permission, from Bodleian MS. Eng. misc. c.390, folio 398):

> Sir,
>
> It is not long since y^{t} by accident I met with a Poem intit: An Essay on Satire occasioned by Mr Pope's death. I own I was much surprised at ye Performance. To say it is the only piece of poetry that has appeared since his Death w^{d} be giving it a very low & invidious co̅mendation. For I think it a masterpiece. The long note on Ridicule is admirable. I am preparing a compleat & very fine Ed^{n} of all Mr Pope's works, & w^{d} by y^{r} leave, & if

it be agreeable to y^{r} inclinations, place it before his works, & discard those insipid pieces wrote in his com̄endation, to give it room. Had poor Mr Pope been alive I know how much he w^{d} have esteem'd such a poem & ye author of it. & in this I sh^{d} be glad to supply his place, & take any opportunity of shewing how much I am,

Sir,

Y^{r} most faithfull humble Servt

W. Warburton

Bedford Row Decr 24
1746

[Note: This letter has been printed, possibly from the same manuscript, in William Darby Templeman's article, "Warburton and Brown Continue the Battle over Ridicule," *Huntington Library Quarterly*, XVII, no. 1 (Nov., 1953), 22.]

Brown accepted the invitation and revised his poem accordingly. The second edition of *An Essay on Satire*, "corrected and enlarged by the author" and "inscribed to Mr. Warburton," was published March 16 or 17, 1749. After the publication of the second edition of the poem, Brown further revised the text, adding fourteen lines near the end of Section II. On October 14, 1749 Warburton wrote to William Bowyer, the printer of the forthcoming edition of Pope's *Works*: "Mr. Knapton tells me he has given Mr. Bowyer Brown's Poem on Satire. Why is it not yet printed? It is to be put at the head of that volume in which the Essay on Man is . . ." (Nichols' *Literary Anecdotes* [London, 1812], II, 228). The revised text, minus the footnote on ridicule, was finally printed at the beginning of Volume III of Warburton's edition of the *Works of Alexander Pope*, first published in nine large octavo volumes June 18, 1751.

Note:

The *Essay on Satire* was certainly the most frequently reprinted of Brown's poems. How many copies—whether in separate editions or collections—were available to the reading public during the author's lifetime?

There does not appear to be any evidence available to indicate the size of either the first edition (1745) or of the second edition (1749).

John Hughs was the printer of Dodsley's *Collection*; but since his business ledgers are not known to exist today, we cannot determine accurately the number of copies he printed. However, in printing some of the editions, Hughs was assisted by other printers. For instance, both William Bowyer (cf. Bodleian MS. DON b.4, folio 142) and William Strahan (cf. British Museum Add. MSS. 48800, folio 83) printed part of the fourth edition (1755), which numbered 1,500 copies. The same source shows that Strahan helped to print the 1,000 copies of the sixth edition (1763).

Editions of 1,000 or 1,500 copies are not unusual for such a work. If one is willing to assume that the first eight editions of Dodsley's *Collection* were published in editions alternating in size between 1,000 and 1,500 copies, then at least 10,000 copies of Brown's poem were available to the London public by 1766 in this form alone.

More specific evidence is available concerning the printing of Warburton's edition of Pope's *Works*. William Bowyer was the sole printer of the first edition, nine volumes in large octavo, 1751. William Strahan began to assist Bowyer in printing the second edition, 1751, and Strahan's share in the printing grew larger until he became sole printer of the editions of 1764 and 1766. The evidence may be seen best in tabular form (see page 12).

These figures were obtained from three ledgers: Bodleian MS. DON b.4, folios 127–128; British Museum Add. MSS. 48800, folio 68; British Museum Add. MSS. 48802A, folios 21, 23, 39, 55, and 61. All twelve editions listed are in Cornell University Library.

As we have seen, there is no way of estimating the size of the first edition (1745), the second edition (1749), or the seventh Warburton edition of Pope's *Works* (1757). If one were to assume that 1,000 copies of each of these three editions were printed, then John Brown lived to see approximately

The Works of Alexander Pope, edited by William Warburton
Authorized London editions only (1751–66)

Number of edition	Number of volumes	Format (as listed in ledgers)	Date	Number of copies printed
1	9	Large 8°	1751	1,500
2	9	Small 8°	1751	3,000
3	9	Large 8°	1752	750
4	9	Small 8°	1753	2,500
5	10	Foolscap 8°	1754	3,000
6	9	Foolscap 8°	1756	3,000
7	10	Very small 8°	1757	?
8	9	Small 8°	1757	2,500
9	9	Large 8°	1760	750
10	6	12°	1764	3,000
11	9	Crown 8°	1766	1,500
12	9	Large 8°	1766	750
Total: 22,250, excluding the seventh edition.				

35,000 copies of the *Essay on Satire* available in some form to the London public.

It is an impressive figure for the 1750's and 1760's. Very few poetical works printed during this period could surpass it: certainly those of Milton and Pope did, and Gray's *Elegy* may have (although I know of no printing statistics for it).

To be sure, one may ask what percentage of the purchasers of Dodsley's *Collection* or of Pope's *Works* chose to read the *Essay on Satire*. But, any attempt to answer that question is indulging in speculation far more uncertain than anything attempted above. One can at least make reasonable estimates of printing figures; the whims and vagaries of readers are unfathomable.

John Brown's Contributions to Dodsley's *Museum*

4.

"*Machinæ Gesticulantes:* THE PUPPET-SHOW. Translated from the *Latin* of Mr. ADDISON." In *The Museum*, I, no. 3 (April 26, 1746), 96–99.

5.

"*CURSUS GLACIALIS:* SCATING, *translated from the* Musæ Anglicanæ." In *The Museum*, I, no. 8 (July 5, 1746), 293–295.

The Museum: or, the Literary and Historical Register.
Three Volumes, 1746–47

Volume title-pages: THE / *MUSEUM:* [red] / OR, THE / Literary and Historical / REGISTER. [red] / VOLUME THE FIRST. [SECOND.] [THIRD.] / [cut] / *LONDON:* [red] / Printed for R. DODSLEY in *Pall-mall.* / [rule] / M. DCC. XLVI. [red; Vols. I, II] [M. DCC. XLVII. (red; Vol. III)]

Volume I

Collation: 8° (in 4's): A^4 a1 ("The Preface," inserted between A1 and A2) B–2G^4 2I–3Y^4 3Z1, pages *1–2* + [2] + *3* 4–40 *41* 42–80 *81* 82–120 *121* 122–160 *161* 162–200 *201* 202–240 *241* 242–280 *281* 282–320 *321* 322–360 *361* 362–400 *401* 402–440 *441* 442–480 *481* 482–521 text, 522–538 Index [i.e., 540 pages]. Page 251 misnumbered 151.

Contents: This periodical was published every other Saturday, starting March 29, 1746. Each issue consists of five octavo gatherings in half-sheets (40 pages). Volume I contains the first thirteen issues (March 29 through September 13, 1746). The thirteenth issue contains 58 pages, because included in it is the Index to Vol. I.

Volume II

Collation: 8° (in 4's): A–3T⁴, pages *1–3* 4–40 *41* 42–80 *81* 82–120 *121* 122–160 *161* 162–184, 149–164 *165* 166–204 *205* 206–244 *245* 246–283, 260 *261* 262–300 *301* 302–340 *341* 342–380 *381* 382–420 *421* 422–450 text, 451–457 *458* 459–460 Index [i.e., 520 pages]. Page 372 misnumbered 327; other pages misnumbered as above.

Contents: Volume II also contains thirteen issues: numbers 14–26 (September 27, 1746 through March 14, 1746/47). As before, each issue consists of five octavo gatherings in half-sheets (40 pages). The twenty-sixth issue also consists of 40 pages, which include the Index to Vol. II.

Volume III

Collation: 8° (in 4's): *A*⁴ B–3T⁴, pages *1–3* 4–40 *41* 42–56, 49–72 *73* 74–112 *113* 114–152 *153* 154–192 *193* 194–232 *233* 234–272 *273* 274–312, *317* 318–356 *357* 358–396 *397* 398–436 *437* 438–476 *477* 478–510 text, 511–516 Index [i.e., 520 pages]. Page 76 misnumbered 67; page 110 misnumbered 101; other pages misnumbered as above.

Contents: Volume III also contains thirteen issues: numbers 27–39 (March 28, 1747 through September 12, 1747). Each issue still consists of five octavo gatherings in half-sheets (40 pages). The last issue also consists of 40 pages, which include the Index to Vol. III.

Copies: This is a very common periodical. *The Union List of Serials* (1965) records 26 complete sets, including those at the University of Chicago; Columbia; Library of Congress; *Cornell; Harvard; University of Illinois; Newberry Library; New York Public Library; and Texas. (*Yale and *D. D. Eddy also have sets.) The *British Union-Catalogue of Periodicals*

(1957) lists five complete sets, including those in the Bodleian; *British Museum (264.l.18–20); Cambridge University Library; and Edinburgh University Library. (The second British Museum copy was destroyed by German bombs.)

Notes:

1. Joseph Addison wrote the Latin poem "Machinæ Gesticulantes," which he first published in the second volume of the *Musarum Anglicanarum analecta* (Oxford, 1699). The collection was popular and went through six editions by 1761, usually published under the title *Musæ Anglicanæ*. For a good discussion of this collection, see Leicester Bradner's *Musae Anglicanae* (New York, 1940).

2. The Latin poem "Cursus Glacialis" probably was written by Philip Frowde and not by Joseph Addison; see Leicester Bradner, "The Composition and Publication of Addison's Latin Poems," *MP*, XXXV, no. 4 (May, 1938), 359–367; and Peter Smithers, *The Life of Joseph Addison* (Oxford: Clarendon Press, 1954), p. 40.

3. That John Brown is the author of the two poems listed above is proved by the following letters he wrote to Robert Dodsley (quoted, with permission, from Bodleian MS. Toynbee d.19):

> Carlisle. Feb: 15th 1745/6
>
> Sr
>
> I have been banished from Carlisle ever since the Rebels took Possession of it till last Night: this is the Reason why I have been so late in receiving and answering Yours. I shall be very ready to throw in my Mite to your Treasury, according to what I have: But I fancy you will not expect very much from me when I assure you I never wrote so many Verses in my whole Life as those I have published, these excepted. I was entirely prevented from proceeding in my late Design, by the Progress of the Rebels, who broke off all our Communication with London for several Weeks. If you think the Essays wch You sent to Mr Dixon will be of any Use to you in any other shape than what they are now in, they are entirely

at your Service: If you will inform me of this, I shall desire him to send them to you. I have been looking among some old Papers, but can find nothing which I think can be for your Purpose except it be a Translation of two latin Poems from the Musæ Anglicanæ, one on Scating the other Mr. Addison's Puppet Show, which were two or three Morning's Amusement last Winter: Strada's Nightingale & the Battle of the Pygmies & Cranes not compleated. If any of these will answer your design, I shall transcribe them & send them when you please. I shall very probably be sending you some small Matters of Amusement now & then. I shall desire to have your Musæum regularly transmitted to me, which you will add to my Account. As our Booksellers here have no very certain Correspondence with London, I should be very glad to have them by the Post in Franks, but whether this be a Proposal which you can conveniently agree to, is what I know not. I wish you success in your Undertaking & am

Sr. Your most humble Servt.,
J: Brown.

Wigton (8 miles from Carlisle) March 4th. [1745/46]

Sr.

I left Carlisle unexpectedly the Day after I wrote to You, & did not receive Yours till last Post: I have enclosed a few Verses which had their Birth here last Week by mere accident: They are at your Service for your Museum, or any other purpose you may think them proper for. You have made an Improvement in your Title Page: I designed to have objected to your *Magazine*. Upon Recollection I believe none of the Essays I mentioned will be for your Purpose, except the third, & perhaps the first Page or so of the second, which may be added to the other: but I have no foul Copies, having been reduced to the Necessity of burning these with several other things of a paralel Nature, when Carlisle surrendered to the Rebels. I shall return thither in two or three Days & will then send you the Translations that are finished. Upon Consideration I find the Proposal I made in my last was somewhat unreasonable, & must therefore revoke it; especially as I imagine the whole Pamphlet cannot be enclosed in one Frank. You may put the first and second Nos. as soon as published, under Covers directed to ye. Bishop of Carlisle at Rose Castle. When you have Leisure, I wish you would favour me with an Answer to a few Questions which follow. Pray by what means, came these Verses of Mr. Pope to Light, on the D. of M.? And who had them in keeping?—What other things do you know or hear of, that Mr. Pope has left behind him? particularly whether ever he made any Progress in, or ever finished the Design he mentions in one of his Letters to D. Swift, *on Knowledge*? I am told he had begun something in the Epic Kind, but don't believe it till I have better Authority. Pray who is the Author of that little Ode to Lord Lonsdale?—And of the Hymn lately published to Liberty, which I have not seen?—What & whose is this last new Tragedy of H. the 7th.?—I have several other Questions which I want to have resolved but I am afraid I shall tire you. I am Sr.

Your most humble Servant
J: Brown

Carlisle Oct: 27th. 1746

Sr.

I send you a few Lines in the adjoyning Page which, if you think them worth their Room, you may insert in your Museum: They were a Morning's Exercise done at fourteen Years old; I think it would be best to insert them as such but as to this take your own Way. As the rambling season is now over with me for a while, I may possibly send you some small matters now & then. . . .

Thus, these letters mention several poems which John Brown sent, or at least offered, to Dodsley for the *Museum*. As indicated above, the only ones positively identified are "Scating" and "The Puppet Show." Several poems in the *Museum* might have been written by a fourteen year old boy, but none are so identified, nor does the Bodleian letter have any verses "in the adjoining Page." The translations of Strada's "Nightingale" and the "Battle of the Pygmies & Cranes" either were never completed or at least never published in the *Museum*.

4. In his book *Robert Dodsley* (London, 1910), pp. 85–86, Ralph Straus suggests that John Brown may have been the author of the "Historical Memoirs" section which was printed at the end of each issue of the *Museum*. Straus says:

> It would appear from a letter of his [i.e., Brown's] dated Oct. 5th, 1745, that he had written further essays for Dodsley on some subject of immediate interest and proposed a rather curious method of publication. "The inclosed Paper," he wrote, "will inform you of my Design, and give You a Specimen of the Manner in which I intend to pursue it. If you chuse to engage in an Affair of this Nature, please to let me Know your Resolution by the first Opportunity. As to the Method in which these Essays may be published, I have not come to any Determination about it. I should like to have one Essay printed every week in a single Sheet, but that I believe would subject them to the Stamp Duty, which must greatly increase the Expence of Printing them. The other Method which I think may be more feasable will be to throw four Essays together once a Month, which will make up at least a sixpenny Pamphlet. If you approve of this Method, I shall be ready to furnish you with four every month, of which You shall have the Liberty to print one Edition of what Number you please, for five Guineas each Month: This I am certain is a very moderate Share of the Profit that must arise from them if they meet with any tolerable Success, and if there is not a probability of this I think they had much better remain unpublished." It seems not improbable that these essays were afterwards issued as the Historical Memoirs which formed part of Dodsley's *Museum*, . . .

Clearly, the essays mentioned in this letter are the same as those discussed in the letters of February 15 and March 4,

1745/46, printed above. Is Straus correct in suggesting that these essays were used by Dodsley in the "Historical Memoirs" section of the *Museum*?

The answer is probably no. In his letter of March 4, 1745/46, Brown himself tells Dodsley that "Upon Recollection I believe none of the Essays I mentioned will be for your Purpose . . . ." Also, four of the "Historical Memoirs" sections are entitled "A Succinct History of the Rebellion"; and although the attribution of these essays to Henry Fielding has been refuted by Rupert C. Jarvis (see *Notes and Queries*, CCI [1956], 391–394, 479–482; CCII [1957], 19–24), there is no evidence for attributing them to John Brown. John Campbell wrote all the remaining essays, which he later revised and reprinted in *The Present State of Europe* . . . (London, 1750); see *Notes and Queries*, CLXI (Oct. 3, 1931), 251; CLXII (Jan. 16, 1932), 47; plus the contents of Campbell's book, which went through numerous editions.

6.

The Mutual Connexion between Religious / Truth and Civil Freedom; / Between Superstition, Tyranny, Irreligion, / and Licentiousness: / CONSIDERED IN / Two SERMONS / Preached in *Septemb.* 1746, / AT THE / Cathedral Church of CARLISLE, / During the ASSIZES held there for the / Trial of the REBELS. / [rule] / *By* JOHN BROWN, *M.A.* / [rule] / [ornament] / *LONDON:* / Printed for R. DODSLEY at *Tully*'s Head in / *Pall-mall*; and sold by M. COOPER in *Pater- / noster Row.* / (Price One Shilling.)

Collation: 4°: A^4 B–F^4

Contents: Page *i* title, *ii* blank, *iii*–iv Dedication to Sir George Fleming, Lord Bishop of Carlisle, *5* 6–26 text of first sermon, *27* 28–48 text of second sermon.

Press figures: 16-2, 21-2, 34-2, 45-2.

Number of copies printed: Probably 250 copies were printed at

Brown's expense. (See Brown's letters to Robert Dodsley in note four, below.)

Size of an uncut copy: $8\frac{5}{8}''$ × $6\frac{5}{8}''$ (Cambridge University Library copy).

Date of publication: January 8, 1747 (*Daily Advertiser; General Advertiser*).

Copies: *British Museum; *Cambridge University Library.

Notes:

1. The text for both sermons is "JOHN, Chap. viii. Ver. 32. *Ye shall know the Truth, and the Truth shall make you free.*"

2. These two sermons are reprinted in Brown's *Sermons on Various Subjects* (1764), pages 67–118.

3. The first sermon only is reprinted, in 12°, in abridged form, in:
THE / ENGLISH PREACHER: / OR, / SERMONS / ON THE PRINCIPAL SUBJECTS OF / RELIGION AND MORALITY, / SELECTED, REVISED, AND ABRIDGED FROM / VARIOUS AUTHORS. / VOLUME THE NINTH. / CONTAINING OCCASIONAL SERMONS. / LONDON: / PRINTED FOR J. JOHNSON, ST. PAUL'S CHURCH-YARD. / MDCCLXXIV.
Brown's sermon is No. VI, pages *113* 114–128.
Copies: *British Museum.

4. Parts of two letters from John Brown to Robert Dodsley —quoted, with permission, from Bodleian MS. Toynbee d.19—give the background of the printing history of these two sermons.

> Carlisle Oct: 27th 1746.
>
> . . . I have some thoughts of printing two Sermons, which I preached in the Cathedral during the rebel Assizes here. The Subject is the mutual Connection between religious Truth & civil Freedom, between Tyranny Superstition, Irreligion, & Licentiousness. They are but short Discourses, & may together be decently extended to about forty Pages, tho' they may be included

I think in thirty. My only Motive of printing them, is to do a little Justice to my Character as a Clergyman, as I know it hath been objected to me, that I should publish Verses, rather than things belonging to my own Profession. As I am very sensible that Sermons above all other things are a mere Drug, I cannot propose printing these in any other Method than at my own Expence: Tho' if you think the Copy when you see it can be of any Use to you, it is very much at your Service: But as I do not think there is any probability of this, the principal thing I want to be informed of is the Expence that will attend printing 2, 3, 4, or 5, hundred Copies. They are not both larger than many single Sermons that appear; but as I hate to multiply words without Reason, I cannot think of enlarging them much. I would desire therefore to know what will be the Expence of printing them as a twelve-penny Pamphlet in Quarto: 2dly what will be the Expence of doing it in a smaller Number of Pages as a sixpenny Pamphlet in the same Size: 3dly what will be the Expence of including them both in one sixpenny Octavo. I would not by any means have them on bad Paper, wch disgraces every thing; a very large margin I should chuse. Please to answer these several particulars as soon as may be; & I shall be preparing a portable Copy in the mean time.

If there is any thing extraordinary likely to appear this Winter in the literary way, I should be glad to hear of it. I am a very lazy Writer, & you are the only Intelligencer I have in town. I am

Sr Your most humble Servt
J: Brown

Carlisle Nov: 8th [1746]

Sr

I received yours, but have not yet had Time to transcribe the Sermons. I would indeed chuse to have them printed as a 12 penny Pamphlet; but I think 7 Pounds is very high for 250 Copies: I am told by a Gentleman pretty well versed in these Affairs, that 4 or 500 Copies may be had, with a good Letter & Paper (especially

> where there is but little Work in a Page) for one Guinea per Sheet: which in this Case, reckoning 40 Pages, would amount to five Guineas, for 4 or 500: there is a very material Difference between this Calculation and yours. You will excuse the Freedom of a Conjecture: I imagine you are accustomed to a greater Profit in printing Poetical Affairs, than those Booksellers have who only deal in plain Prose: If so, I think you must either come down to the Profit of a Sermon Printer, or else I must beg the favour of you to direct me to such a one for this time: But as to any certainty in these particulars, I refer myself entirely to your answer. In short all I want is to have the Sermons handsomely done, & to avoid Expence as far as may be consistent with this. . . .

Brown adds in a footnote: "I propose to be in London in January: & if you think that would be as proper a time for publishing these Sermons, I should be almost induced to let them rest till that time."

The sermons were printed according to Brown's wishes—a twelvepenny quarto pamphlet with wide margins—and were published January 8, 1747.

7.

ON / LIBERTY: [red] / A / POEM, / Inscribed to his Grace the / CHANCELLOR [red] / And to the / University of Cambridge, / On occasion of the / PEACE. [red] / [rule] / By *JOHN BROWN*, M.A. / [rule] / [quotation] / [rule] / *LONDON*, [red] / Printed for C. Davis against *Grey's-Inn* Gate *Holbourn.* / and sold by M. Cooper in *Pater-noster-Row.* / [rule] / MDCCXLIX. [red]

Half-title: ON / LIBERTY: / A / POEM. / [Price Sixpence.]

Collation: 4°: *A*^{4} B^4

Contents: Page *1* half-title, *2* blank, *3* title, *4* blank, *5* 6–16 text of the poem.

Press figures: none.

Size of an uncut copy: 8½″ × 6½″ (University of Toronto copy).

Number of copies printed: William Bowyer printed 750 copies, the first of which were delivered on April 7, 1749 (Grolier Club Ledger 19474, folio 70a).

Date of publication: April 26, 1749 (*Daily Advertiser; Public Advertiser; London Evening-Post*, April 25–27; *Whitehall Evening-Post*, April 25–27).

Copies: *Boston Public Library; *British Museum (2 copies); Cambridge University Library; Harvard; Texas; *University of Toronto.

8.

On the Pursuit of FALSE PLEASURE, *and the* / *Mischiefs of* IMMODERATE GAMING: / [rule] / A / SERMON / Preach'd at the / Abbey-Church at *Bath*, / For Promoting the / CHARITY and SUBSCRIPTION / TOWARDS THE / GENERAL HOSPITAL / In that CITY, / On *SUNDAY*, *April* 22, 1750. / [rule] / Publish'd at the Request of the / GOVERNORS *of the said* HOSPITAL. / [rule] / *By* JOHN BROWN, *M.A.* / [rule] / *BATH:* / Printed for JAMES LEAKE; / And sold by C. HITCH, Bookseller, in LONDON. 1750. / [Price *Six-Pence.*]

Collation: 8° (in 4's): *A*² B–D⁴

Contents: *A*1ʳ title, *A*1ᵛ blank, *A*2ʳ Dedication to the Duke of Bedford, *A*2ᵛ blank, pages *1* 2–21 text of sermon, *22–24* blank.

Press figures: none.

Date of publication: May 11, 1750 (*General Advertiser*, May 11, 1750).

Copies: *Bodleian; *British Museum (2 copies); *General Theological Seminary, New York; *Harvard; *New York Public Library; Northwestern University.

9. *The Second Edition (1752)*

On the Pursuit of FALSE PLEASURE, *and the* / *Mischiefs of* IMMODERATE GAMING: / [rule] / A / SERMON / Preach'd at the / Abbey-Church at Bath, / For Promoting the / Charity and Subscription / TOWARDS THE / GENERAL HOSPITAL / In that CITY, / On *SUNDAY, April* 22, 1750. / [rule] / Publish'd at the Request of the / GOVERNORS *of the said* HOSPITAL. / [rule] / *By* JOHN BROWN, *M.A.* / Chaplain to the Right Reverend the Lord / Bishop of *Carlisle.* / [rule] / The SECOND EDITION. / [rule] / LONDON, / Printed for W. BOWYER; / And sold by C. DAVIS against *Gray's Inn Gate, Holbourn*; / and M. COOPER in *Pater-noster-row.* / MDCCLII. / [Price Six-Pence.]

Collation: 8° (in 4's): A^2 B–D^4

*Contents: A*1^r title, *A*1^v blank, *A*2^r Dedication to the Duke of Bedford, *A*2^v blank, pages 1–23 text of sermon, *24* list of "*BOOKS Printed for* C. DAVIS *and* W. BOWYER."

Press figures: 6-1, 14-1, 21-1.

Number of copies printed: William Bowyer printed 500 copies, half of which were delivered to Mrs. Cooper April 30, 1752 (Bodleian MS. DON b.4, folio 129). The same entry records that on May 1, 1752, single copies were sent to the Bishops of Canterbury, Carlisle, Norwich, Litchfield, Worcester, Bangor, Peterborough, and Chester; on the following day copies were sent to Mr. Jortin, A. Bower, Esq., the Hon. Mr. Charles Yorke, Mr. Warburton, Mr. Alton, and Mr. Garrick.

The sermon did not sell rapidly. Although Mrs. Cooper took 250 copies on April 30, 1752, she returned 100 of them Nov. 13. Bowyer noted that of these returned copies, "19 of them was very dirty" (Bodleian MS. DON b.4, folio 134). Five years later, a few weeks after the *Estimate* was published, the booksellers tried to sell some remaining copies of this sermon. On April 30, 1757 Bowyer sent 25 copies to Mrs. Cooper and 25 to Mr. Baldwin (folio 150). Bowyer's ledgers do not mention the sermon again.

Copies: *Bodleian; *British Museum; Northwestern University; *Sion College Library (B.10.34).

I wish to thank Mr. Richard D. Olson, Curator of Rare Books, for describing the Northwestern University copy for me.

Note:

This sermon is reprinted in Brown's *Sermons on Various Subjects*, 1764, pp. 259–288 (see below).

10.

ESSAYS [red] / ON THE / CHARACTERISTICS. [red] / BY / JOHN BROWN, M.A. [red] / [cut] / LONDON, [red] / Printed for C. DAVIS against *Gray's-Inn-Gate, Holborn.* / [rule] / MDCCLI. [red]

Half-title: ESSAYS / ON THE / CHARACTERISTICS / OF THE / Earl of SHAFTESBURY. / I. On RIDICULE considered as a Test / of Truth. / II. On the Obligations of Man to Virtue, and / the Necessity of *religious Principle.* / III. On *revealed* RELIGION, and CHRISTI- / ANITY.

Collation: 8°: A^4 a^2 B–S^8 *T1 T–$2C^8$ $2D^4$(–2D4). R3 missigned R4.

Contents: *A*1^r title, *A*1^v blank, *A*2^r half-title, *A*2^v blank, pages *i* ii–iii Dedication to Ralph Allen, *iv* blank, *v* vi–viii Contents, *1* 2–107 text of Essay I, *108* blank, 109–239 text of Essay II, *240* blank, 241–272 [271][272] 273–406 text of Essay III. *T1 is numbered [271] and [272].

Press figures: 2-1, 18-1, 40-1, 54-1, 68-1, 82-1, 98-1, 100-5, 122-1, 125-5, 144-4, 148-4, 155-1, 172-1, 186-1, 202-4, 210-1, 224-5, 228-1, 251-4, 253-5, 258-1, 268-4, 276-1, 287-5, 301-1, 338-3, 360-4, 367-1, 372-4, 374-3, 386-3, 397-1, 404-3 or none.

Number of copies printed: William Bowyer printed 750 copies, the first of which were delivered to Davis April 12, 1751 (Bodleian MS. DON b.4, folio 129).

Bowyer's printing ledger contains this entry:

> Mr. Browne's Essays 26 sh & $\frac{1}{4}$ & Title red equal to 27 sh N° 750 at 16:6 with Notes
>
> [£] 22/5/6

This amount was marked "recd in full" December 18, 1751 (Grolier Club Ledger 19474, folio 70a).

Date of publication: April 18, 1751 (*General Evening Post*, April 16–18; *London Evening-Post*, April 16–18; *Whitehall Evening Post*, April 16–18). Advertisements: "On Thursday the 18th of April will be publish'd . . ." (*General Evening Post*, April 6–9, 9–11, and 11–13; *Whitehall Evening Post*, April 6–9, 9–11, and 11–13); "On Thursday next will be published . . ." (*London Evening-Post*, Sat. April 13–Tues. April 16); "This Day is published . . . Price bound 5 s. . . . Printed for C. Davis, opposite Gray's Inn Gate, Holborn; L. Davis, at Lord Bacon's Head, Fleet-street; W. Thurlbourne, at Cambridge; and J. Fletcher, at Oxford" (*General Evening Post*, April 16–18; *London Evening-Post*, April 16–18; *Whitehall Evening Post*, April 16–18).

The *London Advertiser; and, Literary Gazette* prints the "This Day is published" notice in its issue of Wednesday, April 17, but presumably this is a premature publication of the advertisement.

Copies: *Bodleian (2 copies); *British Museum; *Bryn Mawr College; *Library of Congress; *Cornell; Duke; *Harvard; University of Kentucky; *Lambeth Palace Library (copy of Thomas Secker, Archbishop of Canterbury); *Library Company of Philadelphia; National Library of Ireland; National Library of Scotland; *New York Public Library; Princeton (2 copies); *University of Rochester; Texas; Yale; *D. D. Eddy (2 copies).

Notes:

1. Page 109 exists in two states: the first is misnumbered 108 (copies: Bodleian [2 copies]; British Museum; Bryn

Mawr College; Library of Congress; Cornell; Harvard; Lambeth Palace Library; Library Company of Philadelphia; University of Rochester; Yale; D. D. Eddy); the second is correctly numbered (copies: New York Public Library; D. D. Eddy).

2. Page 112 exists in two states: the first is misnumbered 190 (copies: Bodleian [2 copies]; British Museum; Bryn Mawr College; Library of Congress; Cornell; Harvard; Lambeth Palace Library; Library Company of Philadelphia; University of Rochester; Yale; D. D. Eddy); the second is correctly numbered (copies: New York Public Library; D. D. Eddy).

3. The half-title is usually bound following the title, but it is also found elsewhere. In one copy it is even bound after the a gathering—that is, immediately preceding the first page of text. Apparently these are binding variants with no bibliographical significance.

4. Two errata are listed on the bottom of page 406. These are corrected in the second and subsequent editions.

5. The vignette on the title-page is by N. Blakey, engraved by C. Grignion. The titulus is a fragment from Aristotle's *Rhetoric* (III. xviii. 1419b3) which Brown quotes and translates on page 43 of the *Essays*. Brown is saying that he intends to confound the raillery (or ridicule) of his adversaries by serious arguments. The figure is a trophy of Pallas Athena (Wisdom militant), standing triumphant over symbols of crude forms of satire and comedy—a fool's cap, a dunce's cap, and so on.

All the editions of this book, including the Dublin duodecimos (1752), use this vignette (or close copies of it) on their title-pages.

6. Only in this first edition is the third line of the title-page, CHARACTERISTICS., printed in red; in all subsequent editions it is printed in black.

7. No edition of this book prints the number of the edition on the title-page. The second through fifth editions are numbered on the last line of the half-title.

11. *The Second Edition (1751)*

ESSAYS [red] / ON THE / CHARACTERISTICS. / BY / JOHN BROWN, M.A. [red] / [cut] / LONDON, [red] / Printed for C. DAVIS, against *Gray's-Inn-Gate, Holborn,* / [rule] / MDCCLI. [red]

Half-title: ESSAYS / ON THE / CHARACTERISTICS / OF THE / Earl of SHAFTESBURY. / I. On RIDICULE considered as a Test / of Truth. / II. On the Motives to VIRTUE, and the Ne- / cessity of *Religious Principle.* / III. On *Revealed* RELIGION, and CHRISTI- / ANITY. / [rule] / THE SECOND EDITION. / [rule]

Collation: 8°: A^4 a^2 B–H^8($\pm$H7,8) I–2C^8 2D^4

Contents: *A*1^r^ title, *A*1^v^ blank, *A*2^r^ half-title: THE SECOND EDITION, *A*2^v^ blank, pages *i* ii–iii Dedication to Ralph Allen, *iv* blank, *v* vi–viii Contents, *1* 2–107 text of Essay I, *108* blank, 109–239 text of Essay II, *240* blank, 241–408 text of Essay III. Page 378 misnumbered 278.

Press figures: 8-1, 22-4, 42-1 or none, 50-1, 70-3, 84-1, 86-1, 102-1, 126-4, 140-5, 146-1, 168-1, 190-1, 198-1, 212-5, 228-4, 238-3, 248-1, 272-1, 284-1, 297-1, 316-1, 322-5, 342-4, 356-5, 367-1, 382-4, 390-4, 396-1, 407-1.

Number of copies printed: William Bowyer printed 1,000 copies, the first of which were delivered to Davis September 11, 1751 (Bodleian MS. DON b.4, folio 129).

Bowyer's printing ledgers contain this entry directly beneath the entry for the first edition:

> D° reprinted with a ¼ cancelled 26 sh & ½ No. 1000 equal to 27 sheets at 19^s^ (2d Edition)
>
> [£] 25/13/—

This amount was marked "recd in full" February 25, [1752] (Grolier Club Ledger 19474, folio 70a).

Date of publication: September 16, 1751 (*Daily Advertiser*; *General Evening Post,* Sept. 14–17; *London Evening Post,* Sept.

14–17). Each of these newspapers advertises, "This Day was published, The Second Edition, corrected. . . ."

Copies: National Library of Australia; *Columbia; *Cornell (2 copies); Duke; *Harvard; Huntington Library; *Illinois; Indiana; *Newberry Library; *New-York Historical Society; Victoria and Albert (Forster Collection); *D. D. Eddy (2 copies).

Notes:

1. As the quotation from Bowyer's printing ledger indicates, in this second edition a quarter of a sheet was cancelled; these are leaves H7, 8. Presumably, therefore, H7, 8 exist in three states:

a. The original, uncancelled state containing the offending readings. No copy seen.

These leaves contain the first four pages of Essay II, which was revised—including a change of title—in the second edition. I suspect that at this point the compositor probably was setting type from an uncorrected copy of the first edition, and that a few copies of the incorrect second edition were printed before the error was caught. These two leaves were then cancelled.

b. H7, 8 with the corrected text are cancels, inserted on stubs. H7 and H8 are conjugate, with $H7^r$ signed. Copy: D. D. Eddy copy, with H7, 8 loosely inserted, not pasted on the stubs.

c. H7, 8 with the corrected text are not cancels, although $H7^r$ is still signed. After the error was caught and the cancels were printed, the type pages from the cancels were placed in the formes of the H gathering and normal printing of the impression was resumed. Copies: probably all copies examined, except for one D. D. Eddy copy, although in some copies it is difficult to determine cancellation.

2. In this and subsequent editions, the title of the second essay is changed. Certainly "the Motives to Virtue" sounds more persuasive and less authoritarian than "the Obligations of Man to Virtue." Corresponding changes are made in the

text of the second essay. For example, on page 110 of the first edition Brown mentions "that highest and most interesting of all Subjects, *The Obligations of Man to the Practice of Virtue.*" In the second edition the italicized words become "*The Motives to virtuous Action.*"

An examination of the second edition shows many additional substantive, authorial revisions in all three essays. (See the discussion of the text, below.)

3. This second edition text has been reprinted in facsimile by Georg Olms (Hildesheim and New York, 1969).

12. *The Third Edition (1752)*

ESSAYS [red] / ON THE / CHARACTERISTICS. / BY / JOHN BROWN, M.A. [red] / Chaplain to the Right Reverend the Lord / Bishop of CARLISLE. / [cut] / LONDON, [red] / Printed for C. DAVIS, against *Gray's-Inn-Gate, Holborn.* / MDCCLII. [red]

Collation: 8°: A^2 a^4 B–$2C^8$ $2D^4$

Contents: $A1^r$ title, $A1^v$ blank, $A2^r$ half-title: THE THIRD EDITION, $A2^v$ blank, or a list of 19 errata, pages *i* ii–iii Dedication to Ralph Allen, *iv* blank, *v* vi–viii Contents, *1* 2–107 text, *108* blank, 109–239 text, *240* blank, 241–408 text. Page 223 misnumbered 232, and 340 misnumbered 330.

Press figures: 2-1, 4-4, 31-1, 48-1, 64-1, 77-1, 79-3, 82-1, 112-1, 127-3, 140-1, 142-3, 146-4, 157-1, 162-4, 190-1, 208-1, 210-1, 256-1, 272-3, 274-1, 290-3 or none, 317-1, 319-4 or none, 345-4, 377-4, 382-1, 400-1.

Number of copies printed: William Bowyer printed 1,000 copies, the first of which were delivered to Davis June 27, 1752 (Bodleian MS. DON b.4, folio 129).

Bowyer's printing ledgers contain this entry:

> [1752] June 27 Brown's Essays 3^d Edit. 26 shts & $\frac{1}{4}$ N° 1000 at 18^s ($\frac{1}{4}$ sh 5^s)
>
> [£] 23:13:—

On April 20, 1753 Bowyer "recd on acct." £20 for this third edition (Grolier Club Ledger 19474, folios 115 and 70a).

Copies: *British Museum; *Cambridge University Library; *Columbia; *Cornell; *Folger Library; Georgetown University Library; *Harvard (3 copies); Huntington Library; *Illinois; *Indiana (Lilly); *Library Company of Philadelphia; *University of Pennsylvania; Princeton; *D. D. Eddy (2 copies).

Notes:

1. The title and half-title (A^2) are conjugate. The preliminary leaves (a^4) are usually bound after A^2, but in some copies (e.g., the three at Harvard and the one at Cornell) the four leaves of the a gathering are inserted between the title and half-title. This is a binding variant without bibliographical significance.

2. In this third edition there are two states of the half-title. In the first the verso of the half-title is blank (copies: one D. D. Eddy copy); in the second a list of nineteen errata is printed on the verso of the half-title (copies: those listed above, except one D. D. Eddy copy; I am indebted to the librarians who examined copies inaccessible to me). However, in the copy of the Library Company of Philadelphia, the half-title does not have the list of errata printed on the verso; instead, a printed list from another copy has been pasted in.

3. The third edition is a rather inaccurate reprint of the second. Of the nineteen errata listed on the verso of the half-title, all the items except the ninth restore the text of the second edition. The third item on the list is in error: for p. 125 line 25 read p. 120 line 25.

13. *The Fourth Edition (1755)*

ESSAYS [red] / ON THE / CHARACTERISTICS. / BY / JOHN BROWN, D.D. [red] / Chaplain to the Right Reverend the Lord / Bishop of CARLISLE. / [cut] / LONDON, [red] / Printed for C. DAVIS, against *Gray's-Inn-Gate, Holborn.* / MDCCLV. [red]

Collation and press figures: Exactly the same as the third edition.

Contents: $A1^r$ title, $A1^v$ blank, $A2^r$ half-title: THE FOURTH EDITION, $A2^v$ blank, pages *i* ii–iii Dedication to Ralph Allen, *iv* blank, *v* vi–viii Contents, *1* 2–107 text, *108* blank, 109–239 text, *240* blank, 241–408 text. Page 223 misnumbered 232, and 340 misnumbered 330.

Date of publication: January 31, 1755 (*Daily Advertiser*).

Copies: *Library Company of Philadelphia; *Union Theological Seminary, New York; Texas (2 copies); *Yale.

Notes:

1. This "fourth edition" has a new title-page and half-title, but otherwise it is a reissue of the sheets of the third edition. The records of both William Bowyer and James Emonson show that in 1754, possibly on Nov. 9(?), Bowyer's shop printed for Davis "Titles to Brown's Characteristics 1/4 Sht Red & Bl. —/10/6" (Bodleian MS. Eng. misc. c.141, folios 98 and 174).

2. The third edition has an errata list on the verso of the half-title; and although none of these changes are incorporated in the sheets of the "fourth edition," no list of errata is provided.

14. *The Fifth Edition (1764)*

ESSAYS [red] / ON THE / CHARACTERISTICS. / BY / JOHN BROWN, D.D. [red] / Vicar of NEWCASTLE. / [cut] / LONDON, [red] / Printed for L. DAVIS and C. REYMERS, against / *Gray's-Inn-Gate, Holborn,* / Printers to the Royal Society. / MDCCLXIV. [red]

Collation: 8°: A^2 a^4 B–$2C^8$ $2D^4$

Contents: $A1^r$ title, $A1^v$ blank, $A2^r$ half-title: THE FIFTH EDITION, $A2^v$ blank, pages *i* ii–iii Dedication to Ralph Allen, *iv* blank, *v* vi–viii Contents, *1* 2–107 text, *108* blank, 109–239 text, *240* blank, 241–408 text. Page 349 misnumbered 351, and 352 misnumbered 354.

Press figures: 9-4, 14-1, 32-4, 34-2, 54-4, 75-2, 88-4, 105-4, 110-1, 127-4, 140-4, 154-4, 176-1, 192-1, 203-1, 222-1, 238-4, 255-4, 258-4, 278-4, 290-1, 314-1, 322-1, 324-2, 347-2, 349 (misnumbered 351)-1, 358-1, 379-4, 395-2, 400-1, 406-1.

Number of copies printed: William Bowyer printed 500 copies, the first of which were delivered to Davis April 25, 1764 (Bodleian MS. DON b.4, folio 160).

Copies: Bibliothèque Nationale; *British Museum; Brooklyn Public Library; University of Chicago; *Cornell; *Dartmouth; *Harvard (Andover-Harvard Theological Library); *Illinois; Pembroke College, Cambridge; Princeton; Stanford; University of Toronto; *Yale; *D. D. Eddy.

Note:

Once again, the position of the half-title varies in different copies, although presumably it belongs immediately after the title-page. In the British Museum, Illinois, Princeton, and University of Toronto copies, it is bound immediately preceding the title; in the Yale copy, it is the last preliminary leaf and is bound immediately preceding the first page of text. I assume that these are binding variants with no bibliographical significance.

The Printing

William Bowyer's ledgers show that he was the printer of the five London editions published during John Brown's lifetime (Bodleian MS. DON b.4, folios 129 and 160). Charles Davis was the publisher of the first four of these editions. After Davis' death on August 31, 1755, he was succeeded in business by his nephew Lockyer Davis, who was in partnership with Charles Reymers. Bowyer and the Davises were responsible for printing and publishing almost all of the works John Brown wrote during the last fifteen years of his life (1751–66).

When a printer produces five editions of a work, one expects to see some bibliographical similarities among them. In examining books printed in this period, one often finds

Essays on the Characteristics
Press figures in the five London editions, 1751–64

	1		2		3		4		5	
Sig.	(i)	(o)	(i)	(o)	(i)	(o)	(i)	(o)	(i)	(o)
A	—	—	—	—	—	—	Same as		—	—
a	—	—	—	—	—	—	the third		—	—
B	1 [1v]	—	—	1 [4v]	1 [1v]	4 [2v]	edition. It		1 [7v]	4 [5r]
C	1 [1v]	—	4 [3v]	—	1 [8r]	—	is a reissue		—	4 [8v]
D	—	1 [4v]	1 [5v]	—	—	1 [8v]	of third		2 [1v]	—
E	1 [3v]	—	1 [1v]	—	—	1 [8v]	edition		4 [3v]	—
F	—	1 [2v]	3 [3v]	—	3 [8r]	1 [7r]	sheets,		2 [6r]	—
G	1 [1v]	—	1 [3v]	1 [2v]	1 [1v]	—	with a		—	4 [4v]
H	1 [1v]	5 [2v]	1 [3v]	—	—	1 [8v]	new title		1 [7v]	4 [5r]
I	1 [5v]	5 [7r]	4 [7v]	—	3 [8r]	—	and half-		4 [8r]	—
K	—	4 [8v]	—	5 [6v]	3 [7v]	1 [6v]	title.		—	4 [6v]
L	1 [6r]	4 [2v]	1 [1v]	—	4 [1v]	1 [7r]			4 [5v]	—
M	—	1 [6v]	—	1 [4v]	4 [1v]	—			—	1 [8v]
N	1 [5v]	—	1 [7v]	—	1 [7v]	—			—	1 [8v]
O	4 [5v]	—	1 [3v]	—	—	1 [8v]			1 [6r]	—
P	1 [1v]	5 [8v]	—	5 [2v]	1 [1v]	—			1 [7v]	—
Q	—	1 [2v]	3 [7v]	4 [2v]	—	—			4 [7v]	—
R	4 [6r]	5 [7r]	—	1 [4v]	—	1 [8v]			4 [8r]	—
S	1 [1v]	4 [6v]	—	1 [8v]	—	3 [8v]			4 [1v]	—
T	5 [8r]	1 [2v]	—	1 [6v]	1 [1v]	—			4 [3v]	—
U	—	1 [7r]	—	1 [5r]	3 [1v]	—			1 [1v]	—
X	—	—	—	1 [6v]	4 [8r]	1 [7r]			1 [5v]	—
Y	—	—	5 [1v]	—	—	—			1 [1v]	2 [2v]
Z	3 [1v]	—	4 [3v]	—	—	4 [5r]			2 [6r]	1 [7r]
2A	1 [8r]	4 [4v]	1 [8r]	5 [2v]	—	—			1 [3v]	—
2B	3 [3v]	4 [2v]	4 [7v]	—	1 [7v]	4 [5r]			4 [6r]	—
2C	3 [1v]	1 [7r]	4 [3v]	1 [6v]	—	1 [8v]			2 [6r]	1 [8v]
2D	—	3 [2v]	1 [4r]	—	—	—			1 [3v]	—

See G. Thomas Tanselle, "The Recording of Press Figures," *The Library*, XXI, no. 4 (December, 1966), 318–325.

recurrent printing from standing type, several impressions of a single edition, and the bindery's mixing sheets from different impressions and editions. Certainly one has such points in mind when he comes to examine Bowyer's editions of the *Essays*.

The fourth edition has no bibliographical distinction, since it is merely a reissue of third edition sheets, with a new title and half-title.

The fifth edition was printed a dozen years after the third, so it is not surprising that in its printing it bears no relationship to the earlier editions.

The first three editions, however, were printed within a period of fourteen months. Not unexpectedly, they have some press figures in common: the first and second editions have 367-1 in the 2A gathering; the second and third editions have 190-1 in the N gathering; and the first and third editions have 2-1, 82-1, and 210-1 in the B, G, and P gatherings. Strangely enough, a collation of these gatherings shows a completely different setting of type in both the inner and outer formes of each of the gatherings that one would expect to be identical. Evidently Bowyer's pressmen often tended to put their figures in the same position, especially on 1 and 3 verso (inner forme) and 2 and 8 verso (outer forme). In this case such habits have misled our bibliographical expectations, for the identical press figures have no significance in the printing of the first three editions of this book.

Brown revised his text before the printing of the second edition, changing quite a few passages and adding footnotes. To cite just a few examples, he adds new material: page 78 contains four lines of text not in the first edition; and footnotes d (pp. 169–170), k (p. 362), g (p. 381), and q (pp. 384–385) are all new in the second edition. He deletes material: for example, page 381 of the second edition deletes six lines from the first edition. He revises much of his text: he changes the title of the second essay and corresponding passages in the text; he drastically alters the first sentence on page 11; and so on. He often eliminates verbal infelicities: for example, on page 129 of the first edition, Brown says that Truth can produce "a Stream of genuine Lustre, which the most obdurate Prejudice can only withstand by winking hard." The second edition reads: ". . . which the most obdurate Prejudice can hardly withstand." Or, on page 147 of the first edition, a sentence begins: "The first Principle he lays down, or rather takes up, *i.e.* for granted, is . . . ." The second edition merely says "takes for granted."

The third edition is a rather careless reprint of the text of the second. Collation indicates widespread resetting of type. The list of errata in the third edition makes one change in the revised text of the second edition: page 230, line 28: for *anticipated* read *anticipating*. This restores the reading to that of the first edition.

15. *The First Dublin Edition (1752)*

ESSAYS / ON THE / CHARACTERISTICS. / BY / JOHN BROWN, M.A. / [cut] / *DUBLIN:* / Printed by GEORGE FAULKNER in *Essex-street.* / [rule] / MDCCLII.

Collation: 12°: *A* (three leaves) a^2 B–M^{12} N^6

Contents: *A*1^r title, *A*1^v blank, *A*2^r half-title, *A*2^v blank, pages *i*–ii Dedication to Ralph Allen, *v* vi–viii Contents, *1* 2–72 text of Essay I, *73* 74–161 text of Essay II, *162* 163–276 text of Essay III.

Press figures: none.

Copies: *Bodleian; *Cambridge University Library; *Cornell; *D. D. Eddy (2 copies).

Notes:

1. This Dublin edition is a reprint of the accurately printed first London edition. William Bowyer sent one copy of the first edition to Dublin (Bodleian MS. DON b.4, folio 129).

2. The contents listed above are those of the Cambridge University Library copy. In the Bodleian and Cornell copies and in the first D. D. Eddy copy, the half-title is bound before

the title; in the second D. D. Eddy copy, the two leaves of contents (a^2) are bound immediately after the title. Possibly the order of binding should have been: title, pages *i*–ii Dedication, *iii–iv* half-title, *v* vi–viii Contents, *1* 2–276 text.

16. *The Second Dublin Edition (1752)*

ESSAYS / ON THE / CHARACTERISTICS. / BY / JOHN BROWN, M.A. / [cut] / DUBLIN: / Printed by GEORGE FAULKNER, in Essex-street. / MDCCLII.

Collation: 12°: *A* (three leaves) a^2 B–M^{12} N^6

Contents: *A*1^r title, *A*1^v blank, *A*2^r half-title, *A*2^v blank, pages *i*–ii Dedication, *v* vi–viii Contents, *1* 2–72 text of Essay I, *73* 74–161 text of Essay II, *162* 163–276 text of Essay III.

Press figures: none.

Copies: National Library of Ireland (2 copies); *New York Public Library; Texas.

Notes:

1. This second Dublin edition appears to be a hasty reprint of the first; it contains numerous compositorial errors not found in the first edition. Spot collation indicates that the second is a different setting of type from the first: many of the pages show different lineation of the text, the ornaments used on page one are different, and so on. The easiest way to differentiate the two editions is by the distinctive differences in their title-pages.

2. Once again it is possible that the order of binding should have been: title, pages *i*–ii Dedication, *iii–iv* half-title, *v* vi–viii Contents, *1* 2–276 text.

17.

On the USE *and* ABUSE *of* EXTERNALS / *in* RELIGION. / [rule] / A / SERMON. / [rule] / *By* JOHN BROWN, *M.A.* / *Chaplain to the Right Rev. the Lord Bishop of* CARLISLE. / [rule] /

ESSAYS

ON THE

CHARACTERISTICS.

BY

JOHN BROWN, M. A.

Τον δε γελωτα, Σπουδη

DUBLIN:

Printed by GEORGE FAULKNER in *Essex-street*,

MDCCLII.

D. D. EDDY

I. Title-page of no. 15

Size of page: $6\frac{3}{4}'' \times 3\frac{3}{4}''$

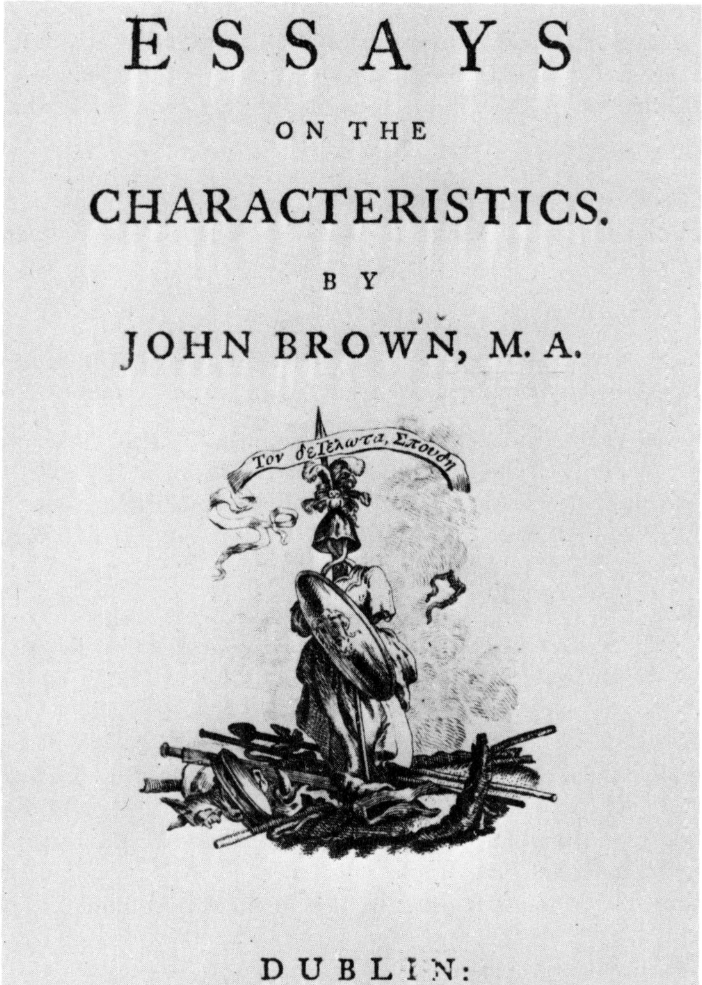

ESSAYS

ON THE

CHARACTERISTICS.

BY

JOHN BROWN, M. A.

DUBLIN:

Printed by GEORGE FAULKNER, in Essex-street.

MDCCLII.

NEW YORK PUBLIC LIBRARY

II. Title-page of no. 16

Size of page: $6\frac{10}{16}'' \times 3\frac{11}{16}''$

PREACHED AT THE / CONSECRATION / OF / *St* JAMES'*s Church in* WHITEHAVEN, / BY THE RIGHT REVEREND / *The* LORD BISHOP *of* CARLISLE. / [double rule] / Printed for C. DAVIS in HOLBORN. 1753. / Price SIX-PENCE.

Collation: 8° (in 4's): π^4($-\pi$4 [= D1 ?]) A–C^4 D1(= π4?)

Contents: $\pi 1^r$ half-title, $\pi 1^v$ blank, $\pi 2^r$ title, $\pi 2^v$ blank, $\pi 3^r$ Dedication to Sir James Lowther, $\pi 3^v$ blank, pages *1* 2–26 text.

Press figures: none.

Size of an uncut copy: 9″ × 5¾″ (Cambridge University Library copy, unbound, stitched, and partially unopened).

Copies: *Bodleian; *Boston Athenaeum; *British Museum (2 copies); *Cambridge University Library; *General Theological Seminary, New York; *Lambeth Palace Library; *Newberry Library; Northwestern University; *Sion College Library (B.10.34); *Yale.

Note:

This sermon is reprinted, in handsome large octavo format, in: THE / FAMILY CHAPLAIN: / BEING A COMPLETE / COURSE OF SERMONS / UPON THE / FESTIVALS AND FASTS / (THROUGHOUT THE YEAR) / AS PRESCRIBED IN / THE BOOK OF COMMON-PRAYER. / . . . [etc.] . . . IN TWO VOLUMES . . . [etc.] . . . LONDON, / Printed for L. DAVIS, in Holborn; and R. BALDWIN, / in Pater-Noster Row. 1775.

Brown's sermon is the first sermon in the first volume, pages 1–18.

Copies: *British Museum.

18.

AN / ACCOUNT / OF / *BARBAROSSA*, / The USURPER of *ALGIERS*. / BEING THE / STORY / On which the / NEW TRAGEDY, / Now in Rehearsal at the / Theatre Royal in

Drury-Lane, / Is FOUNDED. / [rule] / [quotation] / [double rule] / *LONDON:* / Printed and sold by W. REEVE, in *Fleet-Street.* / [double rule] / M.DCC.LV.

Half-title: [row of type ornaments] / THE / STORY / OF THE / NEW TRAGEDY, / CALL'D, / *BARBAROSSA,* / The USURPER of *ALGIERS.* / [row of type ornaments] / [Price Six-pence.]

Collation: 8° (in 4's): A^2 B–C^4

Contents: Page *1* half-title, *2* blank, *3* title, *4* blank, *5* 6–19 text, *20* blank.

Press figures: none.

Date of publication: December 9, 1754 (*Daily Advertiser*; *Public Advertiser*). Price 6d.

Copies: *British Museum 11778.f.8 (lacks half-title); *Folger Library.

Note:

This pamphlet was reviewed briefly in the *Monthly Review,* XI (Dec., 1754), 467. The reviewer states accurately that "the particulars here related concerning *Barbarossa,* are purloined from a book" entitled *A Compleat History of the Piratical States of Barbary* . . . London: Printed for R. Griffiths, 1750. (Copy: *British Museum 9061.ccc.2.)

19.

BARBAROSSA. / A / TRAGEDY. / As it is Perform'd at the / Theatre-Royal in *Drury-Lane.* / [rule] / [ornament] / [double rule] / *LONDON:* / Printed for J. and R. TONSON and S. DRAPER in the *Strand.* / [rule] / MDCCLV. [Price 1 *s.* 6 *d.*

Collation: 8°: A^4 B–E^8 F^4

Contents: Page *1* title, *2* blank, *3–5* Prologue and Epilogue, *6* Dramatis Personae and Advertisement, *7* 8–80 text of the play. Page 8 misnumbered 10.

Press figures: 16-1, 22-3, 33-3, 39-1, 54-1, 56-3, 60-1, 66-3, 79-3.

Size of an uncut copy: $8\frac{3}{4}'' \times 5\frac{5}{8}''$ (D. D. Eddy copy).

Date of first performance: December 17, 1754 at Drury Lane (*Public Advertiser*, December 17, 1754).

Date of publication: December 23, 1754 (*Daily Advertiser*; *Public Advertiser*). Advertisements: "On Monday will be published..." (*Daily Advertiser*, Sat., Dec. 21; *Public Advertiser*, Sat., Dec. 21; *London Evening-Post*, Thurs., Dec. 19–Sat., Dec. 21; *Whitehall Evening Post*, Thurs., Dec. 19–Sat., Dec. 21); "This Day is published . . ." (*Daily Advertiser*, Mon., Dec. 23; *Public Advertiser*, Mon., Dec. 23; *London Evening-Post*, Sat., Dec. 21–Tues., Dec. 24; *Whitehall Evening Post*, Sat., Dec. 21–Tues., Dec. 24).

The advertisement in the *London Evening-Post* of Dec. 21–24, 1754 adds this note: "In Page 42, line 10. for *Steps* read *Steeps*. Some other less material Errors, it is hop'd, the Reader will excuse."

Copies: *Bodleian; *Boston Public Library; *British Museum (2 copies); *Cambridge University Library; University of Chicago (2 copies); *Library of Congress; *Cornell; *Harvard; Huntington Library; *Illinois; *Indiana (Lilly); National Library of Scotland; Newberry Library; *New York Public Library; *University of Pennsylvania; Princeton; Texas; University of Toronto; University of Virginia; Yale; *D. D. Eddy (2 copies).

Manuscripts: David Garrick wrote the prologue and epilogue to this play. Garrick's manuscripts of both pieces are in the Folger Library; they represent early versions of the text, which was revised before printing in the first edition.

A fair copy scribal manuscript of the play (minus the prologue and epilogue) is in the Larpent Collection of the Huntington Library. Dated December 3, 1754, it is the text that Garrick and Lacy submitted to the Lord Chamberlain's office. This text also was revised before printing in the first edition.

Performances: Although the play was quite popular in the 1770's

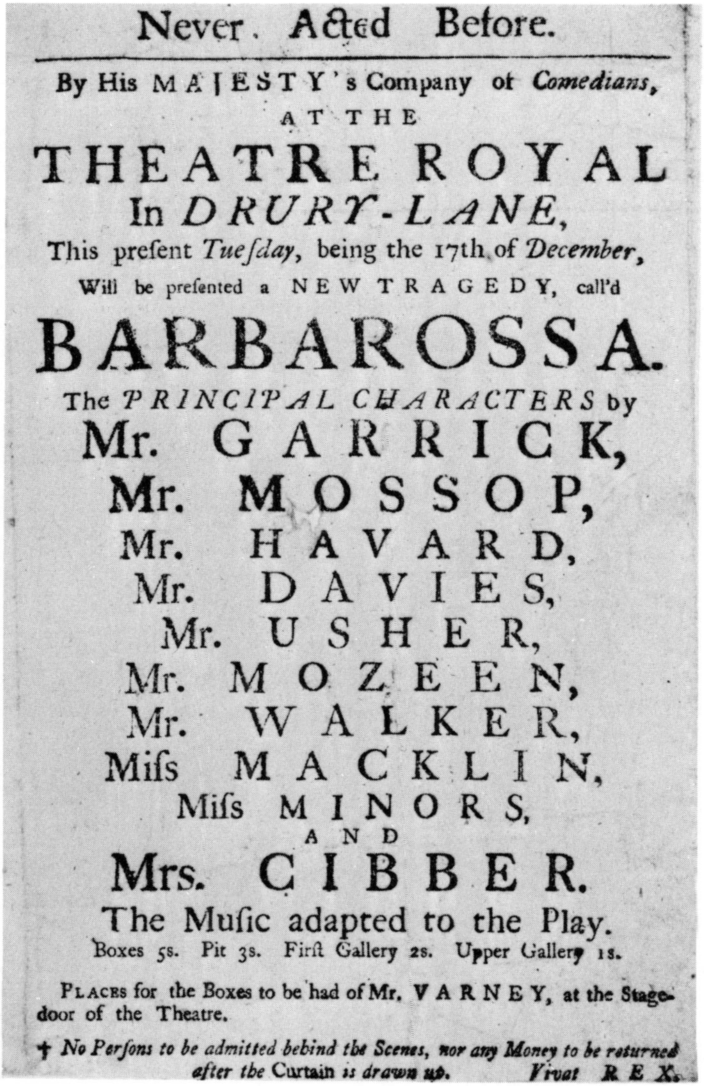

Never Acted Before.

By His MAJESTY's Company of *Comedians*,

AT THE

THEATRE ROYAL

In *DRURY-LANE*,

This preſent *Tueſday*, being the 17th of *December*,

Will be preſented a NEW TRAGEDY, call'd

BARBAROSSA.

The *PRINCIPAL CHARACTERS* by

Mr. GARRICK,

Mr. MOSSOP,

Mr. HAVARD,

Mr. DAVIES,

Mr. USHER,

Mr. MOZEEN,

Mr. WALKER,

Miſs MACKLIN,

Miſs MINORS,

AND

Mrs. CIBBER.

The Muſic adapted to the Play.

Boxes 5s. Pit 3s. Firſt Gallery 2s. Upper Gallery 1s.

PLACES for the Boxes to be had of Mr. VARNEY, at the Stage-door of the Theatre.

† *No Perſons to be admitted behind the Scenes, nor any Money to be returned after the* Curtain *is drawn up.* *Vivat* REX.

HENRY E. HUNTINGTON LIBRARY

III. Playbill for the first performance of *Barbarossa*

Size of playbill: $9\frac{1}{4}'' \times 5\frac{7}{8}''$

and in the early nineteenth century, there were only twenty-five performances at Drury Lane during the lifetime of John Brown, sixteen of them during the initial season of 1754–55. According to the *London Stage* (Part 4: 1747–76, ed. George Winchester Stone, Jr.), these twenty-five performances were on these dates: 1754—Dec. 17, 18, 19, 20, 21, 23, 30, 31. 1755—Jan. 1, 2, 3; Feb. 1, 4, 11, 15; May 27; Dec. 23, 31. 1761—Nov. 21, 23. 1762—Jan. 13; Mar. 8; Dec. 6. 1763—Jan. 3; Nov. 14.

The three Author's Nights were Dec. 19 and 23, 1754 and Jan. 1, 1755. According to the *London Stage*—citing Cross—the box office receipts for those three performances were £170, £190, and £180, respectively, a total of £540. Of this amount, John Brown received £304. The original receipt for this amount, dated Feb. 20, 1755, written and signed by Brown, is in the Forster Collection of the Victoria and Albert Museum.

20. *The Second Edition (1755)*

BARBAROSSA. / A / TRAGEDY. / As it is Perform'd at the / Theatre-Royal in *Drury-Lane*. / [rule] / [ornament] / [rule] / The SECOND EDITION. / [rule] / *LONDON:* / Printed for J. and R. TONSON and S. DRAPER in the *Strand*. / [rule] / MDCCLV. [Price 1 *s.* 6 *d.*

Collation and Contents: The same as the first edition. Page 8 is correctly numbered.

Press figures: 4-2, 6-2, 17-1, 22-3, 30-3, 33-3, 54-2, 56-1, 60-2, 66-3.

Size of an uncut copy: $8\frac{1}{2}'' \times 5\frac{3}{8}''$ (Cornell; Illinois).

Date of publication: February 17, 1755 (*Public Advertiser*; *London Evening-Post*, Feb. 15–18; *Whitehall Evening Post*, Feb. 15–18).

Copies: *Bodleian; *British Museum (11777.f.10); *Cornell; *Folger Library; Huntington Library; *Illinois; *Indiana (2 copies); *New York Public Library (2 copies); *University of Pennsylvania; Texas; *D. D. Eddy (2 copies).

Note:

Brown revised the text of this play before the printing of the second edition. Since collation indicates that he never revised the text again, the second edition is thus very important and worth comparing with the first.

Substantive authorial revisions are found in the second edition in the A, B, D and F gatherings, and both the inner and outer formes of these gatherings are printed from new settings of type. (Although both editions have press figure 3 on page 22 in the B gathering, the figure is located in different positions in the two settings of type.)

The C and E gatherings of the second edition do not contain any substantive textual revisions; and, since the first two editions were published less than two months apart, we should not be surprised to find some similarities between them.

The inner forme of the C gathering is printed from different settings of type in the two editions (P.F. 39-1 in the first edition, 30-3 in the second). The outer forme of the C gathering is a more complex case; for although most of the pages are printed from obviously different settings of type in the two editions, page 33 is identical in both editions and has press figure 3 in exactly the same location.

The inner forme of the E gathering is the same impression of the same setting of type in both editions, with press figure 3 on page 66. The outer forme of the E gathering shows two impressions of the same setting of type (P.F. 60-1 in the first edition, 60-2 in the second).

A critical edition of the text of this play is being prepared by Miss Katherine A. Rankin, to whom I am indebted for information about the textual variants in the different editions.

21. *The Third Edition (1762)*

BARBAROSSA. / A / TRAGEDY. / As it is Perform'd at the / Theatre-Royal in *Drury-Lane*. / [ornament] / [rule] / The THIRD EDITION. / [double rule] / LONDON: /

Printed for J. and R. TONSON in the *Strand.* / [rule] / MDCCL-XII. [Price 1 *s.* 6 *d.*

Collation: 8°: A–E[8]

Contents: Page *1* title, *2* blank, *3–5* Prologue and Epilogue, *6* Dramatis Personae and Advertisement, *7* 8–80 text.

Press figures: none.

Copies: *Bodleian; *British Museum; *Cambridge University Library (lacks title-page); University of Chicago; *Folger Library; Harvard; *Illinois; *Indiana (Lilly); National Library of Ireland; National Library of Scotland; *New York Public Library; Texas; University of Virginia; *D. D. Eddy.

22. *The Fourth Edition (1770)*

BARBAROSSA. / A / TRAGEDY. / As it is Performed at the / THEATRES-ROYAL / IN / *DRURY-LANE* / AND / *COVENT-GARDEN.* / [rule] / The FOURTH EDITION. / [double rule] / LONDON: / Printed for T. CASLON, T. LOWNDES, W. NICOLL, / and S. BLADON. / [rule] / M. DCC. LXX. / [Price One Shilling and Six-pence.]

Collation: 8°: A–E[8]

Contents: Page *1* title, *2* blank, *3–5* Prologue and Epilogue, *6* Dramatis Personae and Advertisement, *7* 8–80 text.

Press figures: 10-3, 13-1, 20-3, 27-1, 34-3, 41-1, 57-1, 59-1, 72-1, 78-3.

Size of an uncut copy: $8\frac{7}{8}'' \times 5\frac{3}{8}''$ (D. D. Eddy copy).

Copies: *Columbia; *Harvard; *Indiana (Lilly); *D. D. Eddy.

23. *The Fifth Edition (1770)*

BARBAROSSA. / A / TRAGEDY. / As it is Performed at the / THEATRES-ROYAL / IN / *DRURY-LANE* / AND /

COVENT-GARDEN. / [rule] / The FIFTH EDITION. / [double rule] / LONDON: / Printed for T. CASLON, T. LOWNDES, W. NICOLL, / and S. BLADON. / [rule] / M.DCC. LXX. / [Price One Shilling and Six-pence.]

Collation: 8°: A–E[8]

Contents: Page *1* title, *2* blank, *3–5* Prologue and Epilogue, *6* Dramatis Personae and Advertisement, *7* 8–80 text.

Press figures: 9-1, 15-3, 18-1, 28-3, 34-3, 41-3, 50-3, 64-1, 72-1, 78-3.

Copies: *Bodleian (2 copies); *British Museum (2 copies); University of Chicago; *Cornell; *Folger Library; *Indiana (Lilly); Texas; *D. D. Eddy.

Note:

Only the E gathering (with press figures 72-1 and 78-3) appears to be the same impression as the E gathering in the fourth edition. Press figure 3 on page 34 is in different locations in the two editions. Also, there are numerous changes in type ornaments and setting of type.

24. *Another Edition of 1770 (?)*

BARBAROSSA. / A TRAGEDY / TAKEN FROM / THE MANAGER'S BOOK, / AT THE / Theatre Royal, Covent-Garden. [this line in black letter] / [double rule] / *LONDON:* / Printed for R. BUTTERS, No. 79, Fleet-street; and sold by all / Booksellers in Town and Country.

Collation: 12° (in 6's): *A*1 B1 C–E[6]

Contents: Page *1* title, *2* Dramatis Personae, *3* 4–40 text.

Press figures: none.

Copies: *Bodleian; *British Museum (11778.b.19); Harvard (17472.7.8); Texas.

Note:

Barbarossa was not performed at Covent Garden before 1770, so this edition cannot have been printed earlier than that date; the British Museum Catalogue is surely incorrect in suggesting a date of 1755. The Covent Garden cast listed in this edition is: Barbarossa—Bensley; Selim—Savigny; Othman—Clarke; Sadi—Hull; Aladin—Gardner; Officer—Fox; Slave—Bates; Zaphira—Mrs. Yates; Irene—Miss Macklin; Slave—Mrs. Poussin. Only the last two names on this list differ from the cast listed in the fifth edition of the play, 1770.

25. *London Edition (1371 [for 1771])*

BARBAROSSA. / A / TRAGEDY. / Now Acting at the / Theatre-Royal in *Covent-Garden.* / [rule] / A NEW EDITION. / [rule] / [ornament] / [rule] / *LONDON:* / Printed for, and Sold by the BOOKSELLERS of / *London* and *Westminster.* MCCC-LXXI. / [Price One Shilling.]

Collation: 12° (in 6's): A–D^6 E^4

Contents: Page *1* title, *2* blank, *3–4* Prologue, *4–6* Epilogue, *6* Dramatis Personae at Covent-Garden, 1771, *7* 8–56 text.

Press figures: none.

Copies: *Bodleian Vet. A 5 e. 1974; *Folger Library (2 copies).

Note:

Except for the Slave, the cast is the same as that of the fifth edition, 1770.

26. *London Edition (1777)*

BARBAROSSA. / A / TRAGEDY. / As it is Acted at the / THEATRES-ROYAL / IN / Drury-Lane and Covent-Garden. / [rule] / By the Rev. Dr. BROWN. / [rule] / [ornament] / [double rule] / LONDON: / Printed for J. WENMAN, No 144, FLEET-STREET; and Sold by all / other Booksellers in Town and Country. / M DCC LXXVII.

Collation: 8° (in 4's): A–B^4

Contents: Page *1* title, *2* Prologue, Epilogue, and Dramatis Personae, *3* 4–15 text, *16* blank. In most copies a plate is bound as a frontispiece; it is "Mrs. Yates in the Character of Zaphira," published by J. Wenman 1 Oct. 1777.

Press figures: none.

Copies: *Bodleian; *British Museum (3 copies); *Columbia; *Cornell; *Folger Library; *Harvard; *Illinois; *New York Public Library; Texas; University of Virginia; Yale; *D. D. Eddy.

Note:

In this edition, the text is printed in double columns.

27. *London Edition (1777)*

BARBAROSSA. / A / TRAGEDY. / Marked with the Variations in the / MANAGER's BOOK, / AT THE / Theatre-Royal in Covent-Garden [black letter] / [ornament] / *LONDON:* / Printed for T. Caslon, T. Lowndes, W. Nicoll, / and S. Bladon. / M. DCC. LXXVII.

Collation: 12°: A–B^{12} C^6

Contents: Page *1* title, *2* note, *3–5* Prologue and Epilogue, *6* Dramatis Personae, *7* 8–58 text, *59–60* Advertisement. A frontispiece, dated Feb. 28, 1777, precedes the title.

Press figures: *4*-1, 23-3, 39-2, 45-1, 54-3.

Copies: *Boston Athenaeum; *Boston Public Library; *Cornell; *Folger Library; *Harvard; Indiana (Lilly); *New York Public Library.

Note:

This edition of *Barbarossa* is also in *The New English Theatre*, Vol. VIII . . . London, Printed for J. Rivington & Sons [and many others], 1776.

28. *London Edition (1778)*

BARBAROSSA, / A / TRAGEDY, / Marked with the Variations in the / MANAGER's BOOK, / AT THE / THEATRE ROYAL IN COVENT-GARDEN. / [ornament] / LONDON. / Printed for the PROPRIETORS, and sold by the Book- / sellers in Town and County. / [rule] / MDCCLXXVIII.

Collation: 12° (in 6's): *A*1 B–E^6 F^4. B1 missigned B2.

Contents: Page *1* title, *2* note, *3–5* Prologue and Epilogue, *6* Dramatis Personae, *7* 8–58 text.

Press figures: none.

Copies: *Folger Library.

Note:

This edition is a close reprint of the London edition of 1777 (see previous entry).

29. *First Dublin Edition (1755)*

BARBAROSSA: / A / TRAGEDY. / As it is Perform'd at the / THEATRE-ROYAL / IN / DRURY-LANE. / [ornament] / DUBLIN: / Printed for J. EXSHAW, R. JAMES, R. MAIN, / and W. WHITESTONE and B. EDMOND, in / Dame-street, Booksellers. MDCCLV.

Collation: 12°: A^6 B–C^{12} D^6. C1–5 are missigned B1–5.

Contents: A1^r half-title, A1^v blank, A2^r title, A2^v blank, A3 Prologue, A4 Epilogue, A5^r An Apology, A5^v–A6^r Advertisement, A6^v Dramatis Personae, pages *1* 2–57 text, *58–60* blank.

Press figures: none.

Copies: *Bodleian (2 copies, one of which [Don.f.281] lacks leaves A3, 4—the Prologue and the Epilogue); *University of Cincinnati; *Indiana (Lilly); National Library of Ireland.

The University of Cincinnati and the Lilly Library copies have the blank leaf D6.

30. *Second Dublin Edition (1756)*

BARBAROSSA: / A / TRAGEDY. / As it is perform'd at the / THEATRE-ROYAL / IN / DRURY-LANE. / [ornament] / DUBLIN: / Printed for WILLIAM DAVIS, at *Newton*'s-*Head*, / on *Temple-Bar*. M, DCC, LVI.

Collation: 12° (in 6's): A^4 B–F^6

Contents: Page *5* half-title, *6* blank, *7* title, *8* blank, *9* An Apology, *10–11* Advertisement, *12* Dramatis Personae, *13* 14–69 text, *70* blank, *71* Advertisement of William Davis, *72* blank.

Press figures: none.

Copies: *National Library of Ireland. (I have examined a Xerox print of the National Library of Ireland copy.)

31. *Third Dublin Edition (1757)*

BARBAROSSA: / A / TRAGEDY. / As it is Perform'd at the / THEATRE-ROYAL / IN / DRURY-LANE. / [rule] / The THIRD EDITION. / [rule] / [ornament] / [rule] / *DUBLIN:* / Printed for J. EXSHAW, A. JAMES, and S. PRICE, / in Dame-street, Booksellers. / MDCCLVII.

Collation: 12°: A^6 B–C^{12} D^6

Contents: $A1^r$ half-title, $A1^v$ blank, $A2^r$ title, $A2^v$ blank, A3 Prologue, A4 Epilogue, $A5^r$ An Apology, $A5^v$–$A6^r$ Advertisement, $A6^v$ Dramatis Personae, pages *1* 2–57 text, *58–60* blank.

Press figures: none.

Copies: *Cambridge University Library; National Library of Ireland.

32. *Dublin Edition (1770)*

BARBAROSSA: / A / TRAGEDY. / As it is Performed at the / THEATRE-ROYAL / IN / DRURY-LANE. / [rule] /

The SIXTH EDITION. / [rule] / [ornament] / [rule] / *DUBLIN:* / Printed for J. EXSHAW, T. DYTON, Booksellers, in / Dame-street, and S. PRICE, in Henry-street. 1770.

Collation: 12°: A–C^{12}

Contents: *A1*^{r} half-title, *A1*^{v} blank, *A2*^{r} title, *A2*^{v} blank, A3 Prologue, A4 Epilogue, A5^{r} An Apology, A5^{v}–A6^{r} Advertisement, A6^{v} Dramatis Personae, pages *1* 2–57 text, *58–60* blank. Pages 37–57 are misnumbered 49–69. In the Lilly Library copy, pages 13–57 are misnumbered 25–69—i.e., the misnumbering begins with the B gathering. Evidently the misnumbering of the B gathering was corrected in the course of printing.

Press figures: none.

Copies: *Bodleian; *British Museum; *Indiana (Lilly); National Library of Ireland (4 copies); Trinity College, Dublin; Yale; *D. D. Eddy.

33. *First Dublin "Wilkinson" Edition*

BARBAROSSA: / A / TRAGEDY, / As it is Perform'd at the / THEATRE-ROYAL / IN / DRURY-LANE. / [ornament] / DUBLIN: / Printed for THOMAS WILKINSON, in *Wineta- / vern-street*, the Corner of *Cook-street*. Where / may be had, all the New Novels, Books of / Entertainment, Plays, Farces, &c. as soon / as Published.

Collation: 12° (in 6's): A–$K^{4/2}$

Contents: Page *1* title, *2* Dramatis Personae, *3* 4–56 text of the play, *57–58* Prologue, *59–60* Epilogue and Advertisement.

Press figures: none.

Copies: *Bodleian Vet. A5 f. 1535; *Indiana (Lilly); National Library of Ireland (3 copies).

Note:

The Advertisement at the bottom of page 60 reads: "*Just Published . . . Price Bound,* 6 s. 6 d. *Sewed,* 5 s. 5 d. A TREATISE ON THE VENEREAL DISEASE. *Translated from the French of* M. Jourdan de Pellerin, *Physician Chemist to his Most Christian Majesty.*" If a copy of this work could be found, its date might help to establish the date of this Dublin edition of *Barbarossa.*

The first edition of E. Jourdan de Pellerin's *Traité sur les maladies vénériennes* . . . was published by M. Jombert in two duodecimo volumes (Paris, 1749); the Bibliothèque Nationale has a copy of this edition.

Apparently the first English translation of this work is *A Treatise on Venereal Maladies . . . translated from the French* . . . by George Arnaud de Ronsil . . . London, 1750. 8°. (This edition is listed in *Die Litteratur über die venerischen Krankheiten* . . . von J. K. Proksch . . . Erster Band. Bonn: Peter Hanstein, 1889, p. 34); a copy is in Dartmouth College Library.

However, I have not been able to locate any later edition, let alone one published in Dublin. The National Union Catalogue does not record any copies.

Mr. Michael O'Neill Walshe, of the firm of Falkner Greirson, informs me that Thomas Wilkinson's addresses, taken from the city directories, were: 40 Winetavern Street (from 1774 to 1796) and 30 Winetavern Street (from 1796 to 1802). Therefore, perhaps the most one can say about the date of this edition of *Barbarossa* is "1774 or later."

34. *Edinburgh Edition (1774)*

BARBAROSSA. / A / TRAGEDY. / BY / DR. BROWNE. / EDINBURGH: / PRINTED AND SOLD BY J. ROBERTSON. / [rule] / M, DCC, LXXIV.

Collation: 12° (in 6's): a^2 A–D^6 E^4

Contents: Page *i* title, *ii* blank, *iii*–iv Prologue, *v* Advertisement, *vi* Dramatis Personae, *7* 8–58 text of the play, *59*–60 Epilogue. An engraved frontispiece precedes the title.

Press figures: iv-1, 16-1, 28-2, 40-2, 52-2.

Copies: *Cornell; *National Library of Scotland. (I have examined a Xerox print of the National Library of Scotland copy.)

Note:

This edition is the first play in the fifth volume of THE TRAGIC THEATRE. IN SEVEN VOLUMES. . . . EDINBURGH: PRINTED AND SOLD BY J. ROBERTSON . . . M, DCC, LXXVI.

35. *First American Edition (1794)*

BARBAROSSA; / A / *TRAGEDY.* / [type ornament] / WITH *ALTERATIONS* AND *AMENDMENTS.* / AS PERFORMED AT THE / Theatre in Boston. [black letter] / [double rule] / PRINTED AT THE Apollo Press, ["Apollo Press" in black letter] IN BOSTON, / FOR DAVID WEST, No. 36, MARLBORO' / STREET, AND JOHN WEST, No. 75, CORNHILL. / MDCCXCIV.

Collation: 12° (in 6's): A–D^6

A3, B3, C3 and D3 missigned A2, B2, C2 and D2; A2, B2, C2 and D2 are not signed.

Contents: Page *1* title, *2* Dramatis Personae, *3*–4 Prologue, *5* 6–47 text, *48* Epilogue.

Press figures: none.

Size of an uncut copy: $7\frac{5}{8}'' \times 4\frac{3}{4}''$ (Harvard copy, unbound, stitched).

Copies: American Antiquarian Society; *Boston Public Library; John Carter Brown; *Columbia; *Cornell; *Harvard; Library Company of Philadelphia; *New York Public Library; Princeton; Texas; University of Virginia; *D. D. Eddy.

Note:

This is Evans 26706. This piece is also included in the first volume of an *American Selection of Plays* (Evans 26559).

36. *Second American Edition (1809)*

BARBAROSSA: / *A TRAGEDY,* / IN FIVE ACTS. / [ornamental rule] / BY DR. BROWN. / [ornamental rule] / *As performed at the* / THEATRE ROYAL, COVENT GARDEN. / (*first published in London,* 1754.) / [double rule] / NEW-YORK: / PUBLISHED BY D. LONGWORTH, / At the Dramatic Repository, / *Shakspeare-Gallery.* / [rule] / 1809

Collation: 12° (in 6's): A–F^6 G^4

A3, B3, C3, D3, E3 and F3 missigned A2, B2, C2, D2, E2 and F2. A2, B2, C2, D2, E2 and F2 not signed.

Contents: Page *1* title, *2* blank, *3* 4–5 Prologue, *6* Dramatis Personae, *7* 8–77 text of play, *78*–79 Epilogue, *80* blank.

Press figures: none.

Copies: American Antiquarian Society; Columbia; *Illinois; New York Public Library; Princeton; Yale; *D. D. Eddy.

Note:

This is Shaw and Shoemaker 17092, which also lists a copy at the University of Minnesota.

This piece is also the second item in the twenty-ninth volume of *The English and American Stage,* New York: D. Longworth, 1809–1812. Forty-one volumes (Shaw and Shoemaker 17456, 17457, 20057, 25347, 25348, 25349). Copies of this set are in the American Antiquarian Society, Princeton, and Yale.

37. *French Translation (1767)*

BARBEROUSSE, / *TRAGÉDIE,* / EN CINQ ACTES, / *Traduite de l'Anglois.* / NOUVELLE ÉDITION. / [cut] / A LONDRES, / Chez JEAN NOURSE. / [double rule] / M.DCC. LXVII.

Half-title: BARBEROUSSE, / *TRAGÉDIE,* / EN CINQ ACTES.

Collation: 12°: π^6 A–E^{12}

Contents: $\pi 1^r$ volume half-title, $\pi 1^v$ blank, $\pi 2^r$ volume title, $\pi 2^v$ blank, $\pi 3^r$ half-title of *Barberousse,* $\pi 3^v$ blank, page *i* title of *Barberousse, ii* blank, iii–v Prologue, Epilogue, Apologie, vi Acteurs, *1* 2–119 text, *120* blank.

Press figures: none.

Copies: Bibliothèque Nationale (2 copies); *Yale; *D. D. Eddy.

Notes:

1. This piece is the first item in the second volume of *Nouveau Théatre Anglois, ou Choix des meilleures pièces de Théatre représentées à Londres depuis quelques années.* A Londres, M.DCC. LXVII. 2 vols. 12°. No table of contents. Each play has its own half-title and title and is separately paginated.

2. The translator of this play has not been identified with certainty. A note in the catalogue of the Bibliothèque Nationale reads: "D'après Paul Lacroix, *Bibliothèque dramatique de M. de Soleinne,* la traduction de cette pièce est due soit à Mme. Thiroux d'Arconville, soit à Pierre Clément."

The B.N. catalogue lists nothing under Clément, however; the translation is listed solely under: Thiroux d'Arconville, Marie Geneviève Charlotte Darlus, Mme. (1720–1805).

3. One should not be misled by the "nouvelle edition" on the title-page, for apparently this is the first edition of this translation of Brown's play.

In the late 1740's, Pierre-Antoine de La Place translated a selection of English plays, with his "Discours sur le Théâtre Anglois," under the title *Le Théatre Anglois.* Londres, 1746–49. 8 vols. 12°.
Copies: Bibliothèque Nationale; British Museum. Twenty years later Mme. Thiroux d'Arconville's (?) translations of a different group of English plays were published as *Nouveau Théatre Anglois,* with the compositor mistakenly printing "nouvelle edition" on the title-pages of the plays.

Equally possible as a source of confusion are the two volumes of *Nouveau théâtre anglois* . . . Paris: Humblot, 1767, an entirely different group of English plays translated by Mme. Marie Jeanne (de Heurles Laboras de Mézières) Riccoboni (1713–92). Another edition was published in Paris in 1769, and these translations are also included in the collected works of Mme. Riccoboni; see Charles Alfred Rochedieu, *Bibliography of French Translations of English Works, 1700–1800* (Chicago: University of Chicago Press, 1948). However, none of the plays translated by Mme. Riccoboni are by John Brown.

38.

ATHELSTAN. / A / TRAGEDY. / As it is ACTED at the / THEATRE ROYAL in *Drury-Lane.* / [rule] / [ornament] / [double rule] / LONDON, / Printed for LOCKYER DAVIS and CHARLES REYMERS, / against *Grays-Inn-Gate, Holbourn*; / And at *Lord Bacon's Head* in *Fleet-Street.* / MDCCLVI. / [Price One Shilling and Six-pence.]

Collation: 8°: A^4 $B–F^8$

Contents: Page *i* title, *ii* quotation from Brumoy, *iii* iv–v Dedication to the Duke of Devonshire, *vi–vii* Prologue, *viii* Dramatis Personae, *1* 2–77 text of the play, *78–79* Epilogue, *80* Advertisement for the second edition of *Barbarossa.*

Press figures: iv-4, 4-2, 15-1, 31-3 or 4 (see note 1, below), 36-3, 43-4, 50-2, 61-4, 66-2, 68-3 or none (see note 2, below).

Size of an uncut copy: $8\frac{7}{8}''$ × $5\frac{3}{4}''$ (Folger Library; D. D. Eddy).

Number of copies printed: William Bowyer printed 4,000 copies, the first of which were delivered to Davis March 6, 1756; John Brown personally paid for the entire costs of the printing and the paper (Grolier Club Ledger 19474, folio 79).

Date of first performance: February 27, 1756 at Drury Lane (*Public Advertiser*).

Date of publication: March 9, 1756 (*Daily Advertiser*; *Public Advertiser*). Advertisements: "The Beginning of next week

Never Acted Before.

By His *MAJESTY*'s Company of Comedians,
AT THE
THEATRE ROYAL
In *DRURY-LANE*,
This present *Friday*, being the 27th of *February*,
Will be presented a TRAGEDY, call'd

ATHELSTAN.

The PRINCIPAL CHARACTERS by
Mr. GARRICK,
Mr. MURPHY,
Mr. ROSS,
Mr. HAVARD,
Mr. DAVIES,
Mr. BURTON,
Mr. JEFFERSON,
Mrs. BENNET,
AND
Mrs. CIBBER.
The PROLOGUE to be spoken
By Mr. HOLLAND,
In the Character of the GENIUS of *ENGLAND*.

Boxes 5s. Pit 3s. First Gallery 2s. Upper Gallery 1s.
PLACES for the Boxes to be had of Mr. VARNEY, at the Stage-door of the *Theatre*.
† *No Persons to be admitted behind the Scenes, nor any Money to be returned after the* Curtain *is drawn up* *Vivat* REX.

HENRY E. HUNTINGTON LIBRARY

IV. Playbill for the first performance of *Athelstan*
Size of playbill: $9\frac{1}{4}'' \times 6\frac{1}{4}''$

will be publish'd . . ." (*Daily Advertiser*, Tues., Mar. 2, and Fri., Mar. 5; *Public Advertiser*, Thurs., Mar. 4, and Fri., Mar. 5); "Tomorrow will be publish'd . . ." (*Daily Advertiser*; *Public Advertiser*, Mon., Mar. 8); "This Day is publish'd . . ." (*Daily Advertiser*; *Public Advertiser*, Tues., Mar. 9; *Whitehall Evening Post*, Mar. 6–9).

Copies: National Library of Australia; *Bodleian (2 copies); *Boston Athenaeum; *Boston Public Library; *British Museum (2 copies); *Cambridge University Library; University of Chicago; *Columbia; *Library of Congress; *Cornell (2 copies); *Folger Library; *Harvard; Huntington Library; *Illinois; Indiana; Newberry Library (4 copies); *New York Public Library (3 copies); *University of Pennsylvania (2 copies); Princeton; National Library of Scotland; Texas (2 copies); University of Toronto; Yale; *D. D. Eddy (3 copies).

Manuscripts: David Garrick wrote the epilogue to this play; his manuscript of it is in the Folger Library. It represents an early version of the text, which was revised slightly before printing in the first edition.

A fair copy scribal manuscript of the play (minus the prologue and epilogue) is in the Larpent Collection of the Huntington Library. Dated February 18, 1756, it is the text that Garrick and Lacy submitted to the Lord Chamberlain's office. This text also was revised before printing in the first edition.

Apparently no manuscript of John Brown's prologue has survived.

Notes:

1. Page 31 has press figure 3 or 4; I have not been able to determine which figure represents the earlier state. The two figures may reflect an interruption in the printing of the inner forme of the C gathering, but both states obviously are printed from the same setting of type.

2. Page 68 has press figure 3 or no press figure; again, I

do not know which "state" is earlier, if one may use the term in this case. The figure may have dropped out accidentally during the course of printing; or, the printing of the outer forme of the F gathering may have been interrupted, with the figure being added or deleted. In any case, both "states" are printed from the same setting of type.

I rechecked approximately a dozen copies, and in each instance 31-4 and 68-3 were found in the same copy, as were 31-3 and 68-none. I suspect, however, that the association of those states is an accident of binding, and that an examination of more copies would discover 31-3 bound with 68-3, and 31-4 with 68-none. In my experience, both states of each page are equally common.

The Bodleian, the British Museum, and D. D. Eddy have copies of both states of pages 31 and 68.

Performances: Athelstan did not enjoy the popularity of *Barbarossa*; in fact, there were only nine performances at Drury Lane during the lifetime of John Brown. According to the *London Stage* (Part 4: 1747–76, ed. George Winchester Stone, Jr.), those performances were on these dates in 1756: Feb. 27, 28; Mar. 1, 4, 6, 9, 11, 15 and 18.

The three Author's Nights were March 1, 9 and 18, 1756. According to the *London Stage*—citing Cross—the box office receipts for those three performances were £160, £140, and £120, respectively, a total of £420. In this instance we do not have Brown's receipt for his profits, but we may make an estimate. "House charges varied over the years. . . . Sixty pounds was normal for an actor, author or small group from 1740 to the mid-fifties, after which the charge mounted to a flat £63" (*London Stage*, Pt. 4, Vol. I, p. cii). Thus, if we assume a charge of £63 for each of the three Author's Nights, then Brown received £231 clear profit.

39. *Another London Edition [1756?]*

ATHELSTAN. / A / TRAGEDY. / As it is ACTED at the / THEATRE ROYAL in *Drury-Lane*. / [double rule] /

LONDON. / Printed for CH. ROBINSON in *St. Paul's Church-yard.*

Collation: 12° (in 6's): π (3 leaves) *A*^{6} B–F^6(–F6)

Contents: $\pi 1^r$ title, $\pi 1^v$ blank, $\pi 2$ Prologue, $\pi 3^r$ blank, $\pi 3^v$ dramatis personae, pages *1* 2–70 text of the play. Page 69 misnumbered 39, and 70 misnumbered 42.

Press figures: none.

Copies: *British Museum 11785.a.2.(3.); *Columbia (820.12 Z85); *Library Company of Philadelphia; Texas; University of Toronto.

Note:

In this edition the dramatis personae agrees exactly with that in the first London edition, 1756. Of course, this is no reliable indication of the date of publication, for the first edition could have been reprinted at any time.

40. *Dublin Edition (1756)*

ATHELSTAN. / A / TRAGEDY. / As it is ACTED at the / THEATRE ROYAL in *Drury-Lane.* / [rule] / By the AUTHOR of BARBAROSSA: / A TRAGEDY. / [rule] / [quotation] / [row of type ornaments] / DUBLIN: / Printed for G. and A. EWING, G. FAULKNER, / J. EXSHAW, and R. JAMES, Booksellers. / [rule] / MDCCLVI.

Collation: 12°: A–F$^{8/4}$

Contents: Page *i* title, *ii* quotation from Brumoy, *iii*–iv (misnumbered v) Dedication "TO HIS GRACE THE Duke of DEVONSHIRE, Lord Lieutenant of *Ireland*," signed by "The Author," *v*–vi Prologue and Dramatis Personae, *7* 8–70 text of the play, *71–72* Epilogue.

Press figures: none.

Copies: *Bodleian Don. f.282; *British Museum 1507/1570;

*Cambridge University Library; National Library of Ireland; Trinity College, Dublin; *D. D. Eddy.

41. *German Translation (1778)*

Athelstan. / [row of type ornaments] / Ein / Trauerspiel / in fünf Aufzügen. / [rule] / Nach dem Englischen bearbeitet. / [double rule] / Aufgeführt / im kaiserl. königl. National-theater. / [ornament] / [horizontal type ornament] / Wien, / zu finden beym Logenmeister. / [horizontal bracket, facing downwards] / 1778.

[Note: This title-page is printed entirely in black letter, and for the umlaut uses superscript e.]

Collation: 8°: a–d^8 e^4 f^2

Contents: Page *1* title, *2* Dramatis Personae, *3* 4–76 text. Page 44 misnumbered 54.

Press figures: none.

Copies: Bibliothèque Nationale; *New York Public Library.

Note:

The catalogue of the Bibliothèque Nationale states that this edition of *Athelstan* was translated by Johann Leonhardi.

42.

AN / ESTIMATE [red] / OF THE / MANNERS / AND / PRINCIPLES [red] / OF THE / TIMES. / [rule] / By the AUTHOR of / ESSAYS on the CHARACTERISTICS, &c. / [rule] / [quotation] / [double rule] / *LONDON*, [red] / Printed for L. DAVIS, and C. REYMERS, in / *Holborn*; Printers to the ROYAL SOCIETY. / MDCCLVII. [red]

Collation: 8°: a^4 B–O^8 P^4

Contents: Page *1* title, *2* blank, *3* Advertisement, *4* blank, 5–8 Contents, *9* special title for Part I, *10* blank, 11–67 text of Part I, *68* blank, *69* special title for Part II, *70* blank,

71–145 (misnumbered 154) text of Part II, *146* blank, *147* special title for Part III, *148* blank, 149–221 text of Part III, *222* blank, *223–224* Advertisement. Page 145 misnumbered 154.

Press figures: 21-4, 23-1, 28-2, 50-2, 64-2, 84-1, 98-4, 117-1, 124-1, 134-2, 138-1, 149-4, 161-2, 167-1, 184-2, 202-1.

Size of an uncut copy: $8\frac{3}{4}''$ × $5\frac{3}{8}''$ (the Yale copy).

Number of copies printed: William Bowyer printed 1,000 copies. Grolier Club Ledger 19474, folio 109 gives this entry under the account of Mr. Lockyer Davis: "Estimate of Manners. 1st Edit. 14 sh at 16s No. 1000. 11:12:—." This charge of £11:12:0 is verified in the account book of James Emonson and William Bowyer, under the entry for March, 1757 (Bodleian MS. Eng. misc. c.141, folio 178). The charge apparently was derived as follows: 14 sheets at 16s. per sheet equals £11:4:0, plus 8s. for red titles equals £11:12:0.

Several times in his listing of charges Bowyer mentions "Title red equal to half a sht" (see, for example, Grolier Club Ledger 19474, folio 70a).

Date of publication: March 31, 1757 (*Public Advertiser*). Advertisements: "Thursday next will be published . . ." (*Public Advertiser*, Sat., March 26, 1757); "This Day is published . . ." (*Public Advertiser*, Thurs., March 31, 1757).

Copies: *Bodleian; *British Museum (2 copies); *Cambridge University Library; *University of Cincinnati; *Cornell; *General Theological Seminary, New York; *Harvard; Huntington Library; *Indiana (Lilly); *Newberry Library; Pennsylvania State University; Texas; *Yale; *D. D. Eddy (2 copies).

43. *The Second Edition (1757)*

AN / ESTIMATE [red] / OF THE / MANNERS / AND / PRINCIPLES [red] / OF THE / TIMES. / [rule] / By the AUTHOR of / ESSAYS on the CHARACTERISTICS, &c. [red] /

[rule] / [quotation] / [rule] / The SECOND EDITION. / [double rule] / LONDON, [red] / Printed for L. DAVIS, and C. REYMERS, in / *Holborn*; Printers to the ROYAL SOCIETY. / MDCCLVII. [red]

Collation and Contents: Exactly the same as the first edition, except that page 145 is correctly numbered.

Press figures: 19-4, 26-2, 53-4, 60-4, 87-1, 98-2.

Number of copies printed: Presumably 1,000 copies were printed, but only six of the fourteen sheets of this edition were printed by William Bowyer. Grolier Club Ledger 19474, folio 109 gives this entry under the account of Mr. Lockyer Davis: "Estimate of Manners . . . 2ᵈ Edit. 6 sh. red Titles. 5:4:—." This same information is given in the account book of James Emonson and William Bowyer (Bodleian MS. Eng. misc. c.141, folios 98 and 178). If we assume the same charge of 16s. per sheet, then the total cost is derived as follows: 6 × 16s. equals £4:16:0, plus 8s. for red titles equals £5:4:0.

I believe the six sheets Bowyer printed are gatherings B through G. It was Bowyer's normal practice to use press figures in works of this size, and B–G are the only gatherings with press figures. Also, the special titles for Parts I and II of the second edition (pages 9 and 69) use the identical type ornaments found in all three special titles of the first edition, while the ornaments on the special title for Part III of the second edition (page 147) are quite different. In a similar manner, a single type ornament is used as the headpiece on the first page of Parts I, II and III of the first edition and Parts I and II of the second edition, while the first page of Part III of the second edition uses a different type ornament.

I have not been able to determine the printer(s) of the other gatherings.

Date of publication: April 14, 1757 (*London Evening-Post*).

Copies: *British Museum (2 copies); *Cambridge University Library; *Cornell; *Harvard; *New York Public Library; Princeton; Texas; *Yale; *D. D. Eddy.

Note:

This is a setting of type different from the first edition; compositorial errors are introduced.

44. *The Third Edition (1757)*

AN / ESTIMATE [red] / OF THE / MANNERS / AND / PRINCIPLES [red] / OF THE / TIMES. / [rule] / By the AUTHOR of / ESSAYS on the CHARACTERISTICS, &c. [red] / [rule] / [quotation] / [rule] / The THIRD EDITION. / [double rule] / LONDON, [red] / Printed for L. DAVIS, and C. REYMERS, / against *Gray's-Inn-Gate, Holborn*; / Printers to the ROYAL SOCIETY. / MDCCLVII. [red]

Collation and Contents: Exactly the same as the first two editions; all numbered pages are numbered correctly.

Press figures: 24-1, 26-1, 33-4, 58-2, 60-4, 84-4, 115-1 or none, 124-1, 134-2, 151-1.

Number of copies printed: Presumably 1,000 copies were printed, but only five of the fourteen sheets were printed by William Bowyer. Grolier Club Ledger 19474, folio 109 gives this entry under the account of Mr. Lockyer Davis: "Estimate of Manners . . . 3[d] Edit. 5 sh red Titles. 4:8:—." The entry in the account book of James Emonson and William Bowyer reads: "Estimate of Manners . . . 3[d] Edit. 5 Sh. & red Title at 16 4:8:—" (Bodleian MS. Eng. misc. c.141, folio 178). Therefore, 5 × 16s. equals £4:0:0, plus 8s. for red titles equals £4:8:0.

Once again, the presence of press figures and distinctive type ornaments—among other reasons—leads me to believe that William Bowyer printed gatherings B, C, E, F and I.

Date of publication: May 5, 1757 (*London Evening-Post*).

Copies: National Library of Australia; *Bodleian; *British Museum; *Cornell; *Folger Library; *Library Company of Philadelphia; Texas; *Yale; *D. D. Eddy (2 copies).

45. *The Fourth Edition (1757)*

AN / ESTIMATE [red] / OF THE / MANNERS / AND / PRINCIPLES [red] / OF THE / TIMES. / [rule] / By the AUTHOR of / ESSAYS on the CHARACTERISTICS, &c. [red] / [rule] / [quotation] / [rule] / The FOURTH EDITION. / [double rule] / LONDON, [red] / Printed for L. DAVIS, and C. REYMERS, against / *Grays-Inn-Gate, Holborn*; / Printers to the ROYAL SOCIETY. / MDCCLVII. [red]

Collation and Contents: Exactly the same as the first three editions; all numbered pages are numbered correctly.

Press figures: 19-1, 33-1, 35-4, 58-4, 60-1, 76-1, 78-4, 92-1, 149-2 or none.

Number of copies printed: Presumably 1,000 copies were printed, but only six of the fourteen sheets of this edition were printed by William Bowyer. Grolier Club Ledger 19474, folio 109 gives this entry under the account of Mr. Lockyer Davis: "Estimate of Manners . . . 4th Edit. 6 sh red Titles 5:4:—." The entry in the account book of James Emonson and William Bowyer reads: "Estimate of Manners . . . 4th Edit. 6 Sh. & red Title at 16 5:4:—" (Bodleian MS. Eng. misc. c.141, folio 178). Therefore, 6 × 16s. equals £4:16:0, plus 8s. for red titles equals £5:4:0.

Once again, the presence of press figures, distinctive type ornaments, and other typographical peculiarities leads me to believe that William Bowyer printed gatherings B, C, E, F and G. The sixth gathering he printed is probably H, I or L; but because these gatherings have the same paper, fonts of type, and headlines, I am unable to differentiate among them.

Date of publication: May 31, 1757 (*Daily Advertiser*).

Copies: *British Museum; *Cornell; *Indiana (Lilly); *New York State Library, Albany; Pembroke College, Oxford; *University of Pennsylvania; University of Toronto; *Union

Theological Seminary, New York; *Yale (Lewis Walpole Library); *D. D. Eddy.

46. *The Fifth Edition (1757)*

AN / ESTIMATE [red] / OF THE / MANNERS / AND / PRINCIPLES [red] / OF THE / TIMES. / [rule] / By the AUTHOR of / ESSAYS on the CHARACTERISTICS, &c. [red] / [rule] / [quotation] / [rule] / The FIFTH EDITION. / [double rule] / LONDON, [red] / Printed for L. DAVIS, and C. REYMERS, against / *Grays-Inn-Gate, Holborn*; / Printers to the ROYAL SOCIETY. / MDCCLVII. [red]

Collation and Contents: The same as the first four editions; all numbered pages are numbered correctly.

Press figures: 19-1, 34-1, 76-1, 92-1.

Number of copies printed: Presumably 1,000 copies were printed, but only seven of the fourteen sheets of this edition were printed by William Bowyer. The entry in the account book of James Emonson and William Bowyer reads: "Estimate of Manners . . . 5th Edit. £6/–/–" (Bodleian MS. Eng. misc. c.141, folio 98). Still assuming 16s. per sheet for 1,000 copies, the total charge would be derived as follows: 7 sheets × 16s. equals £5:12:0, plus 8s. for red titles equals £6:0:0.

Once again, the presence of press figures, distinctive type ornaments, and other typographical peculiarities leads me to believe that William Bowyer printed gatherings a, B, C, D, E, F, G, and P.

Date of publication: July 4, 1757 (*Public Advertiser*).

Copies: *Bodleian; *Boston Public Library; *Bryn Mawr College; *Columbia; Indiana; *Lambeth Palace Library; National Library of Scotland; *New York Public Library; *Union Theological Seminary, New York; Texas; *D. D. Eddy.

Note:

Collation indicates that the fifth edition is a different setting of type from the fourth edition, with the following exceptions: B gathering, inner forme (both have P.F. 19-1); F gathering, outer forme (both have P.F. 76-1); F gathering, inner forme (the fifth seems to be a different impression of the same setting of type as the fourth; the fourth has a press figure, the fifth has none); G gathering, outer forme (both have P.F. 92-1); also, the inner forme of the G gathering seems to be the same (although there are no press figures in either). Everything beyond the G gathering appears to be a different setting of type, with the possible exception of parts of the N and O gatherings.

47. *The Sixth Edition (1757)*

AN / ESTIMATE [red] / OF THE / MANNERS / AND / PRINCIPLES [red] / OF THE / TIMES. / [rule] / By the Author of / Essays on the Characteristics, &c. [red] / [rule] / [quotation] / [rule] / The Sixth Edition. / [double rule] / LONDON, [red] / Printed for L. Davis and C. Reymers, against / *Grays-Inn-Gate, Holborn*; / Printers to the Royal Society. / MDCCLVII. [red]

Collation and Contents: The same as the first five editions. Page 72 is not numbered; all numbered pages are numbered correctly.

Press figures: 19-1, 35-4, 72-1, 92-1, 114-1, 117-1, 124-4, 154-4, 156-1, 177-1.

Number of copies printed: The index to Grolier Club Ledger 19474, folio 14 shows that 1,000 copies of the sixth edition were printed. Apparently Bowyer printed all the gatherings of this edition (see Bodleian MS. DON b.4, folio 159). Certainly the type rules and ornaments in all three parts are Bowyer's.

Date of publication: September 1, 1757 (*Daily Advertiser*).

Copies: *British Museum; University of Chicago; *Columbia; *Harvard (2 copies); *Illinois; *Library Company of Philadelphia; *University of Rochester; Texas; *Virginia State Library, Richmond.

Note:

Collation indicates that the sixth edition is a different setting of type from the fifth edition, with the following exceptions: B gathering, inner forme (both have P.F. 19-1); B gathering, outer forme (although there are no press figures in either); and the D and P gatherings. As in the fourth and fifth editions, the outer forme of the G gathering has press figure 92-1, but it is in a different position on the page and the settings of type are not the same.

The advertisement leaf, P4, is the same in the first five editions, listing eleven items "Printed for L. Davis and C. Reymers." In the sixth edition the contents of the advertisement leaf are changed and twelve items are listed.

48. *The Seventh Edition (1758)*

AN / ESTIMATE [red] / OF THE / MANNERS / AND / PRINCIPLES [red] / OF THE / TIMES. / [rule] / By the Author of / Essays on the Characteristics, &c. [red] / [rule] / [quotation] / [rule] / VOL. I. / [rule] / The Seventh Edition. / [double rule] / LONDON: [red] / Printed for L. Davis and C. Reymers, against / *Grays-Inn-Gate, Holborn*; / Printers to the Royal Society. / MDCCLVIII. [red]

Collation and Contents: The same as the first six editions; all numbered pages are numbered correctly.

Press figures: 22-3, 36-4 or none, 43-3, 49-1, 60-1, 66-3, 74-5, 84-4, 98-3, 104-5, 108-1, 115-5, 131-1, 144-1, 154-1, 157-4, 178-3, 181-4, 192-3, 194-4, 202-2, 204-1, 218-2.

Number of copies printed: William Bowyer printed 1,000 copies, the first of which were delivered to Davis April 15, 1758 (Bodleian MS. DON b.4, folio 159). Bowyer printed all the gatherings of this edition.

An Estimate of the Manners and Principles of the Times
Volume I. Press figures in the seven London editions, 1757–58
All the editions collate a^4 B–O^8 P^4

	1		2		3		4		5		6		7	
Sig.	(i)	(o)	(i)	(o)	(i)	(o)	(i)	(o)	(i)	(o)	(i)	(o)	(i)	(o)
a	—	—	—	—	—	—	—	—	—	—	—	—	—	—
B	1[8r]	4[7r]	4[6r]	—	—	1[8v]	1[6r]	—	1[6r]	—	1[6r]	—	3[7v]	—
C	—	2[2v]	2[1v]	—	1[1v]	4[5r]	4[6r]	1[5r]	1[5v]	—	4[6r]	—	—	4[6v]
D	2[5v]	—	—	4[7r]	—	—	—	—	—	—	—	—	3[2v]	1[5r]
E	—	2[4v]	—	4[2v]	2[1v]	4[2v]	4[1v]	1[2v]	—	—	—	1[8v]	3[5v]	1[2v]
F	—	1[6v]	1[8r]	—	—	4[6v]	4[3v]	1[2v]	—	1[2v]	—	—	5[1v]	4[6v]
G	4[5v]	—	2[5v]	—	—	—	—	1[2v]	—	1[2v]	—	1[2v]	3[5v]	5[8v]
H	—	1[7r]	—	—	1[6r]	—	—	—	—	—	1[5v]	1[7r]	5[6r]	1[2v]
I	2[7v]	1[2v]	—	—	2[7v]	1[2v]	—	—	—	—	—	4[2v]	1[6r]	—
K	1[1v]	4[7r]	—	—	1[8r]	—	—	2[7r]	—	—	—	—	—	1[4v]
L	1[8r]	2[5r]	—	—	—	—	—	—	—	—	4[1v]	1[2v]	1[1v]	4[3r]
M	—	2[8v]	—	—	—	—	—	—	—	—	—	1[5r]	3[5v]	4[7r]
N	—	—	—	—	—	—	—	—	—	—	—	—	4[5v]	3[4v]
O	1[1v]	—	—	—	—	—	—	—	—	—	—	—	2[1v]	1[2v]
P	—	—	—	—	—	—	—	—	—	—	—	—	2[1v]	—

See G. Thomas Tanselle, "The Recording of Press Figures," *The Library*, XXI, no. 4 (Dec., 1966), 318–325.

Date of publication: April 20, 1758 (*London Chronicle*; *Whitehall Evening Post*).

Copies: Bibliothèque Nationale; *Boston Public Library; *British Museum (2 copies); *Cornell; *Library Company of Philadelphia; National Library of Scotland; *University of Pennsylvania; *Texas (2 copies); *D. D. Eddy (2 copies).

Note:

In this edition the advertisements (pages 223–224) are different from those in the first six editions. Also, in this edition "VOL. I." precedes each signature.

49. *First Dublin Edition (1757)*

AN / ESTIMATE / OF THE / MANNERS / AND / PRINCIPLES / OF THE / TIMES. / [rule] / By Dr. BROWN, / AUTHOR of the ESSAYS on Lord SHAFTESBURY'S / CHARACTERISTICS, &c. / [rule] / [quotation] / [double rule] / DUBLIN: / Printed for G. FAULKNER, J. HOEY, and / J. EXSHAW, Booksellers. MDCCLVII.

Collation: 12°: A^4 $B–F^{12}$ G^2

Contents: Page *1* title, *2* blank, *3* Advertisement, *4* blank, 5–*6* Contents, *7* special title for Part I, *8* blank, 9–44 text of Part I, *45* special title for Part II, *46* blank, 47–90 text of Part II, 91–132 text of Part III.

Press figures: none.

Copies: *Cambridge University Library (imperfect: lacks pages 127–128); *D. D. Eddy.

50. *Second Dublin Edition (1757)*

Title: transcription is identical with the first Dublin edition, but it is clearly a different setting of type.

Collation: 12°: $A–E^{12}$ F^6

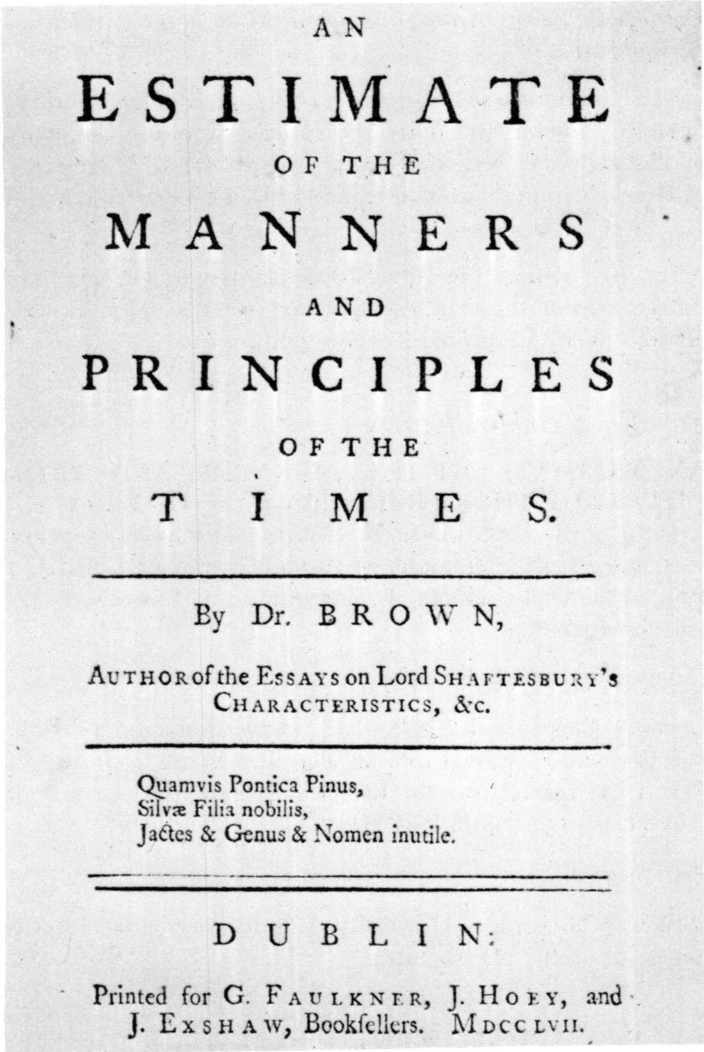

AN

ESTIMATE

OF THE

MANNERS

AND

PRINCIPLES

OF THE

TIMES.

By Dr. BROWN,

AUTHOR of the ESSAYS on Lord SHAFTESBURY's CHARACTERISTICS, &c.

Quamvis Pontica Pinus,
Silvæ Filia nobilis,
Jactes & Genus & Nomen inutile.

DUBLIN:

Printed for G. FAULKNER, J. HOEY, and J. EXSHAW, Booksellers. MDCCLVII.

D. D. EDDY

V. Title-page of no. 49

Size of page: $6\frac{3}{4}'' \times 3\frac{7}{8}''$

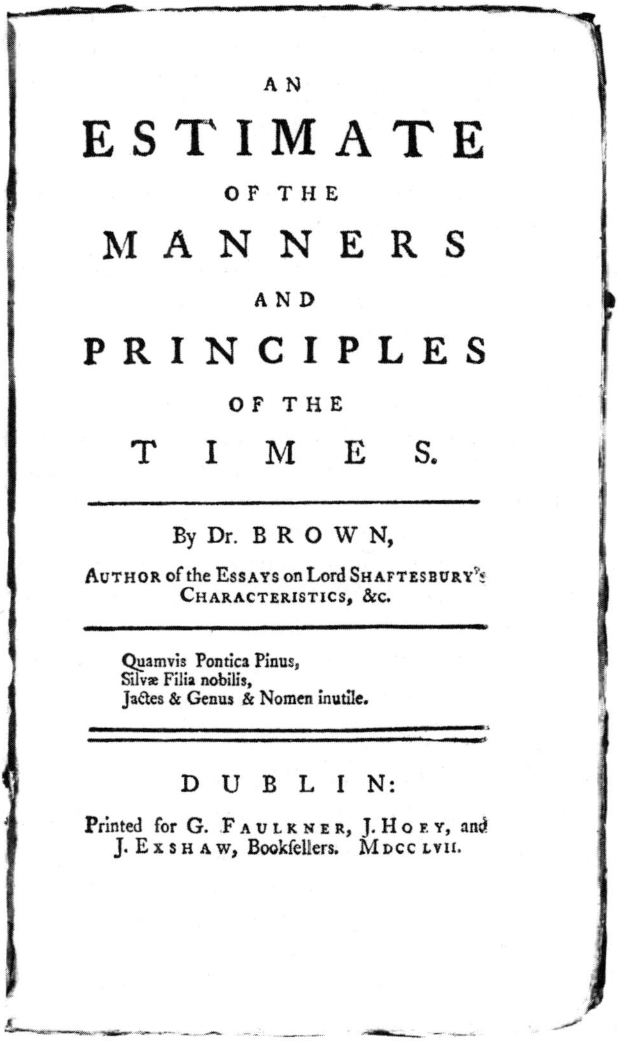

A N

ESTIMATE

OF THE

MANNERS

AND

PRINCIPLES

OF THE

TIMES.

By Dr. BROWN,

AUTHOR of the ESSAYS on Lord SHAFTESBURY's CHARACTERISTICS, &c.

Quamvis Pontica Pinus,
Silvæ Filia nobilis,
Jactes & Genus & Nomen inutile.

DUBLIN:

Printed for G. FAULKNER, J. HOEY, and J. EXSHAW, Bookfellers. MDCCLVII.

PENNSYLVANIA STATE UNIVERSITY

VI. Title-page of no. 50
Size of page: $7\frac{1}{4}'' \times 4\frac{1}{4}''$

Contents: Page *i* title, *ii* blank, *iii* Advertisement, *iv* blank, v–vi Contents, *vii* special title for Part I, *viii* blank, 9–44 text of Part I, *45* special title for Part II, *46* blank, 47–90 text of Part II, 91–132 text of Part III.

Press figures: none.

Size of an uncut copy: $7\frac{1}{4}''$ × $4\frac{1}{4}''$ (Pennsylvania State University copy, in contemporary boards).

Copies: *Library of Congress; *Folger Library; National Library of Ireland (2 copies); New York Public Library; *Pennsylvania State University.

Notes:

1. Although the two editions agree in their title-pages, number of leaves, and pagination, they differ in two respects: (a) their collation; (b) in the first edition, $A3^r$ is numbered "5" and $A3^v$ is not numbered; in the second edition, $A3^r$ is numbered "v" and $A3^v$ is numbered "vi."

2. Collation shows that the type of the second edition has been extensively reset, with the introduction of compositorial changes, especially in the accidentals.

3. The special titles for Parts I and II use different type ornaments in the two editions.

50A. *Third Dublin Edition (1758)*

AN / ESTIMATE / OF THE / MANNERS / AND / PRINCIPLES / OF THE / TIMES. / [rule] / By Dr. BROWN, / AUTHOR of the ESSAYS on Lord SHAFTESBURY'S / CHARACTERISTICS, &c. / [rule] / [quotation] / [double rule] / DUBLIN: / Printed for G. FAULKNER, J. HOEY, sen. and / jun. and J. EXSHAW, Booksellers. / [rule] / MDCCLVIII.

Collation: 12°: A–E^{12} F^6

Contents: Page *i* title, *ii* blank, *iii* Advertisement, *iv* blank, v–vi Contents, *vii* special title for Part I, *viii* blank, 9–44 text of Part I, *45* special title for Part II, *46* blank, 47–90 text of Part II, 91–132 text of Part III.

Press figures: none.

Copies: *D. D. Eddy.

Notes:

1. This is a hasty reprint of the second Dublin edition. The type has been reset, and numerous compositorial changes have introduced errors not found in the first two Dublin editions (e.g., the third edition omits a complete line of text on p. 10).

2. The special titles for Parts I and II use type ornaments different from those in either the first or second Dublin editions.

51. *Belfast Edition (1758)*

AN / ESTIMATE / OF THE / MANNERS / AND / PRINCIPLES / OF THE / TIMES. / [rule] / By Dr. BROWN, / AUTHOR of the ESSAYS on Lord SHAFTSBURY'S / CHARACTERISTICS, &c. / [rule] / [quotation] / [rule] / The SEVENTH EDITION. / [double rule] / BELFAST: / Printed by HENRY and ROBERT JOY. 1758.

Collation: 12° (in 6's): A^2 B–G^6 H^4

Contents: Page *i* title, *ii* blank, iii–iv Contents and Advertisement, 5–26 text of Part I, 27–54 text of Part II, 55–82 text of Part III, *83–84* blank.

Press figures: none.

Copies: *Cambridge University Library; *Folger Library; *Library Company of Philadelphia.

52. *First American Edition (1758)*

AN / ESTIMATE / OF THE / MANNERS / AND / PRINCIPLES / OF THE / TIMES. / [rule] / By *JOHN BROWN*, D.D. / Author of ESSAYS on the CHARACTERISTICS, &c. / [rule] / [quotation] / [rule] / The SEVENTH EDITION. / [double rule] / LONDON, Printed. / *BOSTON*, NEW-ENGLAND; / Re-printed and Sold by GREEN and RUSSELL, at their / Printing-Office in Queen-street. / MDCCLVIII.

Collation: 8° (in 4's): A^2 B–O^4

Contents: Page *5* title, *6* blank, *7–8* Advertisement and Contents, *9* 10–110 text, *111–112* blank. In some copies page 70 is not numbered.

Press figures: none.

Size of an uncut copy: 8⅝″ × 5⅝″ (New-York Historical Society copy, stitched, in original blue paper wrapper).

Copies: American Antiquarian Society; *Bodleian; *Boston Public Library; *British Museum; John Carter Brown; *Library of Congress; *Cornell; Grolier Club Library; *Harvard; *Indiana (Lilly) [imperfect copy]; University of Michigan (William L. Clements); *Newberry Library; *New-York Historical Society; *New York Public Library (2 copies); *Yale (2 copies); *D. D. Eddy (2 copies).

Notes:

1. Evidently the compositor of the B gathering assumed that there were to be four preliminary leaves rather than two, and therefore the first page of text would be numbered 9.
2. This is Evans 8094.

53. *French Translation (1758)*

LES / MOEURS ANGLOISES [red] / OU / APPRECIATION [red] / DES MOEURS ET DES PRINCIPES / QUI / CARACTERISENT ACTUELLEMENT / LA / NATION BRITANNIQUE. [red] / [ornament] / *A LA HAYE,* [red] / Chez PIERRE GOSSE, Junior, / Libraire de S.A.R. / *M. DCC. LVIII.* [red]

Collation: 8°: $*^6$ A–P^8 Q^2. \$5(-*5) signed.

Contents: Page *i* title, *ii* blank, *iii* iv–vi Avertissement, *vii* viii–xii Table des Chapitres, *1* 2–70 *71* 72–154 *155* 156–242 text, *243–244* blank.

Press figures: none.

Size of an uncut copy: $8\frac{3}{4}'' \times 5\frac{1}{2}''$ (D. D. Eddy copy, in original blue paper wrapper).

Copies: Bibliothèque Nationale; *British Museum; *Harvard; *New York Public Library; *Yale; *D. D. Eddy (2 copies).

Note:

According to the British Museum catalogue, this translation was done by Charles Chais.

54. *French Translation. The Second Edition (1758)*

LES / MŒURS ANGLOISES, / *OU* / APPRÉCIATION / *DES MŒURS ET DES PRINCIPES* / QUI CARACTERI-SENT ACTUELLEMENT / *LA NATION BRITANNIQUE.* / [ornament] / *A LA HAYE.* / Chez PIERRE GOSSE, Junior, / Libraire de S.A.R. / [double rule] / M.DCC.LVIII.

Collation: 12°: π^2 A–H^{12} I^2

Contents: Page *i* title, *ii* blank, iii–iv Avertissement, 1–194 text, *195–196* Table des Chapitres. Page 131 misnumbered 13.

Press figures: none.

Copies: *Bodleian; National Library of Scotland; *Newberry Library; Stadtbibliothek, Zürich.

Note:

There may be another edition of this work, in two octavo volumes, dated 1765; see Charles Alfred Rochedieu, *Bibliography of French Translations of English Works, 1700–1800* (Chicago: University of Chicago Press, 1948), p. 35.

55.

AN / ESTIMATE [red] / OF THE / MANNERS / AND / PRINCIPLES [red] / OF THE / TIMES. / [rule] / By the AUTHOR of / ESSAYS on the CHARACTERISTICS, &c. [red] / [rule] / [quotation] / [rule] / VOL. II. / [rule] / LONDON: [red] / Printed for L. DAVIS and C. REYMERS, against / *Grays-Inn-Gate*, *Holborn*; / Printers to the ROYAL SOCIETY. / MDCCLVIII. [red]

Collation: 8°: A^4 B–F^8(±F8) G^8(±G1) H–R^8 S^4

Contents: Page *1* title, *2* blank, 3–8 Contents and list of four errata, *9* special title for Part I, *10* blank, 9–100 text of Part I, *101* special title for Part II, *102* blank, 103–265 text of Part II, *266* blank, *267–270* Advertisements.

Press figures: 15-1, 20-2, 30-2, 32-3, 42-4, 52-5, 58-1, 65-2, 79-3, 84-4, 86-1 or none, 88-5 or none, 92-1, 99-5, 104-3, 114-2, 129-5, 131-4, 144-1, 146-3, 154-2, 160-4, 174-1, 176-5, 193-2, 194-3, 200-5, 211-4, 216-1, 218-2, 242-2, 245-1, 254-2, 256-4, *267*-3.

Size of an uncut copy: 8¾″ × 5⅜″ (Yale).

Number of copies printed: William Bowyer printed 4,000 copies of this volume, the first of which were delivered to Davis April 3, 1758 (Bodleian MS. DON b.4, folio 159).

Date of publication: April 8, 1758 (*London Chronicle*).

Copies: Bibliothèque Nationale; *Bodleian (2 copies); *British Museum (3 copies); *Bryn Mawr College; University of Chicago; University of Cincinnati; Columbia; *Cornell (2 copies); Huntington Library (2 copies); Illinois; Indiana (2 copies); *Lambeth Palace Library (imperfect); *Library Company of Philadelphia (2 copies); National Library of Scotland (2 copies); Newberry Library; New York Public Library; *New York State Library, Albany; *University of Pennsylvania; Pennsylvania State University; *Texas (5 copies); University of Toronto; University of Virginia; *Virginia State Library, Richmond; *Yale (3 copies); *D. D. Eddy (6 copies).

Notes:

1. Page 126 exists in two states: the first is correctly numbered; the second is misnumbered 26 (after the numeral dropped out in the course of printing). Copies of both states are common.

2. Leaf F8 exists in four states. In the first state, F8 is not a cancel and page 85 is not signed "VOL. II. F8." In this original state page 85 contains this sentence, which is not present in all subsequent states: "I am told, that in some great Houses, the Place of Rendezvous for the Servants goes by the Name of *Hell*; a Name, perhaps, not ill suited to the Genius of its Inhabitants: But a Name vilely given in Sport, and in Defiance of Divine Justice." (Copies: *Bodleian Godw. Pamph. 103; *British Museum 8404.de.27.)

3. The second state, with F8 a cancel tipped in on a stub. Page 85 signed "VOL. II. F8" and, as in the first state, page 86 has no press figure. The offending sentence has been removed. Page 86, line 5 reads "Murderers?" (Copies: *Bodleian Godw. Pamph. 2165; *British Museum 8409.h.35; University of Cincinnati; *Lambeth Palace Library; *New York Public Library; *D. D. Eddy.)

4. The third state, with F8 a cancel tipped in on a stub. Page 85 signed "VOL. II. F8" with press figure 1 on page 86. The text of this third state is the same as the text of the second state in both substantives and accidentals, and yet both pages 85 and 86 are of a setting of type different from the second state. (Copies: *British Museum 16219; *University of Texas 309.942 B813e 1758 v.2; *D. D. Eddy.)

5. The fourth state, with F8 a cancel tipped in on a stub. Page 85 signed "VOL. II. F8" while page 86 may or may not have press figure 1. This state is of a setting of type different from the second and third states, and it differs from them even in accidentals: e.g., page 86, line 5 reads "Murderers!" (Copies: *Bryn Mawr College; *Columbia 942.5 B811;

*Library Company of Philadelphia (both copies); *University of Pennsylvania 320.4 B816; *Virginia State Library HN 388.B84 1757 v.2; *D. D. Eddy.)

The designations "second," "third," and "fourth" states are arbitrary, for I have not determined their priority.

6. Leaf G1 presumably exists in four states. The first is the original, uncancelled state, containing the offending reading which necessitated the cancellation. No copy seen.

7. The second state, with G1 a cancel tipped in on a stub. No press figure on page 88. Page 87, line 12 reads "Essays, he." (Copies: *British Museum 8409.h.35; University of Cincinnati; *Lambeth Palace Library; *New York Public Library; *D. D. Eddy.)

8. The third state—exactly the same as the second state, except for clearly being of a different setting of type. (Copies: *British Museum 16219; *University of Texas 309.942 B813e 1758 v.2; *D. D. Eddy.)

9. The fourth state, with G1 a cancel tipped in on a stub. Press figure 5 on page 88. This state is of a setting of type different from the second and third states, even in the accidentals: e.g., page 87, line 12 reads "Essays he." (Copies: *Bodleian Godw. Pamph. 2165; *Bodleian Godw. Pamph. 103; *Columbia 942.5 B811; *University of Pennsylvania 320.4 B816; *Virginia State Library HN 388.B84 1757 v.2; *D. D. Eddy.)

Once again, the designations "second," "third," and "fourth" states are arbitrary, for I have not determined their priority.

56. *First Dublin Edition of Volume II (1758)*

AN / ESTIMATE / OF THE / MANNERS / AND / PRINCIPLES / OF THE / TIMES. / [rule] / By the AUTHOR of / ESSAYS on the CHARACTERISTICS, &c. / [rule] / [quotation] / [rule] / VOL. II. / [double rule] / DUBLIN: / Printed for G. FAULKNER, J. HOEY, sen. and / jun. J. EXSHAW, and R. SMITH, Booksellers. / [rule] / MDCCLVIII.

Collation: 12°: $A^{12}(A1 + \chi^2 + A2\text{–}12)$ B–G^{12} H^4. (Total: 90 leaves, 180 pages.)

Contents: Page *1* title, *2* blank, 3–6 Contents, *3* special title for Part I, *4* blank, 5–66 text of Part I, *67* special title for Part II, *68* blank, 69–174 text of Part II, *175–176* blank.

Press figures: none.

Size of an uncut copy: $7\frac{1}{4}''$ × $4\frac{1}{4}''$ (Pennsylvania State University copy, in contemporary boards).

Copies: *Folger Library; National Library of Ireland; University of Kentucky; *Pennsylvania State University; *D. D. Eddy.

Note:

Two conjugate leaves, χ^2, listing the table of contents, are inserted immediately after the title. These four pages are numbered 3–6. Leaves A2–5 are all signed.

57. *French Translation of part of Volume II (with a fragment from Volume I)*

[Type ornament] / RAPPROCHEMENT HEUREUX, / *OU* / PORTRAIT D'UN GRAND MINISTRE, / [This is followed by text; there is no separate title-page.]

Collation: 8° (in 4's): A^4

Contents: Pages *1* 2–6 text of "Portrait d'un Grand Ministre," 6–7 text of "Réflexion Politique du même Auteur," *8* blank.

Press figures: none.

Date: Unknown; variously estimated from 1789 to 179–.

Copies: Bibliothèque Nationale; *British Museum (2 copies); University of Chicago; *Newberry Library.

Notes:

1. The colophon at the end of page 7 reads, "De l'Imprimerie de VALLEYRE, rue de la Bouclerie."

2. The "Portrait d'un Grand Ministre" is translated from the second volume of Brown's *Estimate*, 1758, pages 252–259. The note at the bottom of page 1 says ". . . nous avons traduit *le Caractere d'un grand Ministre*, que l'on trouve à la fin du second volume."

3. Notes at the bottom of pages *1* and 7 say that the "Réflexion Politique" was translated from the first volume of Brown's *Estimate*, the seventh edition (1758), page 220.

4. The "grand minister" being referred to is Jacques Necker.

58. *French Translation of part of Volume II*

DIALOGUE / *ENTRE* / PHOCION ET MABLY, / *AUX CHAMPS ÉLYSÉES,* / A L'OCCASION DES ÉTATS-GÉNÉRAUX / DE LA FRANCE, / *Suivi de l'Idée d'un Ministre patriote, ou du / Portrait de M. Necker, tracé en 1757, / par un Auteur Anglais; / Ainsi que du Caractère d'un Ecrivain politique / impartial, tiré du même Auteur.* / [ornament] / A ABBEVILLE, / Chez Devérité, Imprimeur du Roi / & de Mgr Comte d'Artois. / *ET SE VEND A PARIS,* / Chez les Marchands de Nouveautés. / [rule] / 1789.

Collation: 8°: A^8 B^4 C^2

Contents: Page *1* title, *2* blank, *3* 4–18 text of "Dialogue entre Phocion et Mably," 19–24 text of "Portrait anticipé de M. Necker, ou Caractere d'un bon Ministre; *tracé en 1757, par un Auteur Anglais,*" 25–27 text of "Caractere de l'écrivain politique impartial; *tiré du même Ouvrage,*" *28* blank.

Press figures: none.

Copies: *British Museum.

Note:

Both the "Caractere d'un bon Ministre" and the "Caractere de l'écrivain politique impartial" are translated from the second volume of Brown's *Estimate*, 1758, pages 252–265.

59. *Walker, George. 1618–1690*

The Power of Protestant religious Principle / *in producing a national Spirit of Defence,* / EXEMPLIFIED IN A / DIARY / OF THE / SIEGE of *LONDON-DERRY.* / Written by / The Rev. *GEORGE WALKER,* D.D. / Who commanded the Garrison during the Siege. / Now published, as a *useful Lesson* to the / PRESENT TIMES. / To which is prefixed, / A PREFATORY ADDRESS to the Public, / By the EDITOR. / [rule] / *Heu, Pietas! Heu, prisca* FIDES! / [rule] / LONDON: / Printed for L. DAVIS and C. REYMERS, / against *Gray's-Inn, Holborn.* MDCCLVIII. / [Price One Shilling and Sixpence.]

Collation: 8° (in 4's): A^2 a^4 $B–L^4$ M^2

Contents: Page *i* title, *ii* blank, *iii* (misnumbered ii) iv–xii Brown's Prefatory Address to the Public, *i* ii–v George Walker's Dedication, *vi* blank, *vii* viii–x A Description of Londonderry, 1–73 text of Walker's diary, *74* Advertisement. Page iii is misnumbered ii.

Press figures: iv-1, xi-4, viii (i.e., $B4^v$)-3, 2-2, 14-4, 18-2, 27-1, 34-2, 42-2, 54-2, 60-4, 69-4.

Size of a slightly trimmed copy: $8\frac{1}{4}'' \times 5\frac{5}{16}''$ (British Museum G.4798.[1.]).

Number of copies printed: William Bowyer printed 1,000 copies, 300 of which were sent to the binder April 29, 1758 (Bodleian MS. DON b.4, folio 159).

Date of publication: May 4, 1758 (*Whitehall Evening Post*).

Copies: *British Museum (2 copies: listed under Walker, George); Cambridge University Library (2 copies); *Harvard; Huntington Library; New York Public Library.

Note:

On page *74*, Davis and Reymers advertise six of Brown's works, three of which were printed years earlier: *On Liberty: A Poem* (1749); *On the Pursuit of false Pleasure . . . A Sermon* [presumably the second edition, 1752]; and *On the Use and Abuse of Externals in Religion. A Sermon* (1753).

John Brown's Prefatory Address continues the arguments expressed in his *Estimate.*

60.

AN / EXPLANATORY DEFENCE / OF THE / ESTIMATE / OF THE / MANNERS / AND / PRINCIPLES / OF THE / TIMES. / BEING / An APPENDIX to that Work, occasioned by the / Clamours lately raised against it among certain / Ranks of Men. / WRITTEN / By the AUTHOR of the ESTIMATE, in a / Series of Letters to a noble FRIEND. / [double rule] / LONDON: / Printed for L. DAVIS and C. REYMERS, against / *Grays-Inn-Gate, Holborn.* MDCCLVIII.

Half-title: [row of type ornaments] / AN / EXPLANATORY DEFENCE / OF THE / ESTIMATE, *&c.* / [row of type ornaments]

Collation: 8°: A^2 $B^8(\pm B3)$ C–F^8 G^2

Contents: $A1^r$ half-title, $A1^v$ blank, $A2^r$ title, $A2^v$ blank, pages 1–84 text.

Press figures: 4-4, 29-4, 38-2, 59-3, 60-4, 76-4.

Size of an uncut copy: $8\frac{7}{8}''$ × $5\frac{5}{8}''$ (Cornell and D. D. Eddy copies, unbound, stitched).

Number of copies printed: William Bowyer printed 1,000 copies, the first 500 of which were delivered to Davis June 15, 1758 (Bodleian MS. DON b.4, folio 159).

Date of publication: June 19, 1758 (*Daily Advertiser*).

Copies: *Bodleian (2 copies); *Boston Athenaeum (2 copies); *British Museum (4 copies); *Cambridge University Library (3 copies); *Columbia; *Cornell; *Harvard (2 copies); Huntington Library (2 copies); *Illinois (2 copies); *Library Company of Philadelphia; National Library of Scotland;

*Newberry Library; *New-York Historical Society; *University of Pennsylvania; Pennsylvania State University; Princeton; Texas; *Yale (2 copies); *D. D. Eddy.

61.

AN ADDITIONAL / DIALOGUE / OF THE / DEAD, / BETWEEN / PERICLES and ARISTIDES: / Being a Sequel to the Dialogue between / PERICLES and COSMO. / [rule] / [quotation] / [double rule] / LONDON, / Printed for L. DAVIS and C. REYMERS, opposite / *Gray's-Inn-Gate*, in *Holbourn*. MDCCLX.

Collation: 8° (in 4's): a[4] B–F[4]

Contents: Page *i* half-title, *ii* blank, *iii* title, *iv* blank, v–viii Advertisement, 9–48 text.

Press figures: 15-4, 24-‡.

Number of copies printed: William Bowyer printed 1,000 copies, the first of which were delivered to Davis May 31, 1760 (Bodleian MS. DON b.4, folio 128).

Date of publication: June 3, 1760 (*Daily Advertiser*; *London Chronicle*). Price 1s.

Copies: *Bodleian; *British Museum; *University of Wisconsin; *D. D. Eddy (lacks half-title). (I have examined a Xerox print of the University of Wisconsin copy.)

Notes:

1. John Brown wrote this pamphlet to refute the political arguments advanced by Lord Lyttelton in his *Dialogues of the Dead*—specifically, Dialogue XXIII, pages 241–259 of the first edition, 1760 (see below, no. 133).

2. Brown was the earliest but not the sole respondent to Lyttelton. For example, on June 19, 1760 an anonymous ninety-four page pamphlet was published: *Candid and Critical Remarks on the Dialogues of the Dead: In a Letter from a Gentleman in London to his Friend in the Country*. London: Printed for George

Kearsly, at the Golden Lion in Ludgate-street, 1760. (Copies: *University of Chicago; *Cornell; New York Public Library; *Yale.)

In his discussion of Dialogue XXIII (pages 62–64), the author of this pamphlet recognizes that "the parallel drawn between these two men is intirely political" (p. 62) and that the reader is meant to see allusions to contemporary politicians. However, he makes no judgement of Lyttelton's comments, let alone the type of sharp criticism made by John Brown in his *Additional Dialogue of the Dead.*

62. *The Second Edition (1760)*

AN ADDITIONAL / DIALOGUE / OF THE / DEAD, / BETWEEN / PERICLES and ARISTIDES: / Being a Sequel to the Dialogue between / PERICLES and COSMO. / [rule] / [quotation] / [rule] / THE SECOND EDITION. / [double rule] / LONDON, / Printed for L. DAVIS and C. REYMERS, opposite / *Gray's-Inn-Gate*, in *Holbourn.* MDCCLX.

Collation, Contents, and Press figures: Exactly the same as the first edition.

Date of publication: June 14, 1760 (*Daily Advertiser*). Price 1s.

Copies: *Bodleian (2 copies); *University of Oregon, Eugene; *D. D. Eddy. (I have examined a Xerox print of the University of Oregon copy.)

Note:

This "edition" has a new title-page, but otherwise it is a reissue of the sheets of the first edition.

63.

On the Natural Duty of a Personal Service, / in Defence of Ourselves and Country. / [rule] / A / SERMON, / PREACHED AT / ST NICHOLAS CHURCH, in *Newcastle,* / ON OCCASION of / A late DANGEROUS INSURRECTION, / at HEXHAM. / To which is prefixed, / A Short and Authentic ACCOUNT of the / INSURRECTION. / [rule] / By JOHN BROWN, D.D. / VICAR of NEWCASTLE. / [rule] / NEWCASTLE UPON TYNE: / Printed by I. Thompson, Esq; and Company. / MDCCLXI.

Collation: 8° (in 4's): *A* (3 leaves) B–D^4 E (three leaves)

Contents: Page *1* title, *2* blank, 3–4 Account of the Insurrection, 7–8 Dedication to Henry Partis, Mayor of Newcastle, 9–38 text of the sermon, with pages 5–36 misnumbered 7–38.

Press figures: none.

Date of publication: At least by March 21, 1761 (*The Newcastle Journal*, March 14–21, 1761; *The Newcastle Courant*, March 21, 1761). "Price Six-pence."

Copies: *University of Minnesota, Minneapolis; Society of Antiquaries of Newcastle upon Tyne. (I have examined a microfilm of the University of Minnesota copy.)

Notes:

1. The Bodleian has a copy of a Newcastle edition which lacks the title-page, so there is no way of telling which edition it is.

2. I wish to thank Miss Thompson, the librarian in charge of the Local Collection in the Newcastle upon Tyne Central Public Library, and Mr. Alistair Elliot, Assistant Librarian in the University of Newcastle upon Tyne Library, for providing me with the dates of publication of the first and fifth Newcastle editions of this sermon.

64. *The Second Newcastle Edition (1761)*

On the Natural Duty of a Personal Service, / in Defence of Ourselves and Country. / [rule] / A / SERMON, / PREACHED AT / ST NICHOLAS CHURCH, in *Newcastle*, / On OCCASION of / A late DANGEROUS INSURRECTION, / at HEXHAM. / To which is prefixed, / A Short and Authentic ACCOUNT of the / IN-

SURRECTION. / [rule] / By JOHN BROWN, D.D. / VICAR of NEWCASTLE. / [rule] / The SECOND EDITION. / [double rule] / NEWCASTLE UPON TYNE: / Printed by I. Thompson, Esq; and Company. / MDCCLXI.

Collation, Contents, and Press figures: Identical with the first Newcastle edition, including the misnumbered pages.

Date of publication: Sometime in the week of March 21–28, 1761 (see the dates of publication for the first and fifth Newcastle editions).

Copies: *Boston Public Library.

Note:

This "edition" has a new title-page, but in all other respects it appears to be either a reissue of first edition sheets or a new impression from standing type.

65. *The Third Newcastle Edition (1761)*

No copy seen, but presumably it would be identical with the other Newcastle editions except for its title-page.

Date of publication: Sometime in the week of March 21–28, 1761 (see the dates of publication for the first and fifth Newcastle editions).

66. *The Fourth Newcastle Edition (1761)*

No copy seen, but presumably it would be identical with the other Newcastle editions except for its title-page.

Date of publication: Sometime in the week of March 21–28, 1761 (see the dates of publication for the first and fifth Newcastle editions).

67. *The Fifth Newcastle Edition (1761)*

On the Natural Duty of a Personal Service, / in Defence of Ourselves and Country. / [rule] / A / SERMON, / PREACHED AT /

St Nicholas Church, in *Newcastle*, / On Occasion of / A late Dangerous INSURRECTION, / at Hexham. / To which is prefixed, / A Short and Authentic ACCOUNT of the / INSURRECTION. / [rule] / By JOHN BROWN, D.D. / Vicar of Newcastle. / [rule] / The FIFTH EDITION. / [double rule] / NEWCASTLE UPON TYNE: / Printed by I. Thompson, Esq; and Company. / MDCCLXI.

Collation, Contents, and Press figures: Identical with the first Newcastle edition, including the misnumbered pages.

Date of publication: At least by March 28, 1761 (*The Newcastle Journal*, March 21–28, 1761; *The Newcastle Courant*, March 28, 1761). "Price Six-pence."

Copies: *British Museum.

Note:

This "edition" has a new title-page, but in all other respects it appears to be either a reissue of first edition sheets or a new impression from standing type.

68. *The First London Edition (1761)*

On the Natural Duty of a Personal Service, in / Defence of ourselves and Country. / [rule] / A / SERMON, / PREACHED AT / St Nicholas Church, in *Newcastle*, / On Occasion of / A late Dangerous INSURECTION, / at Hexham. / To which is prefixed, / A Short and Authentic ACCOUNT of the / INSURRECTION. / [rule] / By JOHN BROWN, D.D. / Vicar of Newcastle. / [rule] / LONDON, / Printed for L. Davis and C. Reymers, against *Grays- / Inn, Holborn.* Mdcclxi.

Collation: 8° (in 4's): A–D^4 E^2

Contents: Page *1* title, *2* blank, 3–4 Account of the Insurrection, 5–6 Dedication to Henry Partis, Mayor of Newcastle, 7–36 text of the sermon. Page 18 misnumbered 20, and 20 misnumbered 8.

Press figures: 15-1, 24-4.

Date of publication: March 31, 1761 (*Whitehall Evening Post*, March 28–31). Price 6d.

Copies: *American Philosophical Society; *Bodleian; *British Museum; *Cambridge University Library; *Columbia; *Northwestern University; Pembroke College, Cambridge; *Sion College Library (B.10.34).

69.

THE / CURE / OF / SAUL. [red] / A / SACRED ODE. / Written by DR. BROWN. [red] / [double rule] / LONDON, [red] / Printed for L. DAVIS and C. REYMERS against *Gray's-Inn, Holbourn.* / Printers to the ROYAL SOCIETY. / MDCCLXIII. [red]

Collation: 4°: *A* (three leaves) B–D^4

Contents: *A*1^r half-title, *A*1^v blank, *A*2^r title, *A*2^v blank, *A*3 The Argument, pages *1* 2–21 text, *22* blank, *23* Advertisement, *24* blank.

Press figures: 8-2, 10-4, 18-4.

Number of copies printed: William Bowyer printed 1,000 copies, the first of which were delivered to Davis January 31, 1763; but the first large shipment (485 copies) was sent February 21, 1763 (Bodleian MS. DON b.4, folio 187).

Date of publication: February 25, 1763 (*Public Advertiser*). Price 1s.

Copies: *British Museum (2 copies: 840.k.8.[10.] and 162.m.35, both of which lack the half-title and advertisement leaf); Duke; *Harvard (Horace Walpole's copy, purchased Feb. 26, 1763); University of Kentucky; National Library of Scotland (A1.1.14[3]); *Newberry Library (lacks half-title and advertisement leaf); Texas; *University of Wisconsin, Madison (imperfect); *Yale; *D. D. Eddy (2 copies).

Subsequent printings, in this form:

1. The poem is reprinted, with a few textual variations, in every edition and translation of Brown's *Dissertation on . . . Poetry and Music* (see below, no. 76 ff.).

2. It was reprinted, with some textual variants from the *Dissertation* version, by George Pearch in all four editions of his *Collection of Poems by Several Hands*: London, 1768 (II, 100–111); London, 1770 (II, 104–115); London, 1775 (II, 104–115); London, 1783 (II, 104–115).

3. Excerpts from Pearch's text of the poem were used by Andrew Kippis in his life of John Brown (*Biographia Britannica*, 2d ed. London, 1780 [II, 660–661]).

4. Pearch's text was reprinted by Robert Anderson in the first collected edition of Brown's poems: *Works of the British Poets*. 13 vols. London and Edinburgh, 1795 (X, 881–884).

5. The poem is reprinted in Thomas Park's *Supplement to the British Poets* . . . London, 1809 (IX, 139–148).

70. *First Oratorio Version (1763)*

THE / CURE / OF / SAUL. / A / SACRED ODE. / As it is performed at the THEATRE-ROYAL in / *Covent-Garden*. / [rule] / Written by DR. BROWN. / [rule] / Set to select *Airs, Duets,* and *Choirs*, from HANDEL, / MARCELLO, PURCEL, and other eminent Composers. / [rule] / [quotation] / [double rule] / LONDON, / Printed for L. DAVIS and C. REYMERS against *Gray's-Inn, Holbourn*. / Printers to the ROYAL SOCIETY. / MDCCLXIII.

Collation: 4°: *A*[4] B–C[4]

Contents: Page *i* half-title, *ii* blank, *iii* title, *iv* Advertisement, *v*–vi The Argument, *7* 8–22 text, *23–24* blank.

Press figures: none.

Date of first performance: March 4, 1763 (*Daily Advertiser*; *Public Advertiser*).

Number of copies printed: William Bowyer printed 500 copies, all of which were delivered to Davis on March 4, 1763 (Bodleian MS. DON b.4, folio 187).

Date of publication: March 4, 1763 (*Daily Advertiser*). Price 1s.

Copies: *Boston Athenaeum; *British Museum (2 copies: 643.k.8.[7.] and 840.k.5.[3.], both of which lack the half-title and final blank leaf); *Cornell; *Folger Library (lacks half-title and final blank leaf); *General Theological Seminary, New York; *Harvard; Huntington Library; *Illinois; *Library Company of Philadelphia (2 copies); National Library of Scotland (2 copies: Ak.3.28 and B.H. Lib. 74); Princeton; *Yale (2 copies); *D. D. Eddy (2 copies).

Notes:

1. The Advertisement on page *iv* states: "*It was found necessary to omit a few Lines in the Ode, for the sake of bringing the Performance to a proper Length of Time: And the Poem is here divided into three Parts, to mark the several Pauses in the Representation.*" In addition to these changes, however, this version contains a number of authorial substantive revisions.

2. The *Public Advertiser* prints the "This Day is published" advertisement in its issue of March 3, 1763; surely this is an error, for Bowyer did not deliver any copies to Davis until the following day.

3. The *Public Advertiser* of Friday, March 4, 1763 has this advertisement:

> At the Theatre-Royal in Covent-Garden,
> This Day will be performed
> The CURE of SAUL,
> A SACRED ODE. By Dr. BROWN.
>
> Adapted (by the Author of the Ode) to select Airs, Duets, and Chorusses, from Handel, Marcello, Purcel, and other eminent Composers.
>
> With a Concerto on the Organ by Mr. STANLEY:
> And a Concerto on the Violin by Mr. HAY.
>
> Pit and Boxes to be put together. No Persons to be admitted without Tickets, which will be delivered this

Day at the Office in the Theatre at half a Guinea each. First Gallery 5s. Second Gallery 3s. 6d.

Galleries to be opened at Half an Hour after Four o'Clock, Pit and Boxes at Five. To begin at Half after Six. Vivant Rex & Regina.

4. *The Cure of Saul* was performed as an oratorio only twice during John Brown's life: at Covent Garden on Friday, March 4, 1763, and at Drury Lane on Wednesday, April 27, 1763 (see next entry).

5. In Part 4 of *The London Stage, 1660–1800*, George Winchester Stone, Jr. erroneously lists the *Cure of Saul* under Samuel James Arnold (see Index, II, xxi). Arnold had nothing to do with the music of this oratorio until the performance of January 22, 1767, four months after John Brown's death (see the descriptions, below, of the third oratorio version). Professor Stone intends to correct this point in the next edition of *The London Stage*.

71. *Second Oratorio Version (1763)*

A revised and expanded version of the *Cure of Saul* was performed in Drury Lane on Wednesday, April 27, 1763. The *Public Advertiser* of that date carries an advertisement very similar to the playbill (q.v.).

Number of copies printed: William Bowyer printed 500 copies of this "second impression"—as Bowyer's ledger describes it—all of which were delivered to Davis on April 21 (or 23), 1763 (Bodleian MS. DON b.4, folio 187).

Date of publication: April 25, 1763 (*Daily Advertiser*).

> *This Day is published, Price* 1 *s.* THE CURE of SAUL. A Sacred Ode, written by Dr. BROWN. Printed as it is to be performed at the Theatre Royal in Drury-Lane on Wednesday next, the 27th instant. . . .

Copies: None located. I suspect that the title-page is very

FOR THE

Benefit of the Colleges of *Philadelphia* and *New York*.

AT THE

Theatre Royal in *Drury-Lane*,

This present *Wednesday*, being the 27th of *April*,
Will be PERFORM'D

The CURE of *SAUL*,

A *SACRED ODE*.

Written by Dr. *BROWN*
Set to select *Airs* *Duets* and *Chorusses*,
From Mr. *HANDEL*,
And other Eminent COMPOSERS.
With the Addition of several *New Songs*.
The VOCAL PARTS by

Mr. *Beard*,	Siga. *Clementina*,
Sig. *Tenducci*,	Miss *Young*,
Mr. *Norris*,	AND
Mr. *Champnes*,	Miss *Polly Young*.

The ORCHESTRA to be led

By Signor GIARDINI,

Who will perform a Concerto on the VIOLIN between the Acts.

‖§‖ PIT and BOXES to be put together.

No Persons to be admitted without Tickets, which will be delivered at the Office in the Theatre at *Half-a-Guinea* each; And also at the following Coffee-houses, *viz.* the *Smyrna*, *Pall-mall*; the *Mount*, *Grosvenor-street*; *George's*, *Temple-bar*; the *Rainbow*, *Cornhill*; the *New York*, *Sweeting's-alley*; and the *Pensylvania*, *Birchin-lane*.

FIRST GALLERY 5s. SECOND GALLERY 3s. 6d.

‡ *Galleries to be opened at half an Hour after Four*, *Pit and Boxes at Five*.
† *To begin at half an Hour after Six.* *Vivant Rex & Regina.*

HENRY E. HUNTINGTON LIBRARY

VII. Playbill for the Drury Lane performance of the *Cure of Saul*
Size of playbill: $9\frac{1}{4}'' \times 5\frac{1}{2}''$

similar to the first oratorio version, except for reading "Drury-Lane" instead of "Covent-Garden." The text is also probably very similar except for the addition of the new songs.

Of course, if Bowyer's ledgers are strictly accurate so that he did in fact print nothing but a second impression of the first oratorio version, then bibliographically this item is a ghost. (I have not discovered any variants among the copies of the first oratorio version.)

Note:

The *Public Advertiser* of Wednesday, April 27, 1763 also contains a review of Robert Maddison's *Examination of the Oratorios which have been performed this Season . . .*, which was published two days earlier. Reprinted are extracts from this work which praise highly the *Cure of Saul*; at the end of the review, the newspaper prints this general notice of the oratorio:

> * * * Since, therefore, this Piece hath never been perform'd but *once* before, the Author having generously reserved its second Performance for the Benefit of the laudable Charity above-mentioned; and as the Managers of the Theatre have most disinterestedly concurred in the Design, and the principal Performers, *vocal* and *instrumental*, offered their Services *gratis*, it is not doubted but these benevolent Intentions will be encouraged and made effectual, by the good Disposition of the Town, especially as the *Weather* is so *cool* and favourable to the Purpose. The Author, we hear also, hath made some Additions and Improvements, to render the Piece still more worthy of the Reception it has met with; and some new Performers are added to the vocal Parts, who, it is thought, will give great Satisfaction.

72. *Third Oratorio Version, First Edition (1767)*

THE / CURE / OF / SAUL. / A / SACRED ODE. / [rule] / Written by Dr. BROWN. / [rule] / The MUSIC composed by Mr. ARNOLD. / [rule] / [quotation] / [double rule] /

THE

CURE

OF

SAUL.

A

SACRED ODE.

Written by Dr. BROWN.

The MUSIC compoſed by Mr. ARNOLD.

Grata Teſtudo! — Laborum
Dulce Lenimen! Mihi cunque ſalve,
Rite vocanti.

LONDON:

Printed for L. DAVIS and C. REYMERS, over-againſt *Gray's-Inn-Gate*, *Holbourn*, Bookſellers to the ROYAL SOCIETY.
MDCCLXVII.

VIII. Title-page of no. 72
Size of page: $9\frac{5}{8}'' \times 7\frac{5}{8}''$

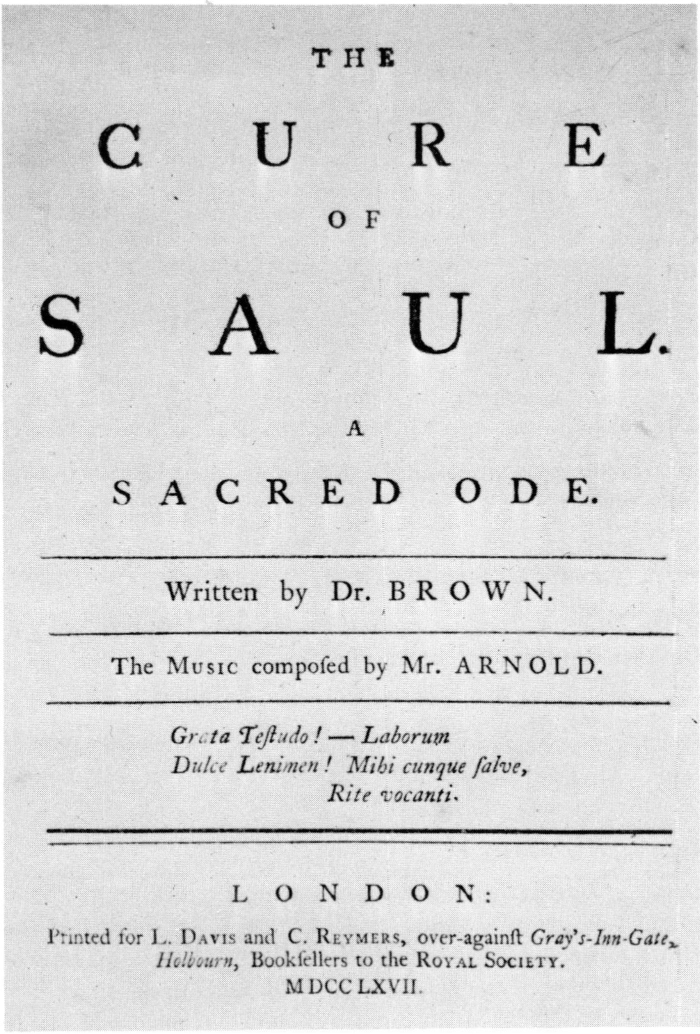

THE

C U R E

OF

S A U L.

A

SACRED ODE.

Written by Dr. BROWN.

The Music composed by Mr. ARNOLD.

Grata Testudo! — Laborum
Dulce Lenimen! Mihi cunque salve,
Rite vocanti.

LONDON:

Printed for L. Davis and C. Reymers, over-against *Gray's-Inn-Gate*, *Holbourn*, Booksellers to the Royal Society.
MDCCLXVII.

NATIONAL LIBRARY OF SCOTLAND

IX. Title-page of no. 73
Size of page: $10\frac{5}{8}'' \times 7\frac{7}{8}''$

LONDON: / Printed for L. DAVIS and C. REYMERS, over-against *Gray's-Inn-Gate*, / *Holbourn*, Booksellers to the ROYAL SOCIETY. / MDCCLXVII.

Half-title: THE / CURE / OF / SAUL. / [Price One Shilling.]

Collation: 4°: *A*^{2} B–C^4. B3 and C3 are signed.

Contents: Page *i* half-title, *ii* Advertisement, "BOOKS Written by Dr. *BROWN*." *iii* title, *iv* Advertisement, *v*–vi (misnumbered iv) The Argument, *7* 8–20 text. Page vi misnumbered iv.

Press figures: none.

Date of first performance: January 23, 1767, at the King's Theatre, with new music composed by Samuel James Arnold.

Copies: *Boston Athenaeum; *British Museum (840.k.10.[5.], lacks half-title); *University of Pennsylvania; Texas.

73. *Third Oratorio Version, Second Edition (1767)*

Title: Same as the first edition of this third oratorio version, but clearly of a different setting of type.

Collation: 4°: *A*^{2} B–C^4. B3 and C3 are *not* signed.

Contents: Page *i* half-title, *ii* Advertisement for books "Printed for L. DAVIS and C. REYMERS," *iii* title, *iv* blank, *v*–vi The Argument, *7* 8–20 text.

Press figures: none.

Copies: *Bodleian; *British Museum (11630.d.4.[17.]); *National Library of Scotland (B.H. Lib. 75). The Bodleian and British Museum copies lack the half-title. I have examined a Xerox print of the National Library of Scotland copy.

Note:

The two editions of the third oratorio version are clearly printed from different settings of type throughout and show compositorial changes. They may be easily differentiated as follows:

(1) The first edition correctly prints the Advertisement on the verso of the title; in the second edition the verso of the title is blank.
(2) In the first edition, $B1^v$ is incorrectly numbered iv; in the second edition it is correctly numbered vi.
(3) In the first edition B3 and C3 are signed; in the second edition they are not.
(4) In the first edition the catchword on page 7 is "By"; in the second edition it is corrected to "Midnight."
(5) The Advertisements on the versos of the half-titles are different; see the Contents, above. Also, in the first edition the last two items advertised on the verso of the half-title are listed under the heading "*Speedily will be published*"; in the second edition these same items are listed as having been published.

74. *Third Oratorio Version, Third Edition (1767?)*

No title-page. This may be an extract from some larger work.

Collation: 8° (in 4's): B–C^4

Contents: Pages 1–15 text, *16* blank.

Press figures: none.

Copies: *Boston Public Library.

Note:

The two works preceding this in a bound volume are operas, in English and Italian, with the imprints "London: Printed for G. Woodfall, at Charing-Cross, 1766" (and 1765). This edition of the *Cure of Saul* has the same format and typography as the two operas, but the text is not printed with an Italian translation. The text has the same distinctive readings as the two quarto editions of 1767, so it is probably part of a work dated 1767 or later (assuming, of course, that the two quarto editions of 1767 preceded the octavo edition and so did not derive their text from it).

75. *Third Oratorio Version, Fourth Edition (1771)*

THE / CURE OF SAUL: / A SACRED ODE. / [rule] / WRITTEN BY DR. BROWN. / [rule] / The MUSIC composed by Mr. ARNOLD. / [rule] / [quotation] / [double rule] / HEREFORD: / PRINTED BY C. PUGH. / [rule] / MDCC-LXXI. / [PRICE SIX-PENCE.]

Collation: 8° (in 4's): A^4 B^4 C^2

Contents: Page *i* title, *ii* Advertisement, *iii*–iv The Argument, *5* 6–18 text, *19–20* blank.

Press figures: none.

Copies: *Bodleian Vet.A5e.4987. (I have examined a Xerox print of the Bodleian copy.)

76.

A / DISSERTATION / ON THE / RISE, UNION, and POWER, [red] / THE / Progressions, Separations, and Corruptions, / OF / POETRY and MUSIC. [red] / To which is prefixed, / The CURE of SAUL. [red] / A / SACRED ODE. / [rule] / Written by DR. BROWN. [red] / [rule] / [quotation] / [double rule] / LONDON, [red] / Printed for L. DAVIS and C. REYMERS against *Gray's-Inn, Holbourn.* / Printers to the ROYAL SOCIETY. / MDCCLXIII. [red]

Collation: 4°: B–2I^4 *K*1

Contents: Page *i* title, *ii* Advertisement, *iii*–iv The Argument of the Ode, *5* 6–19 The Cure of Saul, *20* blank, *21* special title, *22* Errata, *xxiii*–xxiv Contents of the Dissertation, 25–242 text, 243–246 Appendix, *247*–248 (misnumbered 244) An Inscription, Written at a favourite Retirement, in May 1758, *249–250* Advertisements. Page 231 misnumbered 131 and 248 misnumbered 244.

Press figures: 15-1, 31-4, 32-2, 37-2, 39-4, 46-2, 53-2, 62-4, 69-2, 74-2, 76-5, 88-2, 96-5, 101-4, 108-4, 111-2, 114-4, 120-2, 124-5, 136-5, 140-5, 149-5, 150-4, 159-2, 164-2, 166-4,

172-2, 182-2, 189-4, 194-2, 202-2 or none, 205-2, 212-4, 214-1, 222-1, 231 (misnumbered 131)-1, 238-2, 240-2, *247*-2.

Size of an uncut copy: $11\frac{3}{8}'' \times 8\frac{7}{8}''$ (British Museum 1502/100, in original blue boards; Harvard; Wellesley College copy, in contemporary boards; D. D. Eddy copy, in contemporary marbled boards).

Number of copies printed: William Bowyer printed 1,000 copies, the first of which were delivered to Davis February 23, 1763; but the first large shipment (248 copies) was sent to Davis March 15, 1763 (Bodleian MS. DON b.4, folio 187).

Date of publication: March 17, 1763 (*London Chronicle*, Mar. 15–17; *The St. James's Chronicle*, Mar. 15–17). "Price sewed in Boards 8s. 6d."

Copies: *Bodleian; *Boston Public Library (2 copies); *British Museum (2 copies); *Cambridge University Library; University of Chicago; *Library of Congress (2 copies, the first of which is inscribed "For William Ord Esq[r]. From the Author."); *Cornell; *Folger Library; *Harvard (2 copies); Huntington Library; *Illinois; *Indiana; *Lambeth Palace Library; *Library Company of Philadelphia; National Library of Scotland; Newberry Library; Pembroke College, Cambridge; Princeton; University of Toronto; *Union Theological Seminary, New York; *Wellesley College; *Yale; *D. D. Eddy.

Notes:

1. The *Dissertation* reprints the *Cure of Saul* in a slightly revised version of the poem rather than the later oratorio version. In fact, Davis received his first printed copies of the *Dissertation* three days before he published the first edition of the *Cure of Saul.* It is quite possible that by the time Brown sent the manuscript of the *Dissertation* to the printer he had not yet revised the poem to make the oratorio.

2. On the day the *Dissertation* was published, the *London Chronicle* contained a long review of it (March 15–17, 1763, pages 260–261).

3. The *Dissertation* contains the first appearance in print of Brown's poem, "An Inscription written at a favourite Retirement in May, 1758." It is contained in all English language editions of the *Dissertation.*

The "Inscription" is reprinted by George Pearch in all four editions of his *Collection of Poems by Several Hands*: London, 1768 (II, 111–112); London, 1770 (II, 115–116); London, 1775 (II, 115–116); London, 1783 (II, 115–116).

It is reprinted in Andrew Kippis' life of Brown in the *Biographia Britannica* (II [1780], 659) and in William Hutchinson's *History of the County of Cumberland* . . . Carlisle, 1794 (II, 472). It is also reprinted, under the short title "INSCRIPTION," in the first collected edition of Brown's poems: Robert Anderson's *Works of the British Poets.* 13 vols. London and Edinburgh, 1795 (X, 887–888). It is reprinted in Thomas Park's *Supplement to the British Poets* . . . London, 1809 (IX, 160–161).

77. *The Second Edition (1773)*

A / DISSERTATION / ON THE / RISE, UNION, and POWER, / THE / Progressions, Separations, and Corruptions, / OF / POETRY and MUSIC. / To which is prefixed, / The Cure of SAUL. / A / SACRED ODE. / [rule] / Written by Dr. BROWN. / [rule] / THE SECOND EDITION. / [rule] / [quotation] / [double rule] / LONDON: / Printed for J. Murray, No. 32, opposite St. Dunstan's Church, Fleet-Street. / M DCC LXXIII.

Collation, Contents, and Press figures: Exactly the same as the first edition.

Copies: Northwestern University; *Texas. (I have examined a microfilm of the Texas copy.)

Note:

This "second edition" has a new title-page printed all in black, otherwise it is a reissue of the sheets of the first edition.

78. *The First Dublin Edition (1763)*

A / DISSERTATION / ON THE / RISE, UNION, and POWER, / THE / Progressions, Separations, and Corruptions, / OF / POETRY and MUSIC. / To which is prefixed, / The CURE of SAUL. / A / SACRED ODE. / [rule] / Written by Dr. BROWN. / [rule] / [quotation] / [double rule] / DUBLIN: / Printed by G. FAULKNER, on the *Blind-Quay*. / [rule] / MDCCLXIII.

Collation: 12°: A–H^{12} I^{6}

Contents: Page *i* title, *ii* Advertisement, *iii* special title, *iv* blank, v–vi The Argument of the Ode, 7–15 The Cure of Saul, *16* blank, *17* special title, *18* The Contents of the Dissertation, 19–198 text of the Dissertation, 199–202 Appendix, *203*–204 An Inscription written at a favourite Retirement, in May, 1758.

Press figures: none.

Copies: *British Museum; *Cambridge University Library; University of Chicago; *D. D. Eddy.

79. *Selections from Brown's* Dissertation *(1768)*

THE LYRIC MUSE / REVIVED IN EUROPE / OR A CRITICAL DISPLAY / OF THE OPERA IN ALL / ITS REVOLUTIONS. / [rule] / LONDON, PRINTED FOR L. DAVIS AND / C. REYMERS. MDCCLXVIII.

Collation: 8°: a^{4} b–k^{8} $l^{4}(-l4)$

Contents: $a1^{r}$ title, $a1^{v}$ blank, page *i* ii–iii Preface, *iv* blank, *v*–vi A Table of Chapters, *1* 2–149 text, *150* blank. Pages 129–149 misnumbered 127–147.

Press figures: 14-1, 22-1, 47-1, 54-4, 61-1, 70-1, 88-4, 107-1, 124-3, 127-1, 140 (misnumbered 138)-3, 143 (misnumbered 141)-4, 148 (misnumbered 146)-4.

Copies: *Cambridge University Library.

Note:

Most of the material in chapters V–VIII (pages 45–90) is extracted from the writings of John Brown, especially his *Dissertation on . . . Poetry and Music* (1763). The other chapters are extracted from the writings of Martinelli, Antonini, Antoniotti, and so on.

80. *German Translation (1769)*

Dr. Brown's / Betrachtungen / über die / Poesie und Musik, / nach ihrem Ursprunge, ihrer / Vereinigung, Gewalt, Wachsthum, / Trennung und / Verderbnisz. / Aus dem Englischen übersetzt, mit Anmerkungen / und zween Anhängen begleitet, / von / Johann Joachim Eschenburg. / [rule] / Leipzig, / bey Weidmanns Erben und Reich, / 1769.
[Note: This title-page is printed entirely in black letter, and for the umlaut uses superscript e.]

Collation: 8°:)(^{8} (–)(8 [= *I*1 ?]) A–2H^8 *I*1(=)(8?)

One plate, the frontispiece, is tipped in before the title.

Contents: Frontispiece, *)(*1^r title, *)(*1^v blank,)(2^r–)(6^v Foreword of the translator (signed: Braunschweig, den 11. April, 1769. Johann Joachim Eschenburg),)(7^r special title,)(7^v blank, pages *1* 2–394 text of the *Dissertation*, *395* special title: Erster Anhang. / Die Heilung Sauls, / eine Ode / von Dr. Brown. *396* blank, 397–399 Contents of the *Cure of Saul* (German only), 400–431 text of the *Cure of Saul* (English and German on facing pages), *432* blank, *433* special title: Zweyter Anhang, / welcher noch einige weitläuftigere / Anmerkungen / und / Erinnerungen / zu dem Werke / des Herrn Brown enthält. *434* blank, *435* 436–494 text, *495–496* Contents, *497* Errata, *498* blank. Page 5 misnumbered 9, 9 misnumbered 5, and 406 misnumbered 460.

Press figures: none.

Size of an uncut copy: 7″ × 4⅛″ (Library of Congress copy).

Copies: *British Museum; *University of Chicago; *Library of Congress; Stadtbibliothek, Zürich.

Note:

Pages 435–494 contain mainly quotations (in German translation) from *Some Observations on Dr. Brown's Dissertation*... (London, 1764) and from Brown's reply, *Remarks on some Observations* . . . (London, 1764).

81. *Italian Translation (1772)*

DELL' ORIGINE, UNIONE, E FORZA / PROGRESSI, SEPARAZIONI, E CORRUZIONI / *DELLA* / POESIA, E DELLA MUSICA / *DISSERTAZIONE* / DEL DOTTOR GIOVANNI BROWN / *Tradotta in lingua Italiana dall' Originale Inglese,* / ED ACCRESCIUTA DI NOTE / DAL DOTTOR PIETRO CROCCHI / SENESE / ACCADEMICO FISIOCRITICO / *A CUI SI AGGIUNGE* / LA CURA DI SAULE / ODE SACRA DELL' ISTESSO AUTORE / *Tradotta fedelmente in Poesia Italiana di metro / irregolare a confronto del Testo Inglese* / DA ORESBIO AGIEO P.A. / [rule] / [quotation] / [rule] / IN FIRENZE)(MDCCLXXII. / [row of type ornaments] / NELLA STAMPERIA BONDUCCIANA / *Con Approvazione.*

Collation: 8°: π^2 A–P^8 Q^4

Contents: $\pi 1^r$ title, $\pi 1^v$ quotation, $\pi 2$ Dedication to Milord Gio. Child Tylney, signed Gio. Francesco Bartolini, pages 1–213 text of the *Dissertation,* 214–247 the *Cure of Saul* (English and Italian on facing pages), 248 Index. Page 240 misnumbered 140.

Press figures: none.

Size of an uncut copy: $8\frac{1}{2}'' \times 5\frac{3}{4}''$ (British Museum and D. D. Eddy copies, in original boards; Newberry Library copy, rebound).

Copies: Bibliothèque Nationale (2 copies); *British Museum;

*Library of Congress; *Newberry Library; University of Virginia; *D. D. Eddy.

82.

ON RELIGIOUS LIBERTY: / A / SERMON / PREACHED AT / St. PAUL's CATHEDRAL, / ON / SUNDAY the 6th of MARCH, 1763. / On Occasion of the BRIEF for the Establishment of / the COLLEGES of *Philadelphia* and *New York.* / Published at the Request of the MANAGERS of the Charity. / To which is prefixed / An ADDRESS to the principal INHABITANTS / of the *North American* Colonies, / On OCCASION of the PEACE. / [rule] / By JOHN BROWN, D.D. / VICAR of NEWCASTLE. / [rule] / LONDON, / Printed for L. DAVIS and C. REYMERS against *Gray's-Inn, Holbourn,* / Printers to the ROYAL SOCIETY, 1763. / [Price One Shilling.]

Collation: 4°: *A*1 a⁴ b² B–C⁴ D1

Contents: *A*1ʳ title, *A*1ᵛ blank, pages i–xii "AN ADDRESS . . ." dated April 20, 1763, 1–18 text of the sermon.

Press figures: vii-2, 6-2, 16-1.

Size of an uncut copy: 10½″ × 8½″ (New York Public Library copy, in original blue paper wrapper, stitched).

Number of copies printed: William Bowyer printed 500 copies, all of which were delivered to Davis April 23, 1763 (Bodleian MS. DON b.4, folio 187). [N.B. In this instance the ledger does not list the number of copies printed; it merely states: "Used for Sermon 4° 4 Shts 4 (Rx)." Thus, 500 copies.]

Date of publication: April 26, 1763 (*London Chronicle,* Apr. 23–26).

Copies: *Bodleian; *Boston Public Library; John Carter Brown; *Cambridge University Library; *Columbia; *Cornell; *Harvard; *Historical Society of Pennsylvania; Huntington Library; *Library Company of Philadelphia (imperfect: lacks pages i–xii); University of Michigan (William L. Clements); *Newberry Library; *New York Public Library; *University of Pennsylvania; *Sion College Library; *Yale; *D. D. Eddy.

Notes:

1. The entire conclusion to the sermon (pages 12–18) was printed in the *London Chronicle*, March 5–8, 1763 (pages 227–228) just two days after the sermon was preached.

2. This sermon was reprinted in Philadelphia (see next entry); it is also contained in Brown's *Sermons on Various Subjects* (1764), pages 291–341.

83. *First American Edition (1763)*

ON RELIGIOUS LIBERTY: / A / SERMON, / PREACHED at St. PAUL's Cathedral, / On SUNDAY the 6th of MARCH, 1763. / On Occasion of the BRIEF for the Establish- / ment of the COLLEGES of / PHILADELPHIA and NEW-YORK. / Publish'd at the Request of the MANAGERS of the Charity. / TO WHICH IS PREFIXED / AN ADDRESS / To the principal Inhabitants of the / NORTH AMERICAN COLONIES, / On Occasion of the PEACE. / [triple rule] / By JOHN BROWN, D.D. vicar of NEWCASTLE. / [triple rule] / LONDON: / Printed by DAVIS and REYMERS, Printers to the Royal- / Society, Price 1 s. 6 d. / PHILADELPHIA: / Re-printed by ANDREW STEUART, at the Bible-in-Heart, / in Second-street. Price only 6 d. 1763.

Collation: 8° (in 4's): A^4 B–C^4

Contents: Page *i* title, *ii* blank, iii–x An Address to the principal Inhabitants of the North American Colonies, 11–23 text of the sermon, *24* blank.

Press figures: none.

Size of an uncut copy: 8″ × 5½″ (Historical Society of Pennsylvania copy).

Copies: American Antiquarian Society; *Historical Society of Pennsylvania; *New-York Historical Society.

Note:

This is Evans 9356.

84.

SERMONS / ON / VARIOUS SUBJECTS. / [rule] / By JOHN BROWN, D.D. / VICAR of NEWCASTLE. / [double rule] / LONDON, / Printed for L. DAVIS and C. REYMERS, / against *Grays-Inn, Holborn,* / PRINTERS to the ROYAL SOCIETY. / MDCCLXIIII.

Collation: 8°: A^4 ($\pm A1$) B–E[8] *E[4] *F[2] F–Y[8] Z[4]. Note: The title does not appear to be a cancel in the Bodleian copy.

Contents: Page *i* title, *ii* blank, *iii* Dedication, "To the Right Reverend Richard Osbaldeston, D.D. Lord Bishop of London," *iv* blank, *v* vi–viii Contents, *1* special title, *2* blank, *3* 4–32 On the First Principles of Education. Sermon I, *33* special title, *34* blank, *35*, 34–53 On the First Principles of Education. Sermon II, *54* blank, *55* special title, *56* blank, *57*, 54–60, 57–66 On the First Principles of Education. Sermon III, *67* special title, *68* blank, *69*, 68–90 The Mutual Connexion between Religious Truth and Civil Freedom. Sermon I, *91* special title, *92* blank, 93–118 The Mutual Connexion between Religious Truth and Civil Freedom. Sermon II, *119* special title, *120* blank, *121* 122–140 On the Duty of Charitable Distribution. Sermon I, *141* special title, *142* blank, *143* 144–167 On the Duty of Charitable Distribution. Sermon II, *168* blank, *169* special title, *170* blank, *171* 172–192, 197–203 On the Use and Abuse of Externals in Religion, *204* blank, *205* special title, *206* blank, *207* 208–212, 209–231 On the Natural Duty of a Personal Service, in Defence of ourselves and Country, *232* blank, *233* special title, *234* blank, *235* 236–257 On the different Provinces of Goodness, Justice, and Mercy, *258* blank, *259* special title, *260* Advertisement, *261* 262–288 On the Pursuit of false Pleasure, and the Mischiefs of immoderate Gaming, *289* special title, *290* blank, *291* 292–310 *311* 312–341 On Religious Liberty, *342* blank, *343–344* Advertisements. Page 100 misnumbered 00; other pages misnumbered as above.

Press figures: 16-1, 27-2, 43-2, 52-2, 78-1, 84-5, 86-2, 109-5, *121*-1, 130-4, 150-4, 156-1, 172-4, 189-1, 202-1, 212-1, 240-1, 249-1, 267-1, 281-4, 283-1, 296-4, 312-4, 328-1, 334-2, 338-5.

Number of copies printed: William Bowyer printed 1,056 copies (including waste); the first 50 copies were delivered to Davis March 15, 1764 (Bodleian MS. DON b.4, folio 189).

Date of publication: March 29, 1764 (*The St. James's Chronicle*, March 27–29, 1764). "Price bound 5 s."

Copies: *Bodleian; *British Museum; John Carter Brown; Cambridge University Library; *Columbia; *University of Pennsylvania; *Yale; *D. D. Eddy.

Note:

It is possible that the first three sermons may have been issued separately. The newspaper advertisements certainly emphasize them—e.g., the *London Chronicle* lists the book as: "SERMONS on various SUBJECTS (three of them on the first Principles of Education). By JOHN BROWN, D.D." (March 13–15, 1764). In addition to its complete volume, Columbia University Library has a separate copy of the first three sermons (call number 320.1 B81). Its distinctive collation (B–E^8 *E^4 *F^2), pagination, and press figures show that it is part of the same impression of the same edition as the corresponding sections of the complete book. It has no title-page. Of course, such a copy may exist by accident—i.e., without any intention on the part of the publisher. Yet the unusual nature of the collation of these three sermons suggests that Bowyer was deliberately printing them to form a separate unit.

85.

THE / HISTORY / OF THE / RISE and PROGRESS / OF / POETRY, / Through it's several SPECIES. / [rule] / *Written by Dr.* BROWN. / [rule] / [quotation] / [double rule] / NEWCASTLE: Printed by J. WHITE and T. SAINT, / for L. DAVIS and C. REYMERS, against *Gray's- / Inn-Gate, Holborn, London.* / [rule] / MDCCLXIV.

Collation: 8°: A^4 B–R^8 S^2. A3 and A4 missigned A2 and A3; $N7^v$ missigned N4.

Contents: Page *i* title, *ii* blank, *iii* Advertisement, *iv* blank, *v* vi–vii Contents, *viii* blank, *9* 10–266 text, *267–268* Advertisements.

Press figures: none.

Date of publication: April 14, 1764 (*London Chronicle,* April 12–14; *The St. James's Chronicle,* April 12–14). "Price 3 s. 6 d. sewed in Boards"

Copies: National Library of Australia; *Bodleian; *British Museum; University of Chicago; University of Cincinnati; *Columbia; *Cornell; *Dartmouth; *Folger Library; *Harvard; Huntington Library; *Illinois; *Indiana (Lilly); *New York Public Library; Pembroke College, Cambridge; Princeton; University of Toronto; *D. D. Eddy (2 copies).

Note:

The Advertisement on page *iii* reads: "It is thought proper to inform the Purchasers of the '*Dissertation on the Rise, Union, &c. of Poetry and Music,*' that the Substance of *this* Volume is contained in *That;* which is now thrown into the present Form, for the Sake of such classical Readers as are not particularly conversant with Music."

86. *French Translation (1768)*

HISTOIRE / DE L'ORIGINE / *ET DES* / PROGRÈS DE LA POÉSIE, / DANS SES DIFFÉRENS GENRES. /

Par *le Docteur* BROWN. / Traduite de l'Anglois par M. E. & augmentée / de Notes historiques & critiques. / [rule] / [quotation] / [rule] / [ornament] / *A PARIS*, / Chez H. C. DE HANSY le jeune, Libraire, / rue saint Jacques, à sainte Therese. / [double rule] / M. DCC. LXVIII. / *Avec Approbation & Privilége du Roi.*

Collation: 8°: π^2 A–U[8]

Contents: $\pi 1^r$ half-title, $\pi 1^v$ blank, $\pi 2^r$ title, $\pi 2^v$ blank, pages *1* 2–315 text, 316–317 Table des Sections, *318–319* "Approbation" and "Privilege du Roi," *320* blank.

Press figures: none.

Copies: Bibliothèque Nationale; *Library of Congress.

Notes:

1. According to the Library of Congress catalogue, this work was translated by Marc Antoine Eidous.
2. According to the "Privilege du Roi" (p. 318), this work was published by Honoré Clément de Hansy le jeune.
3. According to the colophon (p. 319), this work was printed by P. Al. Le Prieur.

87.

REMARKS / ON / SOME OBSERVATIONS / ON / Dr. BROWN'S DISSERTATION / ON / POETRY and MUSICK. / In a LETTER to the AUTHOR of the / OBSERVATIONS. / [double rule] / LONDON, / Printed for L. DAVIS and C. REYMERS, against / *Gray's-Inn-Gate, Holborn,* / Printers to the Royal Society. / MDCCLXIV.

Collation: 8°: *A*1 (= E8?) B–E[8] (–E8[= *A*1?]). C4 missigned B4.

Contents: *A*1[r] title, *A*1[v] blank, pages *1* 2–62 text.

Press figures: 2-4, 32-4.

Number of copies printed: William Bowyer printed 500 copies, all of which were delivered to Davis May 9, 1764 (Bodleian MS. DON b.4, folio 165).

Date of publication: May 12, 1764 (*The St. James's Chronicle*, May 10–12). Price 1s.

Copies: *Bodleian (2 copies); *British Museum; *Cambridge University Library; *Newberry Library; *Yale.

88.

THOUGHTS / ON / CIVIL LIBERTY, / ON / LICENTIOUSNESS, / AND / FACTION. / [rule] / By the AUTHOR of / ESSAYS on the CHARACTERISTICS, &c. / [rule] / [quotation] / [double rule] / *NEWCASTLE UPON TYNE:* / Printed by J. WHITE and T. SAINT, / For L. DAVIS and C. REYMERS, against / *Gray's-Inn-Gate, Holborn, London;* / Printers to the ROYAL SOCIETY. / MDCCLXV.

Collation: 8° (in 4's): *A*[4] B–T[4] W[4] [sic] X[4]. G2 missigned F2.

Contents: Page *1* title, *2* blank, *3* 4–7 Contents, *8* blank, *9* 10–167 text, *168* Advertisement: . . . "With all Convenient Speed, Will be Published, Principles of Christian Legislation."

Press figures: none.

Size of an uncut copy: 9″ × 5⅞″ (Cambridge University Library copy, in marbled boards; Pierpont Morgan Library; Yale copy, in original blue boards).

Date of publication: February 1, 1765 (*Daily Advertiser*). "Price sewed in Boards 2s. 6d." Advertisements: "On Friday next [i.e., Feb. 1] will be published . . ." (*Daily Advertiser*, Jan. 29; *The St. James's Chronicle*, Jan. 26–29; Jan. 29–31). "This Day is published . . ." (*Daily Advertiser*, Feb. 1; *The St. James's Chronicle*, Jan. 31–Feb. 2).

Copies: Australian National University, Acton; *Bodleian (2 copies); *British Museum; *Cambridge University Library, inscribed "To David Lewis Esq; From the Author"; University of Chicago; *Indiana; *Lambeth Palace Library (copy of Thomas Secker, Archbishop of Canterbury); University of Michigan (William L. Clements); *Newberry Library (2 copies); Pembroke College, Cambridge; *Pierpont Morgan Library; Princeton; University of Toronto; *Yale.

89. *The Second Edition (1765)*

THOUGHTS / ON / CIVIL LIBERTY, / ON / LICENTIOUSNESS, / AND / FACTION. / [rule] / By the AUTHOR of / ESSAYS on the CHARACTERISTICS, *&c.* / [rule] / [quotation] / [rule] / THE SECOND EDITION. / [double rule] / *LONDON:* / Printed for L. DAVIS and C. REYMERS, / opposite *Gray's-Inn-Gate, Holborn,* / Printers to the ROYAL SOCIETY. / MDCCLXV.

Collation: 8°: A^4 B–L^8

Contents: Page *1* title, *2* blank, *3* 4–7 Contents, *8* blank, *9* 10–167 text, 168 Advertisements. Page 152 misnumbered 150.

Press figures: 21-1, 37-1, 50-4, 65-4, 71-1, 85-1.

Size of an uncut copy: $8\frac{7}{8}''$ × $5\frac{11}{16}''$ (D. D. Eddy copy, unopened, in original blue paper boards).

Number of copies printed: William Bowyer printed 1,032 copies (including waste), the first of which were delivered to Davis February 14, 1765 (Bodleian MS. DON b.4, folio 162).

Date of publication: February 19(?), 1765. Advertisements: "On Saturday next [i.e., Feb. 16] will be published . . ." *Daily Advertiser*, Thurs., Feb. 14, 1765; "This Day is published . . ." *Daily Advertiser,* February 19, 1765; *London Chronicle,* Feb. 16–19, 1765. "Price 2 s. 6 d. in Boards."

Copies: Bibliothèque Nationale; *Bodleian; *Boston Public

Library; *British Museum; *Cambridge University Library; *Columbia; *Cornell; *Free Library of Philadelphia; *Harvard (gift of Thomas Hollis, in a brown calf Hollis binding); Huntington Library; *Library Company of Philadelphia; *New York Public Library (3 copies); National Library of Scotland; Yale; *D. D. Eddy.

Note:

In the first edition of this work, Brown made a factual error in the footnote on page 155: he attributes two books to one author, presumably John Cleland. Apparently this same erroneous reading was continued in the early stages of the printing of the second edition; the printing was stopped; the footnote corrected; the offending leaf, L2, was canceled in those copies already printed; and printing was resumed for the rest of the edition with L2 in its corrected state.

Presumably, therefore, leaf L2 exists in three states:

(1) The original, uncanceled state, with the footnote on page 155 containing the erroneous reading of the first edition. No copy seen.

(2) Leaf L2 is a cancel, pasted in on a stub. The error in the footnote has been corrected. *Copies:* Bodleian; Free Library of Philadelphia; New York Public Library (one copy: SEB); D. D. Eddy.

(3) Leaf L2 is not a cancel, but the footnote on page 155 has the corrected text. (The Columbia copy is loosely bound, and L2 is clearly conjugate with L7.) *Copies:* British Museum; Cambridge University Library; Columbia; Cornell; Library Company of Philadelphia; New York Public Library (2 copies).

90. *Dublin Edition (1765)*

THOUGHTS / ON / CIVIL LIBERTY, / ON / LICENTIOUSNESS / AND / FACTION. / [rule] / BY DR. BROWN, / Author of the ESSAYS on Lord SHAFTSBURY'S / CHARACTERISTICS, &c. / [rule] / [quotation] / [double rule] /

DUBLIN: / Printed for A. LEATHLEY, J. EXSHAW, / W. WATSON, and S. WATSON, Booksellers. / M.DCC.LXV.

Collation: 12° (in 6's): A^{6} (−A6[= S1?]) B–R^{6} S1(= A6?). B5 is missigned B3.

Contents: Page *1* half-title, *2* blank, *3* title, *4* blank, 5–10 Contents, *1* 2–194 text, with 193 misnumbered 191, and 194 misnumbered 192.

Press figures: none.

Size of an uncut copy: $7\frac{1}{2}'' \times 4\frac{5}{8}''$ (Allegheny College copy, in original half-sheep with marbled-paper boards).

Copies: *Allegheny College, Meadville, Pa.; British Museum; *Library of Congress; *Cornell; *Harvard Law School; *Library Company of Philadelphia; Texas; *D. D. Eddy. The Library of Congress, Harvard Law School, Texas, and D. D. Eddy copies have the half-title.

91. *German Translation (1771)*

Gedanken / von der / Bürgerlichen Freyheit. / Der Ausgelassenheit und Zweytracht in / freyen Staaten entgegengesetzt. / Aus dem Englischen übersetzt. / [cut; signed with initials S. G.] / [rule] / [quotation] / [rule] / Zürich, / bey Orell, Geszner, Füeszlin und Comp. 1771.

Collation: 8°: A–M^{8} N^{4}

Contents: Page *I* title, *II* blank, *III* IV–VIII Vorbericht, *9* 10–193 text, *194–196* Innhalt, *197–199* Druckfehler, *200* blank. Page 18 misnumbered 19.

Press figures: none.

Copies: *Library of Congress; Stadtbibliothek, Zürich.

Note:

In this work the title-page (except for the quotation) and the entire text are printed in black letter; superscript e is used for the umlaut.

92. *French Translation (1789)*

DE / LA LIBERTÉ CIVILE, / *ET* / DES FACTIONS. / [rule] / [quotation] / [rule] / [center of title-page is blank] / [double rule] / 1789.

Collation: 8°: π^2 A–F[8]

Contents: Page *i* title, *ii* blank, iii–iv Tables des Sections, *1* 2–96 text.

Press figures: none.

Size of an uncut copy: 8½″ × 5⅝″ (Cornell copy).

Copies: Bibliothèque Nationale; *British Museum (2 copies); *Cornell.

93.

On the Female Character and Education: / A SERMON, / PREACHED / On THURSDAY the 16th of MAY, 1765, / AT / THE ANNIVERSARY MEETING / OF / THE GUARDIANS OF THE ASYLUM / FOR DESERTED FEMALE ORPHANS. / [rule] / BY JOHN BROWN, D.D. / Vicar of NEWCASTLE, and Chaplain in Ordinary to His MAJESTY. / [double rule] / LONDON, / Printed for L. DAVIS and C. REYMERS, against *Gray's-Inn-Gate, Holborn.* / Printers to the Royal Society. MDCCLXV. / [Price One Shilling.]

Collation: 4°: *A*[2] B–C[4] D[2] E[4]

Contents: Page *1* title, *2* blank, *3* Dedication to "The Earl of Litchfield, President; the Vice-Presidents, and Stewards, of the Asylum," *4* blank, 5–23 text of the sermon, *24* Advertisement, 25–31 "An Appendix, Relative to a proposed Code of Education," *32* blank.

Press figures: 11-1, 18-4, 22-4, 26-2.

Date of publication: May 23, 1765 (*The St. James's Chronicle*, May 21–23).

Copies: *British Museum.

Note:

The Advertisement on page 24 says that "*This* SERMON *is to be considered as a Sequel to the Three already published by the Author, on the general Subject of Education.*"

94.

A / LETTER / TO THE / Rev. Dr. LOWTH, / OCCASIONED BY HIS LATE / LETTER / To the Right Rev. AUTHOR of / The DIVINE LEGATION of MOSES. / [rule] / By the AUTHOR of / ESSAYS on the CHARACTERISTICS. / [rule] / [quotation] / [double rule] / *NEWCASTLE UPON TYNE:* / Printed by J. WHITE and T. SAINT, / For L. DAVIS and C. REYMERS, against / *Gray's-Inn-Gate, Holborn, London:* / Printers to the ROYAL SOCIETY. / MDCCLXVI.

Collation: 8° (in 4's): *A*1 B–F[4] G1. B2 and C2 not signed.

Contents: Pages *1* title, *2* blank, *3* 4–44 text. The end of the text (p. 44) is dated Dec. 19, 1765.

Press figures: none.

Date of publication: January 7, 1766 (*The St. James's Chronicle*, Jan. 4–7). Price 1s.

Copies: *Boston Athenaeum; *British Museum; *Cambridge University Library (8.36.41); *Cornell; *Folger Library; Huntington Library; *Illinois; *New-York Historical Society; *New York Public Library; University of Toronto; *Yale (4 copies); *D. D. Eddy.

95. *The Second Edition (1766)*

A / LETTER / TO THE / Rev. Dr. LOWTH, / OCCASIONED BY HIS LATE / LETTER / To the Right Rev. AUTHOR of / The DIVINE LEGATION of MOSES. / [rule] / By the AUTHOR of / ESSAYS on the CHARACTERISTICS. / [rule] / [quotation] /

[rule] / The SECOND EDITION. / [double rule] / *NEWCASTLE UPON TYNE:* / Printed by J. WHITE and T. SAINT, / For L. DAVIS and C. REYMERS, against / *Gray's-Inn-Gate, Holborn, London:* / Printers to the ROYAL SOCIETY. / MDCC-LXVI.

Collation and Contents: same as the first edition.

Press figures: none.

Date of publication: January 10, 1766 (*Daily Advertiser*). Price 1s.

Copies: *British Museum (1509/1164); *Cambridge University Library (2.74.3[3]); *Yale; *D. D. Eddy.

Note:

This "edition" has a new title-page, but in all other respects it is either a reissue of first edition sheets or a reimpression from standing type.

96. *The Third Edition (1766)*

A / LETTER / TO THE / Rev. Dr. LOWTH, / OCCASIONED BY HIS LATE / LETTER / To the Right Rev. AUTHOR of / The DIVINE LEGATION of MOSES. / [rule] / By the AUTHOR of / ESSAYS on the CHARACTERISTICS. / [rule] / [quotation] / [rule] / The THIRD EDITION. / [double rule] / *NEWCASTLE UPON TYNE:* / Printed by J. WHITE and T. SAINT, / For L. DAVIS and C. REYMERS, against / *Gray's-Inn-Gate, Holborn, London:* / Printers to the ROYAL SOCIETY. / MDCC-LXVI.

Collation and Contents: the same as the first and second editions.

Press figures: none.

Size of an uncut copy: 9″ × 6″ (Yale copy: unbound, stitched).

Date of publication: January 18, 1766 (*The St. James's Chronicle*, January 16–18; *The Gazetteer and New Daily Advertiser*, January 18). Price 1s.

Copies: *Bodleian; *British Museum; *Cambridge University Library; Huntington Library; *Yale.

Note:

This "edition" has a new title-page, but in all other respects it is either a reissue of first edition sheets or a reimpression from standing type.

97. *The Fourth Edition (1766)*

A / LETTER / TO THE / Rev. Dr. LOWTH, / OCCASIONED BY HIS LATE / LETTER / To the Right Rev. AUTHOR of / The DIVINE LEGATION of MOSES. / [rule] / By the AUTHOR of / ESSAYS on the CHARACTERISTICS. / [rule] / [quotation] / [rule] / The FOURTH EDITION. / [double rule] / *NEWCASTLE UPON TYNE:* / Printed by J. WHITE and T. SAINT, / For L. DAVIS and C. REYMERS, against / *Gray's-Inn-Gate, Holborn, London:* / Printers to the ROYAL SOCIETY. / MDCCLXVI.

Collation and Contents: the same as the first three editions.

Press figures: none.

Date of publication: January 27, 1766 (*The Gazetteer and New Daily Advertiser*, Jan. 27). Price 1s.

Copies: *Bodleian; *Sion College Library (B.10.26).

Note:

This "edition" has a new title-page, but in all other respects it is either a reissue of first edition sheets or a reimpression from standing type.

97A. *[A Description of the Lake at Keswick . . . Newcastle upon Tyne, 1767]*

Copies: None located.

Notes:

1. This prose description is, presumably, printed from a

letter (now lost) which Brown wrote to Lord Lyttelton in the late 1750's, certainly sometime before 1760 when Brown quarreled with Lyttelton in a political dispute. The same letter also contained Brown's well-known poetical rhapsody, "Now sunk the Sun . . .," which was first printed by Richard Cumberland in his *Odes* (London, 1776)—see below, no. 101.

2. William Hutchinson mentions this work and reprints it in its entirety in his *Excursion to the Lakes, in Westmoreland and Cumberland, August 1773* (London, 1774), pages 107–113, and in his more familiar and greatly expanded version of the same work (London, 1776), pages 127–130. In both editions Hutchinson entitles the reprint, "Dr. Brown's Letter, printed at Newcastle in the year 1767." Extensive searching has failed to uncover any Newcastle printing of 1767.

3. However, there is reason to believe that Hutchinson was correct in his statement. Brown's *Description* was reprinted by George Pearch in all four editions of his *Collection of Poems by Several Hands*: London, 1768 (I, 36–39); London, 1770 (I, 36–39); London, 1775 (I, 49–52); London, 1783 (I, 52–55). Pearch prints Brown's piece as a footnote to John Dalton's well-known *Descriptive Poem, Addressed to Two Ladies*, first published in 1755. I infer from Pearch's introduction that he is *reprinting* Brown's *Description*; since the first edition of Pearch's *Collection* was published in 1768, Hutchinson's date of 1767 seems very possible.

4. Brown's *Description* is reprinted in 1770, without identifying its author, in *The Literary Register: or, Weekly Miscellany*... Newcastle: Printed for the Benefit of the Subscribers to the Journal, by the Compilers of that News-Paper. Vol. II (for the Year 1770), no. XLIX, pp. 299–300. At the end of the reprint is this note: "N.B. It is desired that no copy of this paper be given or taken." Copy examined: Yale.

98. *The First(?) Separate Edition (1770)*

A / DESCRIPTION / OF THE / LAKE / AT / KESWICK, / (And the adjacent COUNTRY) / IN / CUMBERLAND. /

COMMUNICATED IN / A LETTER TO A FRIEND. / BY A LATE / POPULAR WRITER. / [rule] / *KENDAL*: / PRINTED BY J. ASHBURNER. / [rule] / M, DCC, LXX.

Collation: 8° (in 4's): A^4

Contents: Page *1* title, *2* blank, *3* 4–8 text.

Press figures: none.

Copies: *Bodleian.

99. *The Second(?) Separate Edition (1771)*

A / DESCRIPTION / OF THE / LAKE / AT / KESWICK, / (And the adjacent COUNTRY) / IN / CUMBERLAND. / COMMUNICATED IN / A LETTER TO A FRIEND, / BY A LATE / POPULAR WRITER. / [rule] / *KENDAL:* / PRINTED BY W. PENNINGTON. / Sold by J. HODGSON at the *Queen*'s *Head* in *Keswick.* / [rule] / M DCC LXXI.

Collation: 8° (in 4's): π^4

Contents: Page *1* title, *2* blank, *3* 4–8 text.

Press figures: none.

Copies: *British Museum; *Cornell (Wordsworth Collection).

100. *The Third(?) Separate Edition (1772)*

A / DESCRIPTION / OF THE / LAKE / AT / KESWICK, / (And the Adjacent Country) / IN / CUMBERLAND. / In a LETTER to a FRIEND. / [double rule] / LONDON, / PRINTED BY T. SHERLOCK. / MDCCLXXII.

Collation: 4° (in half-sheets): B^6. The recto of the third leaf is missigned B2; it is the only leaf signed.

Contents: Page *1* title, *2* blank, *3* dedication "To the Gentlemen of Cumberland . . . by the Editor," *4* blank, *5* 6–11 text, *12* blank.

Press figures: none.

Copies: *British Museum.

Note:

The watermarks on the paper indicate clearly that this twelve-page pamphlet is made up of three pairs of conjugate leaves: 1 and 6, 2 and 5, 3 and 4.

Subsequent printings, listed chronologically [In this instance, I list only those copies I have examined personally]:

1. Hutchinson, William. *An Excursion to the Lakes, in Westmoreland and Cumberland, August 1773* (London, 1774), pp. 107–113. (Copy: Cornell.)

2. Hutchinson, William. *An Excursion to the Lakes in Westmoreland and Cumberland; with a Tour through Part of the Northern Counties, in the Years 1773 and 1774* (London, 1776), pp. 127–130. (Copies: Cornell; D. D. Eddy.)

3. Nicolson, Joseph, and Burn, Richard. *The History and Antiquities of the Counties of Westmorland and Cumberland.* London, 1777 (II, 83–85). (Copy: Cornell.)

4. Kippis, Andrew. "John Brown," in *Biographia Britannica.* The Second Edition. London, 1780 (II, 673–674), entitled "Extract of a letter to Lord Lyttelton." (Copy: Cornell.)

5. West, Thomas. *A Guide to the Lakes, in Cumberland, Westmorland, and Lancashire.* The Second Edition. London, 1780, pp. 193–196. (Copies: British Museum; Cornell.)
   (a) 3d ed., 1784 (Copies: British Museum; Cornell).
   (b) 4th ed., 1789 (Copy: British Museum).
   (c) 5th ed., 1793 (Copies: British Museum; Cornell).
   (d) 6th ed., 1796 (Copies: British Museum; Cornell).
   (e) 7th ed., 1799 (Copies: British Museum; Cornell).
   (f) 8th ed., 1802 (Copy: British Museum).
   (g) 9th ed., 1807 (Copy: Cornell).
   (h) 10th ed., 1812 (Copies: British Museum; Cornell).
   (i) 11th ed., 1821 (Copies: British Museum; Cornell).

Note: The first edition of Thomas West's *Guide to the Lakes* (London, 1778—copies: British Museum and two copies in Cornell) does not reprint Brown's *Description of the Lake. . . .*

However, after the death of Thomas West on July 10, 1779, his *Guide to the Lakes* was revised, edited, and greatly expanded by that industrious writer and enthusiastic admirer of the lake district, William Cockin (1736–1801). For an account of his life and writings, see the introduction to Cockin's *The Rural Sabbath* (London, 1805—copy: Cornell).

6. Gilpin, William. *Observations, Relative Chiefly to Picturesque Beauty, made in the Year 1772* . . . London, 1786, 2 vols. Brown's *Description* quoted and cited (I, 86, 183). (Copy: Cornell.)

(a) 2d ed., 1788 (Copy: Cornell).

(b) 3d ed., 1792 (Copy: Cornell).

(c) "Third edition," [sic], 1808 (Copy: Cornell).

7. Clarke, James. *A Survey of the Lakes of Cumberland, Westmorland, and Lancashire* . . . London: Printed for the Author . . . 1787, pp. 71–72. (Copies: two in Cornell.)

Clarke introduces an extensive quotation from Brown's *Description* by saying, "When I visited this place, I had with me Dr Brown's elegant description of it; and it would be only exposing my own weakness were I to attempt to describe it after him; I shall therefore give it in his own words."

Clarke, however, is no Romantic poet. In a later section he quotes from Thomas Gray's journal, but adds, "Mr Gray's description is pretty accurate, but this sublime way of writing (as Mr West calls it) is not my province; a guide ought, in my opinion, to be merely narrative" (p. 120).

8. Hutchinson, William. *The History of the County of Cumberland* . . . Carlisle, 1794. 2 vols. (II, 159–160). (Copy: Cornell.)

9. West, Thomas. *The Descriptive Part of Mr. West's Guide to the Lakes* . . . (Kendal, 1809), quotes Brown's *Description*, in part, on p. 94. (Copies: British Museum; Cornell.)

101. *Cumberland, Richard. 1732–1811*

ODES, / By RICHARD CUMBERLAND, Esq; / [ornament] / LONDON: / PRINTED FOR J. ROBSON, NEW BOND STREET. / MDCCLXXVI.

Collation: 4° (in 2's): *A*1 B–G^2 *H*1

Contents: Page *1* title, *2* blank, *3* 4–10 "To Mr. George Romney," *11* 12–20 "ODE I. *To the* SUN." 21–27 "ODE II. TO Dr. ROBERT JAMES." *28* Advertisements.

Press figures: none.

Copies: *Bodleian; *British Museum (2 copies); *Cornell; *Harvard (2 copies); *Haverford College; Illinois; Newberry Library; University of Pennsylvania; Texas; Yale; *D. D. Eddy.

Note:

Cumberland discusses John Brown in his introduction (pp. 4–6), and it is clear that he has seen Brown's letter to Lord Lyttelton (see above, no. 98, note 1). Cumberland does not intend to reprint Brown's *Description of the Lake at Keswick,* but he does print another unpublished part of the letter containing Brown's poem, "Now sunk the Sun . . . ." The pertinent passages in Cumberland's introduction are reprinted here.

> I have been favoured with a Manuscript of the late ingenious Dr. Browne, which I had the priviledge of inserting in this publication, and should so have done, but that I found it had already got forth into the world, and was in print: It is touched with great spirit, and in a glowing stile, which gradually kindles till it breaks forth into the following rhapsody, which I believe hath hitherto escaped publication:
>
> *Now sunk the Sun, now Twilight sunk, and Night*
> *Rode in her zenith; nor a passing breeze*
> *Sigh'd to the groves, which in the midnight air*
> *Stood motionless, and in the peaceful floods*
> *Inverted hung: For now the billow slept*
> *Along the shore, nor heav'd the deep, but spread*
> *A shining mirror to the Moon's pale orb,*
> *Which, dim and waining, o'er the shadowy clifts,*
> *The solemn woods and spiry mountain-tops*
> *Her glimmering faintness threw: Now every eye,*
> *Oppress'd with toil, was drown'd in deep repose;*

Save that the unseen shepherd in his watch,
Propt on his crook, stood list'ning by the fold,
And gaz'd the starry vault and pendant moon;
Nor voice nor sound broke on the deep serene,
But the soft murmur of swift-gushing rills,
Forth-issuing from the mountain's distant steep,
(Unheard till now, and now scarce heard) proclaim'd
All things at rest, and imag'd the still voice
Of quiet whispering to the ear of Night.

In fine, says Dr. BROWNE, *this accumulation of beauty and immensity tends not only to excite rapture but reverence; for my part I make an annual voyage to Keswick, not only as an innocent amusement, but a religious act. I walk forth in this stupendous scene, as into the grandest earthly temple of the Creator; and as I take my progress thro' its several parts, often break forth with the divine Psalmist in that grateful exclamation*—"O LORD, how manifold are thy works; in wisdom hast thou made them all."

What I have here inserted is taken from a letter to a friend, and is a valuable specimen of the author. . . .

102. *Dublin Edition (1776)*

ODES, / BY RICHARD CUMBERLAND, Esq; / [ornament] / DUBLIN: / Printed for S. PRICE, W. WHITESTONE, W. WAT- / SON, J. SHEPPARD, J. POTTS, S. WATSON, / J. WILLIAMS, W. COLLES, J. ARMITAGE, / G. BURNET, C. JENKIN, W. WILSON, / R. MONCRIEFFE, T. WALKER, / and P. HIGLY. / [rule] / MDCCLXXVI.

Collation: 8° (in 4's): A–D^4

Contents: Page *1* title, *2* blank, *3* 4–12 "TO MR. GEORGE ROMNEY," *13* 14–22 "ODE I. *To the* SUN." *23* 24–30 "ODE II. TO DR. ROBERT JAMES." *31–32* blank.

Press figures: none.

Copies: *British Museum 12330.aaa.11.(4.); *Cambridge University Library Hib. 7. 776. 15[1].

Subsequent printings [Once again, I list only those copies I have examined personally]:

1. West, Thomas. *A Guide to the Lakes, in Cumberland, Westmorland, and Lancashire.* The Second Edition. London, 1780, pp. 115–116. (Copies: British Museum; Cornell.)

(a) 3d ed., 1784 (Copies: British Museum; Cornell).
(b) 4th ed., 1789 (Copy: British Museum).
(c) 5th ed., 1793 (Copies: British Museum; Cornell).
(d) 6th ed., 1796 (Copies: British Museum; Cornell).
(e) 7th ed., 1799 (Copies: British Museum; Cornell).
(f) 8th ed., 1802 (Copy: British Museum).
(g) 9th ed., 1807 (Copy: Cornell).
(h) 10th ed., 1812 (Copies: British Museum; Cornell).
(i) 11th ed., 1821 (Copies: British Museum; Cornell).

Note: The first edition of West's *Guide to the Lakes* (London, 1778—copies: British Museum and two copies in Cornell) does not reprint Brown's poem, "Now sunk the Sun . . ." (see above, no. 100, note 5).

2. Hutchinson, William. *The History of the County of Cumberland* . . . Carlisle, 1794. 2 vols. (I, 444). (Copy: Cornell.)

3. Anderson, Robert, M.D. *THE WORKS OF THE BRITISH POETS. WITH PREFACES, BIOGRAPHICAL AND CRITICAL.* 13 vols. London and Edinburgh, 1795. In volume X, pages 867–888 contain "THE POETICAL WORKS OF JOHN BROWN, D.D. . . . To which is prefixed, *THE LIFE OF THE AUTHOR* . . . EDINBURGH: PRINTED BY *MUNDELL AND SON*, ROYAL BANK CLOSE. *Anno* 1794." This is the first collected edition of Brown's poems, and the poem "Now sunk the Sun . . ." is printed on page 887 under the title "FRAGMENT OF A RHAPSODY, WRITTEN AT THE LAKES IN WESTMORELAND." (Copy: Cornell.)

4. West, Thomas. *The Descriptive Part of Mr. West's Guide to the Lakes* . . . (Kendal, 1809), pp. 95–96. (Copies: British Museum; Cornell.)

5. Park, Thomas (ed.). *Supplement to the British Poets* . . . London, 1809 (IX, 159–160). (Copy: British Museum.)

6. Wordsworth, William. *A DESCRIPTION OF THE SCENERY OF THE LAKES IN THE NORTH OF ENGLAND.* Fourth Edition. London: Longman, Hurst, Rees, Orme, and Brown, 1823. (Copy: Cornell.)

In this book, the material beginning on p. 31 with the paragraph "It has been said . . ." through p. 35 is all new to this edition—at least, it is not present in the third edition of 1822. Part of the new material is a reprint of Brown's poem "Now sunk the Sun . . ." on p. 35, which Wordsworth introduces by saying, ". . . I will conclude this section with a night-scene suggested by the Vale of Keswick. The Fragment is well known; but it gratifies me to insert it, as the Writer was one of the first who led the way to a worthy admiration of this country" (p. 34).

In the fifth edition of Wordsworth's book, published in 1835 under the new title *A GUIDE THROUGH THE DISTRICT OF THE LAKES*, this same section is reprinted on pages 35–36. (Copy: Cornell.)

BROWNIANA

INTRODUCTION

John Brown's proud, contentious spirit prompted him to join in many controversies—religious, political, musical, literary, and purely personal. Most of the pieces Brown wrote in the last fifteen years of his life—from the publication of *Essays on the Characteristics* in 1751 through the *Letter to Dr. Lowth* in 1766—caused numerous responses, both favorable and unfavorable. (From the very nature of controversies, it is to be expected that the majority of the replies are unfavorable. Most men do not feel compelled to answer arguments with which they agree.)

From the vast array of materials available, it was necessary to form some set of standards for inclusion or exclusion. Listed below, therefore, are all separately published pieces, of whatever length, which deal wholly or substantially with Brown's writings or which prompted Brown's writings. Excluded are all items in serials and periodicals, including book reviews; but after noting the date of publication of one of Brown's works in the main section of the bibliography, it is easy to locate the reviews in periodicals such as the *Gentleman's Magazine*, the *Monthly Review*, or the *Critical Review*.

Included are works such as Lyttelton's *Dialogues of the Dead* (1760) which immediately prompted a reply from Brown, yet works such as Shaftesbury's *Characteristicks* (1711) are excluded even though it was the subject of Brown's finest piece of writing. The *Characteristicks* was such a popular (if controversial) classic by the 1750's that including it in a list of Browniana would be analogous to including editions of Shakespeare in a list of Johnsoniana.

Although some readers undoubtedly will quarrel with the inclusion of certain items in this section, a great many more certainly will object to the omissions. What is one to do with the dozens of interesting pieces in the shadowy area bordering the *terra cognita* of true Browniana? What, specifically, is one to do with the host of replies, imitations, and attacks which followed the publication of Brown's *Estimate* in 1757? For example, the following description is of a pamphlet which I finally rejected from the Browniana section:

THE / TEN PLAGUES / OF / *ENGLAND*, / Of worse Consequence than those of / *EGYPT*, / DESCRIBED / Under the following HEADS: /

I. Disregard to our own Productions.	VI. Hypocrisy.
II. Luxury and Waste in great Families.	VII. Drunkenness.
III. Effeminacy.	VIII. Avarice and Usury.
IV. Gaming.	IX. Pride. and,
V. Love of Novelty.	X. Idleness.

The whole intended to shew, / That whatever CRIMES or FOIBLES in- / fect the Minds of a PEOPLE, are far / more injurious to a NATION than / bodily PLAGUES. / [rule] / By a Well-wisher to GREAT-BRITAIN. / [double rule] / *LONDON:* / Printed for R. WITHY and Co. Book and Print- / sellers, at *Hogarth*'s *Head*, opposite *Salisbury*- / *Court*, *Fleet-Street*. / [rule] / MDCCLVII.

Collation: 8° (in 4's): A^2 B–F^4

Contents: $A1^r$ half-title, $A1^v$ blank, $A2^r$ title, $A2^v$ blank, pages *1* 2–40 text.

Press figures: none.

Date of publication: Probably May, 1757. It was "reviewed" in the May issue of the *Monthly Review* (see note below).

Copies: *Harvard; University of Minnesota; *D. D. Eddy.

Note:

This is a vulgar pamphlet, apparently written in imitation of Brown's *Estimate*. It is accurately reviewed in the *Monthly*

Review, XVI (May, 1757), 455–456; I quote the entire review verbatim: "A low illiterate catch-penny."

In the two months following March 31, 1757, Brown's *Estimate* was published in four separate editions in London (see items no. 42–45 above), and the *Ten Plagues of England* is one of the many pieces published during that period which I believe was produced as a direct response to the *Estimate.* My belief is based on many points of internal evidence, both thematic and stylistic, but as I read pamphlets such as this I always hear a small voice whispering to me, "Can you *prove* that this piece is directly related to John Brown?" In this case the answer is "no," so it was rejected. I decided that for a piece to be included it must mention John Brown (or one of his works) by name and discuss the work to a degree that would considerably exceed a passing mention—usually anything in excess of two pertinent pages would suffice.

The following description, also rejected, presents a slightly different but related problem:

Cockin, William. 1736–1801.

ODE / TO THE / GENIUS OF THE LAKES / IN THE / NORTH OF ENGLAND. / [rule] / [quotation] / [double rule] / LONDON: / Printed for the Author; / And sold by RICHARDSON and URQUHART, under the Royal Exchange; / J. ROBSON, New Bond Street; and W. PENNINGTON, Kendal. / 1780.

Half-title: ODE / TO THE / GENIUS OF THE LAKES. / [Price two Shillings.]

Collation: 4° (in 2's): *A*² B–E² *F*² G–H²

Contents: *A*1ʳ half-title, *A*1ᵛ blank, page *1* title, *2* blank, *3* Advertisement, *4* blank, *5* 6–18 text of the poem (dated February, 1780 on p. 18), *19* special title: THREE / OCCASIONAL NOTES. *20* blank, *21* 22–30 text of the notes.

Press figures: none.

Size of an uncut copy: $11\frac{1}{4}'' \times 8\frac{3}{4}''$ (D. D. Eddy copy, in paper wrapper).

Copies: *Wellesley College (lacks half-title); *D. D. Eddy.

Subsequent printings:

This poem is reprinted on pages 135–165 of William Cockin's *The Rural Sabbath . . . and other Poems* (London, 1805). An uncut copy in original boards is in the Cornell Wordsworth Collection (Healey no. 1933).

Note:

In the reprint of this poem in *The Rural Sabbath*, a footnote on page 137 says, "A few quarto copies of this Ode were printed and thrown into the way of *actual tourists* in 1780. . . ."

This piece praises John Brown and includes an interesting biographical note about him, but the references are all biographical and do not discuss Brown's writings. Such information will be presented in my biography of Brown, but the personal references contained, for example, in Cockin's *Ode* or in John Brown's letters printed in contemporary periodicals are excluded from this bibliography.

The following descriptions of fifty-one pieces of Browniana are listed chronologically, except that all items pertaining to the *Estimate* and the *Explanatory Defence* (nos. 109–132) are grouped together but are chronologically listed within that unit. In most instances the title of the work sufficiently describes the relationship of the item to John Brown; if it does not, the information is given in a note.

The Browniana items present many problems of attribution of authorship. For example, did Robert Maddison write *An Examination of the Oratorios . . .* (no. 138)? There is some evidence that he did, so I list it under his name. Did Robert Andrews or Robert Colvill write the *Animadversions on Mr. Brown's Three Essays . . .* (no. 104)? I could find no evidence for either author, so I list the item by its title. Various libraries solve this problem in different ways, and this is one of the reasons why copies of the Browniana items are often difficult to locate in libraries. The reader should be warned, therefore, that the lists of copies in this section of the bibliography are less reliable than those for the writings of John Brown.

Once again, those copies which I have examined personally are marked with an asterisk.

Four Responses to the *Essays on the Characteristics*

(listed chronologically)

103. *Bulkley, Charles. 1719–1797*

A / VINDICATION / Of my / Lord *Shaftesbury*, / On the Subject of / RIDICULE. / BEING / Remarks upon a Book, intitled, / Essays *on the* Characteristics. / [rule] / [quotation] / [double rule] / *LONDON:* / Printed for John Noon, at the *White- / Hart*, in *Cheapside*, near the *Poultry*. / MDCCLI. / [Price 6 *d*.]

Collation: 8° (in 4's): A^4 B–E^4. B2 missigned B3.

Contents: Page *1* title, *2* blank, 3–39 text, *40* Advertisement.

Press figures: 4-⸸, 37-⸸.

Date of publication: August, 1751 (*Gentleman's Magazine*, XXI [August, 1751], 382).

Copies: *Bodleian; *Boston Public Library; *British Museum (2 copies); *Cambridge University Library; *Harvard (2 copies: Houghton Library; Andover-Harvard Theological Library); *Newberry Library; Princeton; Texas; *Yale; *D. D. Eddy.

Notes:

1. In the D. D. Eddy and Boston Public Library copies and in one of the British Museum copies (1087.c.31.[1.]), the last line of the title-page reads "[Price 6 *d*.]"; in the other seven copies examined the final bracket is not present.

2. A list of errata for this work is printed on page 100 of Bulkley's *Vindication of my Lord Shaftesbury on the Subjects of Morality and Religion* (London, 1752).

104.

Animadversions / ON / Mr. BROWN's / THREE ESSAYS / ON THE / Characteristicks. / [rule] / [quotation] / [rule] / [ornament] / [double rule] / *LONDON:* / Printed for J. NOON, at the *White-Hart* in the / *Poultry*. MDCCLII. / [Price One Shilling.]

Collation: 8° (in 4's): *A*[4] B–G[4] H[2]

Contents: Page *1* title, *2* blank, *3–4* Preface, *5* 6–60 text.

Press figures: none.

Date of publication: January 1, 1752 (*Daily Advertiser*). "Sold by Richard Baldwin, at the Rose in Pater-noster-Row."

Copies: *Bodleian; *Cambridge University Library; *University of Michigan; *Newberry Library; Tulane University.

Notes:

1. The *Whitehall Evening Post* of Tues., Dec. 24–Thurs., Dec. 26, 1751 advertises that this work will be published "on Monday next"—i.e., December 30. However, apparently there are no advertisements of publication earlier than January 1.

2. The authorship of this anonymous pamphlet has never been established beyond the fact that it was written by the author of *Eidyllia: or, Miscellaneous Poems . . . by the Author of Animadversions upon the Reverend Doctor Brown's Three Essays on the Characteristics* . . . Edinburgh, 1757. 4°. The authorship of *Eidyllia* has been attributed to Robert Andrews of Bridgnorth (British Museum Catalogue; *DNB*) and also to Robert Colvill, Minister of Dysart (Bodleian Library Catalogue; Halkett and Laing). However, there are no discernible reasons for attributing *Eidyllia* to either man.

The only obvious course of action was to see if any of the poems in *Eidyllia* were contained in later collections of poetry by either Andrews or Colvill. I wish to thank Miss Fiona Macmillan for making these comparisons with the appropriate books in the British Museum; however, there were no similarities to the poems by either author. I also thank J. D. Fleeman of Pembroke College, Oxford for making similar comparisons in the Bodleian—unfortunately, with the same results.

105. *Bulkley, Charles. 1719–1797*

A / VINDICATION / OF MY / Lord *Shaftesbury*, / On the Subjects of / Morality and Religion. / Being Farther Remarks on a Book / INTITLED, / ESSAYS *on the* Characteristics. / [rule] / [quotation] / [rule] / By CHARLES BULKLEY. / [rule] / LONDON: / Printed for JOHN NOON, at the White / Hart, near the Poultry, in Cheapside; and / R. BALDWIN, at the Rose in Paternoster- / Row. MDCCLII. / [Price 1 *s.* 6 *d.*]

Collation: 8° (in 4's): A–M^4 N^2

Contents: Page *1* title, *2* blank, 3–100 text. List of Errata on page 100.

Press figures: none.

Size of an uncut copy: $8\frac{13}{16}''$ × $5\frac{3}{8}''$ (University of Chicago copy).

Date of publication: May 12, 1752 (*General Advertiser*). Advertisements: "Next week will be published . . ." (*General Advertiser*, May 8, 1752); "This Day is published . . ." (*General Advertiser*, May 12, 1752).

Copies: *Bodleian; *Cambridge University Library; *University of Chicago; *Columbia; *Harvard (2 copies: Houghton Library; Andover-Harvard Theological Library); *D. D. Eddy.

106. *Ramsay, Allan, the younger. 1713–1784*

AN / ESSAY / ON / RIDICULE. / [quotation] / [ornament] / LONDON: / Printed for A. MILLAR in the Strand. / MDCCLIII.

Collation: 8°: *A*⁴(−*A*4[= G1?]) B–F⁸ G1(= *A*4?). But, in the University of Michigan copy, B4 and F4 are cancels; see note 2, below.

Contents: *A*1^r title, *A*1^v blank, pages *i*–ii Advertisement, *iii* Contents, *iv* blank, 1–82 text. In the University of Michigan copy, on cancelled leaf F4 the page number 72 is misprinted 27.

Press figures: 32-4, 45-3, 73-2. Also, in the University of Michigan copy page 72 (misnumbered 27) has press figure 3.

Size of an uncut copy: $8\frac{3}{4}'' \times 5\frac{5}{8}''$ (University of Michigan copy, in original marbled-paper wrapper).

Number of copies printed: William Strahan printed 500 copies of this pamphlet ($5\frac{1}{2}$ sheets) for Andrew Millar (British Museum Add. MSS. 48800, folio 84).

Date of publication: June 1, 1753 (*Daily Advertiser*; *Public Advertiser*). Advertisements: "In a few Days will be published . . ." (*Public Advertiser*, May 25 and 26); "On Friday next will be published . . ." (*Public Advertiser*, Wed., May 30 and Thurs., May 31); "This Day is published, Price 1 s. 6 d. sewed in Marble Paper . . ." (*Daily Advertiser*, June 1; *Public Advertiser*, June 1).

Copies: *British Museum; *University of Cincinnati; *University of Michigan; University of Toronto; *D. D. Eddy.

Notes:

1. In spite of Watt's attribution, accepted by Halkett and Laing and others, this book was not written by William Whitehead, and it is not the second edition of Whitehead's poem, *An Essay on Ridicule* (London: R. Dodsley, 1743).

2. The University of Michigan copy is Allan Ramsay's own copy, extensively annotated in ink. On the front fly-leaf Ramsay says that this copy "began to be corrected for some future edition."

Leaf B4 is a cancel. The text of page 7 (B4^r) is thoroughly revised. For instance, in the original state the first two lines read, "*of shewing that to be ridiculous which is really so.*" In the cancel this is corrected to read, "*of shewing that to be ridiculous which is imagined to be so.*" Page 8 ($B4^v$) is reset with some changes in punctuation but no substantive revisions.

Leaf F4 (pp. 71–72) is a cancel. Both pages are completely reset, but there is only one textual correction. Page 71, line 13 in the original state reads "*which is really so,*" and in the cancel this is corrected to "*which is imagined to be so.*"

In addition to the two cancels, the Michigan copy contains dozens of corrections in Ramsay's hand, some of them quite extensive.

3. In the D. D. Eddy copy B4 and F4 are not cancels, but the two textual changes described above have been made in ink in Ramsay's handwriting.

4. Ramsay reissued this piece as the first of four essays in a collection entitled *The Investigator* (London, 1762), copies of which are in the British Museum, University of Michigan, and Yale. In this collection the *Essay on Ridicule* is a reissue of the sheets of the first edition, except that B4 and F4 are cancels, as described above. None of Ramsay's manuscript corrections in the Michigan copy are incorporated in the text of the essay in *The Investigator.*

107.

CRITICAL REMARKS / ON THE / Tragedy of ATHELSTAN. / WITH / RULES necessary to be Observed / BY ALL / DRAMATIC POETS. / [rule] / BY / The Author of the STATE-FARCE. / [rule] / [quotation] / [rule] / [ornament] / [double rule] / *LONDON:* / Printed for MARY COOPER, at the *Globe* in / *Pater-Noster-Row.* / [rule] / MDCCLVI. / [Price Six Pence.]

Collation: 8° (in 4's): *A*1 B–E^4 F1

Contents: Page *1* title, *2* author's note, 3–36 text.

Press figures: none.

Date of publication: March 26, 1756 (*Daily Advertiser*).

Copies: *Boston Public Library; *British Museum; *Cambridge University Library; *Harvard; Indiana (Lilly).

108.

TURNCOAT, / A / PARODY / Of the TRAGEDY of / *ATHELSTAN.* / [rule] / In One ACT. / [rule] / [ornament] / [double rule] / *LONDON:* / Printed and Sold by PAUL VAILLANT, facing / *Southampton-Street* in the *Strand.* MDCCLVI. / [Price One Shilling.]

Collation: 8° (in 4's): A–F^4 G^2

Contents: Page *i* title, *ii* blank, iii–iv Dedication: TO THE AUTHOR OF *ATHELSTAN*, v–ix A Prefatory Discourse on Parodies, *x* Dramatis Personae, *11* 12–52 text. Page 14 misnumbered 41.

Press figures: none.

Date of publication: June 29, 1756 (*Public Advertiser*). "An unforeseen Accident has hitherto delay'd the Publication of this Parody, which is the first Dramatic one ever attempted in the English Language."

Copies: *British Museum; *Cambridge University Library; *Folger Library; Huntington Library; *Yale.

Replies to, and Imitations of, the *Estimate* (Volumes I and II) and the *Explanatory Defence*

Short Title	Date of publication of the first edition
1. *The Real Character of the Age . . .*	June 3, 1757
2. *The Prosperity of Britain . . .*	October 11, 1757
3. *Friendly Admonitions . . .*	January 10, 1758
4. Ralph's *The Case of Authors . . .*	February 15, 1758
5. Wallace's *Characteristics . . .*	March 11, 1758
6. Temple's *Vindication of Commerce. . . .*	April 4, 1758
7. *Letters to the Estimator . . .*	May 2, 1758
8. *Some Doubts occasioned by the Second Volume . . .*	May 11, 1758
9. *A Letter to the Author of the Estimate . . .*	July 18, 1758
10. *An Essay to prove the Superiority . . .*	January 10, 1759
11. *A Letter to the Reverend Dr. Br—n*	January 15, 1759
12. Gordon's *New Estimate . . .* Parts I and II	April 10, 1760
13. Gordon's *New Estimate . . .* Part III	April 23, 1761
14. *An Estimate of the Manners . . . of the Modern French*	February 11, 1767
15. *Another Estimate of the Manners and Principles . . .*	1769
16. *An Estimate of the Manners of the Present Times*	1782

109.

THE REAL / CHARACTER / OF THE / AGE. / IN A / LETTER to the Rev. Dr. BROWN. / Occasioned by / His ESTIMATE of the MANNERS and / PRINCIPLES of the TIMES. / [ornament] / LONDON: / Printed for M. COOPER, at the Globe, in Pater- / Noster-Row. / [rule] / MDCCLVII.

Half-title: [Row of type ornaments] / THE REAL / CHARACTER / OF THE / AGE. / [row of type ornaments] / [Price One-Shilling.]

Collation: 8° (in 4's): A^2 B–G⁴

Contents: $A1^r$ half-title, $A1^v$ blank, $A2^r$ title, $A2^v$ blank, pages *1* 2–47 text, *48* blank.

Press figures: 5-8, 16-1, 24-3, 39-1.

Size of an uncut copy: $8\frac{7}{8}'' \times 5\frac{3}{8}''$ (General Theological Seminary, New York).

Date of publication: June 3, 1757 (*Public Advertiser*; *London Evening-Post*, June 2–4).

Copies: *Bodleian; *British Museum (2 copies); *Cornell (lacks half-title); *General Theological Seminary, New York (lacks half-title); Huntington Library; *New York Public Library (2 copies); Princeton; *D. D. Eddy.

Note:

The end of this letter (p. 47) is signed "C. L. St."

110. *The Second Edition (1757)*

THE REAL / CHARACTER / OF THE / AGE. / IN A / LETTER to the Rev. Dr. BROWN. / Occasioned by / His ESTIMATE of the MANNERS and / PRINCIPLES of the TIMES. / THE SECOND EDITION. / [ornament] / LONDON: / Printed for M. COOPER, at the Globe, in Pater- / Noster-Row. / [rule] / M DCC LVII.

Half-title: [row of type ornaments] / THE REAL / CHARACTER / OF THE / AGE. / [row of type ornaments] / [Price One-Shilling.]

Collation: 8° (in 4's): A^2 B–G^4

Contents: $A1^r$ half-title, $A1^v$ blank, $A2^r$ title, $A2^v$ blank, pages *1* 2–47 text, *48* blank.

Press figures: 18-6, 32-8.

Size of an uncut copy: 9″ × 5⅞″ (Newberry Library copy).

Copies: *Library of Congress (lacks the half-title); *Newberry Library.

111. *Dublin Edition (1757)*

THE REAL / CHARACTER / OF THE / AGE. / IN A / *Letter* to the Rev. Dr. BROWN. / Occasioned by / His ESTIMATE of the MANNERS and / PRINCIPLES of the TIMES. / [ornament] / DUBLIN: / Printed by JAMES HOEY Sen. and JAMES HOEY Jun. / at the Mercury in Skinner-Row. / [bracket facing vertically] / MDCCLVII.

Collation: 12° (in 6's): *A*1 (= E4?) B–D^6 E^4(–E4[= *A*1?])

Contents: Page *1* title, *2* blank, *3* 4–43 text, *44* Advertisement for the Dublin edition of the first volume of Brown's *Estimate* —"*Just Published by the Printers hereof.* . . ."

Press figures: none.

Date of publication: later than June 3, 1757.

Copies: *Folger Library.

112.

THE / PROSPERITY of BRITAIN, / Proved from the / Degeneracy of its People. / A / LETTER to the Rev. Dr. BROWN, / ON HIS / ESTIMATE of MANNERS. / WITH / Some Thoughts on his ANSWERER / in the REAL CHARACTER. / [double rule] / LONDON: / Printed for R. BALDWIN, in *Pater-noster-Row.* / MDCCLVII. [Price 1 s.

Collation: 8° (in 4's): A–E^4 F^2

Contents: Page *1* title, *2* blank, *3* 4–43 text, *44* blank.

Press figures: 7-2, 12-1, 23-4, 26-2, 39-4.

Date of publication: October 11, 1757 (*Public Advertiser*; *London Evening-Post*, Oct. 8–11).

Copies: *British Museum; *Cornell; Huntington Library; *New York Public Library; Texas; *D. D. Eddy.

Note:

The end of this letter (p. 43) is signed "A NAMELESS FRIEND."

113.

FRIENDLY ADMONITIONS / TO THE / INHABITANTS / OF / GREAT-BRITAIN, in general; / AND TO THE / CLERGY of the CHURCH of ENGLAND, / in particular. / [rule] / By BRITANNICUS. / [rule] / [ornament] / [double rule] / LONDON: / Printed for R. BALDWIN, at the Rose, in Pater-noster- / Row, 1758.

Half-title: [row of type ornaments] / FRIENDLY ADMONITIONS / TO THE / INHABITANTS / OF / GREAT-BRITAIN, in general, &c. / [row of type ornaments] / [Price ONE SHILLING.]

Collation: 8° (in 4's): A^2 B–H^4

Contents: $A1^r$ half-title, $A1^v$ blank, $A2^r$ title, $A2^v$ blank, pages *1* 2–56 text.

Press figures: 2-2, 23-3, 30-3, 40-2, 45-3, 50-3.

Date of publication: January 10, 1758 (*Daily Advertiser*).

Copies: British Museum; *Cornell; *Yale.

Notes:

1. This entire pamphlet is concerned with the problems raised by Brown's *Estimate*, which is specifically mentioned and discussed on pages 41 ff.

2. A good review of this pamphlet is found in the *Monthly Review*, XVIII (Feb., 1758), 189–191; one argument of the pamphlet is answered by a letter in the *London Chronicle*, Feb. 16–18, 1758, p. 166.

114. *Ralph, James. 1705?–1762*

THE / CASE / OF / AUTHORS / BY / PROFESSION OR TRADE, / STATED. / WITH REGARD TO / BOOKSELLERS, the STAGE, and the PUBLIC. / No Matter by Whom. / [rule] / [quotation] / [rule] / [ornament] / [double rule] / *LONDON:* / Printed for R. GRIFFITHS, Bookseller, in *Pater-noster-* / *Row.* MDCCLVIII.

Collation: 8° (in 4's): A^2 B–K^4 L^2

Contents: $A1^r$ title, $A1^v$ blank, $A2^r$ dedication, $A2^v$ Advertisement, pages *1* 2–76 text. Pages 73–76 misnumbered 65–68.

Press figures: 18-3 or none, 26-3, 44-3, 53-3.

Date of publication: February 15, 1758 (*Public Advertiser*; *London Evening-Post*, Feb. 14–16). "Price 1 s."

Copies: National Library of Australia; *Bodleian; *British Museum; University of Chicago; Harvard; Indiana (Lilly); *Newberry Library; *New York Public Library (imperfect: lacks pp. 73–76); Yale; *D. D. Eddy.

Note:

Ralph wrote this work in response to Brown's *Estimate*, which he specifically attacks on pages 13–18. Andrew Kippis, in his biography of Brown, describes Ralph as a formidable adversary.

The Yale copy of this edition of the *Case of Authors* has been reproduced in photofacsimile with an introduction by Philip Stevick. It was published in Gainesville, Florida: Scholar's Facsimiles & Reprints, 1966.

115. *The Second Edition (1762)*

THE / CASE / OF / AUTHORS / BY / PROFESSION OR TRADE, / STATED; / WITH REGARD TO / BOOKSELLERS, the STAGE, and the PUBLIC. / By JAMES RALPH, Esq; / [rule] / [quotation] / [rule] / [ornament] / [double rule] /

LONDON: / Printed for R. GRIFFITHS, Bookseller, in the *Strand*, 1762. / [Price One Shilling and Six-pence.]

Collation, Contents, and Press figures: Exactly the same as the first edition.

Copies: *British Museum; Harvard; *Illinois; Newberry Library; New York Public Library.

Note:

The two preliminary leaves are of a new setting of type in this "edition"; otherwise it is a reissue of sheets of the first edition.

116. *Wallace, Robert. 1697–1771*

CHARACTERISTICS / OF THE / Present Political State / OF / GREAT BRITAIN. / [quotation] / LONDON: / Printed for A. MILLAR in the Strand. / MDCCLVIII.

Collation: 8°: A^2 B–D^8(±D7) E–N^8(±N1,2) O–R^8. B1 is not signed; see note, below. F1–3 and N3 are also cancels in some copies.

Contents: *A*1^r half-title, *A*1^v blank, *A*2^r title, *A*2^v blank, pages *i–ii* Contents and Errata, *iii* iv–xviii Advertisement, *19* 20–49 text of Part I, *50* blank, *51* 52–111 text of Part II, *112* blank, *113* 114–181 text of Part III, *182* blank, *183* 184–191 text of Part IV, *192* blank, *193* 194–256 text of Part V.

Press figures: xiv-4, 24-2, 52-4, 66-2, 77-8, 95-1, 109-8, 138-4, 141-5, 154-1, 175-4, 200-6, 202-5, 218-8, 226-6, 232-2, 255-*.

Number of copies printed: William Strahan printed 750 copies for Andrew Millar (British Museum Add. MSS. 48800, folio 107).

Date of publication: March 11, 1758 (*Public Advertiser*; *Daily Advertiser*; *London Evening-Post*; *Whitehall Evening Post*). "Price 4 s. bound."

Copies: National Library of Australia; *Bodleian; *British

Museum; University of Chicago; *Columbia (3 copies); *Harvard (The Kress Library); *Illinois (2 copies); Indiana (Lilly); *Newberry Library; *New York Public Library; National Library of Scotland (2 copies); *Yale (Franklin Collection).

Notes:

1. The contents listed above are a description of the British Museum, Harvard, and the first Illinois copies. In the Bodleian, Columbia, second Illinois, Newberry Library, New York Public Library and Yale copies the first three leaves are in this order: title, contents, half-title. None of these first three leaves is signed.

2. Brown's *Estimate* is quoted and discussed throughout this book, but especially in Part V, "Of the National Genius and Capacity for Self-Defence." Although Wallace differs considerably from Brown in his opinions, Brown acknowledged in 1758 that Wallace was "the only candid and decent adversary who hath yet appeared against him" (*An Explanatory Defence of the Estimate* . . . London, 1758, p. 35).

117. *The Second Edition (1758)*

CHARACTERISTICS / OF THE / Present Political State / OF / GREAT BRITAIN. / [quotation] / [rule] / The SECOND EDITION, / With Corrections and Additions by the Author. / [double rule] / LONDON: / Printed for A. MILLAR in the Strand. / MDCCLVIII.

Collation: 12°: *A*^{2} B–K^{12} L^{6}

Contents: *A*1^{r} title, *A*1^{v} blank, *A*2 Contents and Errata, pages *i* ii–xiv Advertisement, *15* 16–40 *41* 42–94 *95* 96–156 *157* 158–164 *165* 166–227 *228* text.

Press figures: *15*-2, 24-4, 34-2, 50-2, 60-1, 87-4, 104-2, 111-1, 132-8, 135-2, *157*-2, 166-8, 170-2, 189-8, 215-8, 227-3.

Number of copies printed: William Strahan printed 1,000 copies

(10 sheets) for Andrew Millar (British Museum Add. MSS. 48800, folio 107).

Size of an uncut copy: 7½″ × 4½″ (D. D. Eddy copy, in original boards).

Date of publication: July 13, 1758 (*Daily Advertiser*; *Public Advertiser*; *London Evening-Post*, July 11–13). "With Corrections and Additions, by the Author . . . Price 2 s. 6 d. bound in Twelves."

Copies: National Library of Australia; *Columbia (2 copies); *Library of Congress; *Cornell; *Harvard Law School; Illinois; *Library Company of Philadelphia; *Newberry Library; National Library of Scotland; *Yale; *D. D. Eddy.

118. *Dublin Edition (1758)*

CHARACTERISTICS / OF THE / Present Political State / OF / GREAT BRITAIN. / [rule] / [quotation] / [rule] / [ornament] / [double rule] / DUBLIN: / Printed for L. FLIN, at the Bible in *Castle-street.* / [rule] / M, DCC, LVIII.

Collation: 12°: A^2 B–G^{12} H^4. G3 missigned F3.

Contents: *A*1^r title, *A*1^v blank, *A*2^r "Copy of a Letter to the Editor of this *Dublin* Edition of the CHARACTERISTICS, *&c.*" dated Dublin, March 30, 1758 and signed "R.C." *A*2^v Contents, pages *i* ii–x Advertisement, *11* 12–28 *29* 30–65 *66* 67–106 *107* 108–111 *112* 113–151 Contents, *152* blank. Page vii misnumbered vi, ix misnumbered xi, and x misnumbered v.

Press figures: none.

Copies: *Bodleian; *Illinois.

118A. *French Translation (1759)*

CARACTERISTIQUES / DE / L'ETAT POLITIQUE [red] / DU ROYAUME / DE LA / GRANDE-BRETAGNE [red] / SUR LE PIED / QU'IL EST AUJOURD'HUI. /

Ouvrage traduit sur la Quatrième / Edition de l'Anglois. / [ornament] / *A LA HAYE,* [red] / CHEZ PIERRE GOSSE JUNIOR, / *Libraire de S.A.S. le Prince Stadhouder / des Provinces-Unies &c.* / M. DCC. LIX. [red]

Collation: 8°: π1(= X6?)A–V^{8}X^6(–X6[= π1?]). $5(–K5, X5) signed.

Contents: $\pi 1^r$ title, $\pi 1^v$ blank, pages *1* 2–330 text.

Press figures: none.

Copies: *National Library of Scotland (NE. 508. d. 3.). (I have examined a Xerox print of this copy.)

Note:

I have not been able to locate any copy of the "fourth English edition" which, according to the title-page, is the basis of this translation.

119. *Temple, William, of Trowbridge*

A VINDICATION / OF / COMMERCE / AND THE / ARTS; / Proving that they are the SOURCE of the / Greatness, Power, Riches and Populousness / of a State. / BEING / An Examination of Mr. BELL'S *Dissertation* upon / Populousness, read in the Schools, and honoured / with the Lord Viscount *Townshend*'s PRIZE, by / the UNIVERSITY of CAMBRIDGE. / Wherein Mr. *Bell*'s Calumnies on TRADE are an- / swered, his Arguments refuted, his System ex- / ploded, and the principal causes of *Populosity* / assigned. / With a large APPENDIX, / Containing REMARKS on that part of the Estimate of the / Manners and Principles of the Times, which relates to / TRADE and COMMERCE. / [rule] / By I—— B——, M.D. / [rule] / [quotation] / [rule] / *LONDON:* / Printed for J. NOURSE at the *Lamb* opposite / *Katherine-Street* in the *Strand.* MDCCLVIII.

Half-title: A / VINDICATION / OF / COMMERCE / AND THE / ARTS, *&c.* / Price Two Shillings.

Collation: 8°: A–F^8 G^6 H–K^8

Contents: Page *i* half-title, *ii* blank, *iii* title, *iv* blank, *v* vi–x Dedication "To the Right Honourable the Lord Visc^t. *Townshend,*" *xi* xii–xvi Preface, *1* 2–92 text, 93–96 Remarks, *97* special title: AN / APPENDIX / CONTAINING / Some REMARKS upon that part of the Esti- / mate of the Manners and Principles of the / Times, which relates to TRADE and COM- / MERCE. / [2 quotations] / [rule] / By I—— B——, M.D. / [rule], *98* blank, *99* 100–137 text of the Appendix, *138* Errata, *139–140* blank.

Press figures: vi-1, xvi-1, 2-1, 4-1, 22-2, 34-1, 41-1, 60-1, 62-1, 66-2, 90-1, 107-1, 108-1, 123-2, 135-3.

Date of publication: April 4, 1758 (*Daily Advertiser,* April 4, 1758).

Copies: National Library of Australia; *Cornell; *Harvard (The Kress Library); Indiana (Lilly); National Library of Scotland.

Note:

For the authorship of this tract, see the letter of Josiah Tucker to Lord Kames, dated July 6, 1758: "... I was extremely hurt in observing with what arrogance and indecency Mr H. [i.e., David Hume] was treated by that superficial writer, the author of the *Estimate.* He is himself below Mr H's notice; and just vengeance has been taken on him by several writers; particularly one, who has wrote the *Vindication of Commerce,* styling himself J. B. *M.D.* This *M.D.* is no other than a clothier of Trowbridge, one *Temple,* who has immense erudition in his way,—understands the principles of commerce extremely well, but pushes some of them too far ..."—see Alexander Fraser Tytler, lord Woodhouselee, *Memoirs of the Life and Writings of the honourable Henry Home of Kames* ... In Two Volumes (Edinburgh, 1807), Appendix to Vol. II, p. 6.

120.

LETTERS / TO THE / ESTIMATOR / OF THE / MANNERS and PRINCIPLES / of the TIMES. / [rule] / By ONE who has served the STATE. / [rule] / [quotation] / [double rule] / LONDON: / Printed for J. COOTE, opposite Devereux-court, / in the Strand. MDCCLVIII. / [Price one Shilling.]

Collation: 8° (in 4's): *A*1 (= G4?) B–G^4(–G4[=*A*1?])

Contents: *A*1^r title, *A*1^v blank, pages *1* 2–46 text. The end of the last letter (p. 46) is signed: Swithin Swing. Rope-Alley, Newgate-Street, April 27th, 1758.

Press figures: none.

Date of publication: May 2, 1758 (*Public Advertiser*; *Whitehall Evening Post*).

Copies: *Bodleian (2 copies); *British Museum; *Lambeth Palace Library; *Newberry Library; Texas; *Yale; *D. D. Eddy.

121. *The Second Edition (1758)*

LETTERS / TO THE / ESTIMATOR / OF THE / MANNERS and PRINCIPLES / of the TIMES. / [rule] / By ONE who has served the STATE. / [rule] / SECOND EDITION. / [rule] / [quotation] / [double rule] / Printed for J. COOTE, opposite Devereux-court, / in the Strand. MDCCLVIII. / [Price one Shilling.]

Collation: 8° (in 4's): A^4 C–G^4. No gathering signed B.

Contents: Page *1* title, *2* blank, *3* 4–48 text. (No part of this edition is dated.)

Press figures: none.

Date of publication: May 10, 1758 (*Daily Advertiser*).

Copies: *Harvard (The Kress Library); *Illinois.

122. *The Third Edition (1758)*

LETTERS / TO THE / ESTIMATOR / OF THE / MANNERS and PRINCIPLES / of the TIMES. / [rule] / By ONE who has served the STATE. / [rule] / THIRD EDITION. / [rule] / [quotation] / [double rule] / Printed for J. COOTE, opposite Devereux-court, / in the Strand. MDCCLVIII. / [Price one Shilling.]

Collation, Contents, and Press figures: Same as the second edition.

Size of an uncut copy: $8\frac{3}{4}'' \times 5\frac{3}{4}''$ (Harvard copy, unbound, stitched).

Date of publication: June 27, 1758 (*Public Advertiser*). "The Estimator is advised to enlarge his Defence one half, as there are two or three odd Objections here which my Lord forgot to make and his Reverence to answer." [This note in the newspaper advertisement refers to Brown's *Explanatory Defence* . . ., published June 19, 1758.]

Copies: *Harvard (The Kress Library).

Note:

This "edition" has a new title-page, but in all other respects it appears to be either a reissue of second edition sheets or a new impression from standing type.

123.

SOME / DOUBTS / Occasioned by the / SECOND VOLUME / OF AN / ESTIMATE / OF THE / MANNERS and PRINCIPLES / OF THE / TIMES. / Humbly proposed to the Author or to the Public. / [double rule] / *LONDON:* / Printed for W. SANDBY, in *Fleet-street.* / MDCCLVIII.

Collation: 8°: A^2(=F7, 8?) B–F^8(−F7, 8[=*A*1, 2?])

Contents: *A*1^r title, *A*1^v blank, *A*2 Contents, pages 1–76 text.

Press figures: none.

Date of publication: May 11, 1758 (*Daily Advertiser*).

Copies: *Bodleian; *British Museum (2 copies); *Columbia; *Newberry Library; Princeton; Texas; *Yale.

124. *The Second Edition (1758)*

SOME / DOUBTS / Occasioned by the / SECOND VOLUME / OF AN / ESTIMATE / OF THE / MANNERS and PRINCIPLES / OF THE / TIMES. / Humbly proposed to the Author or to the Public. / [rule] / The SECOND EDITION. / [double rule] / *LONDON:* / Printed for W. SANDBY, in *Fleet-street.* / M DCC LVIII. / [Price One Shilling.]

Collation: 8°: *A*1 B–E[8] F1. A1 and F1 are a conjugate, wrap-around leaf.

Contents: *A*1[r] title, *A*1[v] blank, pages *1–2* Contents, 3–66 text.

Press figures: none.

Size of an uncut copy: 8¾″ × 5¾″ (Harvard copy, unbound, stitched).

Date of publication: July 20, 1758 (*Daily Advertiser*).

Copies: *Boston Athenaeum; *British Museum (2 copies); *Harvard (The Kress Library); *Illinois.

125.

A / LETTER / TO THE / AUTHOR / OF THE / ESTIMATE, / On that Part of his / EXPLANATORY DEFENCE / Which relates to the / UNIVERSITIES. / [Quotation, from Brown's *Essays on the Characteristics*] / [ornament] / *LONDON:* / Printed for J. PRIDDEN, at the *Feathers,* near / *Fleet-Bridge, Fleet-Street.* 1758.

Half-title: A / LETTER / TO THE / AUTHOR / OF THE / ESTIMATE, *&c.* / [Price Sixpence.]

Collation: 8° (in 4's): *A*[2] B–C[4] D[2]

Contents: *A*1[r] half-title, *A*1[v] blank, *A*2[r] title, *A*2[v] blank, pages 1–19 text, *20* blank. Page 15 misnumbered 14.

Press figures: 8-4, 16-2.

Size of an uncut copy: 8½″ × 5½″ (Harvard copy, unbound, stitched).

Date of publication: July 18, 1758 (*Public Advertiser*).

Copies: *Bodleian; *Boston Athenaeum; *British Museum; Huntington Library; *Harvard (The Kress Library); *Illinois; *New York Public Library; *Yale.

Note:

The beginning of the letter (page 1) is dated "29th *June*, 1758."

126.

AN / ESSAY / To prove the / SUPERIORITY / OF THE / Present Age and Nation / Over that of any former. / IN / ANSWER / To the ingenious, but malevolent Writer, of / An ESTIMATE of the MANNERS / and PRINCIPLES of the TIMES. / [rule] / *By* BRITANNICUS. / [rule] / [quotation] / [double rule] / *LONDON:* / Printed for THOMAS HOPE, Successor to the late Mr. / *E. Comyns*, at the Sign of the *Bible and Anchor*, the / Corner of *Bartholomew-lane, Threadneedle-street;* and / sold by *Samuel Trimmer*, at *Derby*; and *John Palmer*, / at *Bristol*. MDCCLIX. / [Price Six-pence.]

Collation: 8° (in 4's): A–D⁴

Contents: Page *1* title, *2* blank, 3–22 text, *23* publisher's advertisement, *24* blank.

Press figures: none.

Date of publication: January 10, 1759 (*Daily Advertiser*).

Copies: *Folger Library.

Note:

"A Rhapsody of nonsense" is the entire "review" of this item in the *Monthly Review*, XX (Jan., 1759), 83.

127. *A Letter to the Reverend Dr. Br—n. London: J. Townsend, [1758 or 1759]*

Date of publication: January 15, 1759 (*Daily Advertiser*). "Printed for J. Townsend, at the Corner of White-Fryars Gateway, in Fleet-Street." Price 6d. 8°.

Copies: none located.

Notes:

1. "The wit of this very little piece lies chiefly in the type, which is made unusually large, with wide spaces between the lines, to ridicule the loose manner in which the Doctor's works are printed . . ." (*Monthly Review*, XX [Jan., 1759], 82).

2. The review in the *Gentleman's Magazine*, XXIX (Jan., 1759), 35 is as follows:

> This is a burlesque congratulation of the Doctor, on the improvement he has made in the art of printing.
>
> I thought, says the author, at the first opening of your book, I saw a discernment quick to find out, and a desire ever ready to please the publick appetite; methought you had perceived how great the prevalence of ostentation was in reading, as in everything else; how much fonder the people were, in general, of turning over a variety of books, than of studying any much; and that, perceiving it, you had endeavoured, to the very utmost of your power, to gratify it; and gave us in *two* volumes, what, in the old stile of printing, could never have been extended to more than *one*.—Whatever honours others may lay claim to, as having exceeded you, and carried your improvements to a still greater degree of excellence, than it had ever before arrived at—Still are you the person to whom we stand indebted for the first thought.—The fountain, from whence these overflowings of profit derive their source originally, and in whom therefore all praises, on this account, should ultimately terminate. And may the practice long continue! So shall we authors increase our profit without

any additional labour, and the public extol our works. —Why?—Merely because they pay dear for them.—I am, Sir, ever proud to follow your example.

This piece contains only one sheet and a quarter, with only 15 lines of a very large character on a page, so faithfully has the author followed the example he commends, which, it is hoped, he will not find it his interest to repeat.

128. *Gordon, John. Archdeacon of Lincoln*

A NEW / ESTIMATE / OF / MANNERS and PRINCIPLES: / Being a COMPARISON between / Ancient and Modern TIMES, / In the three Great Articles / OF / *Knowledge*, *Happiness*, and *Virtue*; / Both with Respect / To MANKIND at Large, / AND TO / This KINGDOM in Particular. / [rule] / [quotation] / [double rule] / *CAMBRIDGE*, / Printed by J. BENTHAM, Printer to the UNIVERSITY; / for W. THURLBOURN and J. WOODYER, in *Cambridge*; / and sold by A. MILLAR in the *Strand*, R. & J. DODSLEY / in *Pall Mall*, & J. BEECROFT in *Pater-noster Row*, *London*. / [rule] / M.DCC.LX.

Collation: 8°: a–c^8 A–G^8 H^2 $*^2$

Contents: Page *i* title, *ii* blank, *iii* iv–xiv An Apology to the Author of the former *Estimate*, *i* ii–xxx (misnumbered xxix) An Explanation of the Design of this Estimate (dated March 20, 1760), *xxxi–xxxiii* Contents, *xxxiv* Advertisement, *1* special title for Part I, *2* blank, *3* 4–44 text of Part I, *45* special title for Part II, *46* blank, *47* dedication, *48* blank, *49* 50–115 text of Part II, *116* Errata, *117–120* Advertisements. Page xxx is misnumbered xxix.

Press figures: 14-4, 18-4, 34-4, 54-4, 66-4.

Date of publication: April 10, 1760 (*Daily Advertiser*). "Price 2s. sew'd"

Copies: *Bodleian; *British Museum (2 copies); *Cambridge University Library; Folger Library; Newberry Library; Texas; *Yale; *D. D. Eddy.

129. *Gordon, John. Archdeacon of Lincoln*

A NEW / ESTIMATE / OF / MANNERS and PRINCIPLES: / Or a COMPARISON between / Ancient and Modern TIMES, / In the three Great Articles / OF / *Knowledge*, *Happiness*, and *Virtue*. / Part III. / OF HAPPINESS; / IN WHICH / Some Principles of Mr. ROUSSEAU / are examined. / [rule] / [quotation] / [double rule] / *CAMBRIDGE*, / Printed by J. BENTHAM, Printer to the UNIVERSITY; / for W. THURLBOURN and J. WOODYER, in *Cambridge;* / and sold by A. MILLAR in the *Strand*, R. & J. DODSLEY / in *Pall-Mall*, and J. BEECROFT in *Pater-noster Row*, *London*. / [rule] / M.DCC.LXI.

Collation: 8°: a–b^8 c^4 *A–*C^8 D^8 *E–*H^8

Contents: Page *i* title, *ii* blank, *iii* dedication to Robert Shafto, *iv* blank, *v* vi–xxxv An Apology to the Reader (dated March 18, 1761), *xxxvi* blank, *xxxvii* special title for Part III, *xxxviii* blank, *xxxix–xl* Contents, *1* 2–125 text of Part III, *126* Advertisement, *127–128* blank.

Press figures: xi-4, xxvii-4, xxxiv-4 or none, 6-4 or none, 26-4, 34-4, 59-4, 78-3, 95-4, 106-4, 123-2.

Date of publication: April 23, 1761 (*Whitehall Evening Post*, April 21–23). "Price 2 s. sewed"

Copies: *Bodleian; *British Museum (2 copies); Folger Library; Newberry Library; *D. D. Eddy.

Note:

The Advertisement on page *126* states that "Parts the IVth and Vth of this ESTIMATE . . . will be published some time next Winter." Presumably they were never published.

130. *Helvétius, Claude Adrien. 1715–1771. (pseudonym)*

AN / ESTIMATE / OF THE / MANNERS / AND / PRINCIPLES / OF THE / MODERN FRENCH. / [rule] / BY /

MONSIEUR HELVETIUS, / AUTHOR OF / THE ESSAY ON SPIRIT. / [double rule] / WITH NOTES, / BY / THE TRANSLATOR. / [double rule] / LONDON: / Printed for F. NEWBERY, in Pater-Noster-Row. / [rule] / MDCCLXVII.

Half-title: [row of type ornaments] / ESTIMATE / OF THE / MANNERS / AND / PRINCIPLES / OF THE / MODERN FRENCH. / [row of type ornaments] / (Price Two Shillings.)

Collation: 8°: A^2 B–G^8 H^2

Contents: *A*1ʳ half-title, *A*1ᵛ blank, *A*2ʳ title, *A*2ᵛ blank, pages 1–44 text, *45* 46–100 Notes. Pages 65–100 misnumbered 81–116.

Press figures: none.

Date of publication: February 11, 1767 (*Daily Advertiser*). Advertisement: "... Printed for F. Newbery, at No. 15, in Pater-noster-Row; W. Gisborne, at his Circulating Library, in Great Russel-Street, Bloomsbury; and A. Yates, at the Bible, in Brewer-Street, Golden-Square."

Copies: British Museum; Northwestern University; *Yale.

Note:

The supposed translation of the "French" *Estimate* occupies the first forty-four pages of this work, while the notes on pages 45–100 consist mainly of a comparison between the French *Estimate* and John Brown's *Estimate*, a comparison very much in Brown's favor.

The following are some extracts from the *Monthly Review*, XXXVI (March, 1767), 234–235:

> What does the Translator mean by stiling Mons. Helvetius author of the Essay on Spirit?—We have a famous tract under that title, written by the late excellent Dr. Clayton, bishop of Clogher, in Ireland; and we know of no other: we suppose, however, that the Englisher

of this Estimate refers to the celebrated work entitled *De L'Esprit*, written by M. Helvetius; but if he does, he is not very fortunate in his translation of that title.

With respect to this flimsy Estimate, it was, probably, intended as an imitation of Dr. Brown's Estimate of the Manners and Times of *this* Country. . . .

Since writing the above remark, we have seen in the News-papers, a public *disavowal* of this Estimate, on the part of M. Helvetius. Indeed, we were surprized at the appearance of so poor a performance, under the sanction of so respectable a name; for, whatever may be thought of Mr. H.'s principles, by those who differ from him on certain points of speculation, he is, undoubtedly, possessed of very great as well as very agreeable talents.

131.

ANOTHER / ESTIMATE / OF THE / MANNERS / AND / PRINCIPLES / OF THE / PRESENT TIMES. / [ornament] / LONDON: / Printed for G. KEARSLY, at No. 1, Ludgate-Street. / MDCCLXIX.

Collation: 8°: *A*1 B–H^8 I^2

Contents: *A*1^r title, *A*1^v blank, pages *1* 2–115 text, *116* blank.

Press figures: none.

Copies: *British Museum T. 708.(5.); *Yale.

Note:

Page 113 exists in two states: in the first it is misnumbered 100 (copies: British Museum); in the second it is correctly numbered (copies: Yale).

132.

AN / ESTIMATE / OF THE / MANNERS / OF THE / PRESENT TIMES. / [rule] / *LONDON:* / PRINTED IN THE YEAR MDCCLXXXII.

Collation: 8° (in 4's): A–C^4

Contents: Page *1* title, *2* blank, *3* 4–23 text, *24* blank.

Press figures: none.

Size of an uncut copy: $7\frac{13}{16}''$ × $4\frac{7}{8}''$ (D. D. Eddy copy, unbound, stitched).

Copies: Bodleian; *British Museum; University of Chicago; *Cornell; Lambeth Palace Library; Newberry Library; *Yale; *D. D. Eddy.

133. *Lyttelton, George Lyttelton, first baron. 1709–1773*

DIALOGUES / OF THE / DEAD. / [rule] / [ornament] / [double rule] / *LONDON:* / Printed for W. SANDBY, in Fleet-street. / [rule] / M.DCC.LX.

Collation: 8°: A^4 a^2 B–C^8(±C1, 4–6) D–X^8

Contents: Page *i* title, *ii* blank, iii–vii Preface, *viii* blank, ix–xii Contents, 1–320 text of the 28 dialogues.

Press figures: vi-8, 12-3, 34-4, 50-2, 68-3, 93-4, 100-3, 120-4, 137-3, 138-8, 156-2, 158-3, 162-4, 189-3, 204-3, 210-4, 232-2, 242-3, 256-4, 258-8, 265-9, 286-4, 288-8, 296-8, 302-4, 316-8.

Size of an uncut copy: $8\frac{3}{4}''$ × $5\frac{5}{8}''$ (D. D. Eddy copy, in original blue boards).

Date of publication: May 17, 1760 (*Daily Advertiser*). Advertisements: "On Saturday next will be publish'd . . ." (*Daily Advertiser*, Tues., May 13, Wed., May 14, and Thurs., May 15, 1760); "Tomorrow will be publish'd . . ." (*Daily Advertiser*, Fri., May 16, 1760); "This Day are publish'd, Price 4 s. in blue Covers . . ." (*Daily Advertiser*, Sat., May 17, 1760).

Copies: *Bodleian (2 copies: Vet. A5e.2317 and Vet. A5e. 3452); *British Museum (716.c.1); *Harvard (inscribed "The Gift of the Author to Mary Hume 1760"); *Newberry Library; *D. D. Eddy.

Variants of the first edition:

I. Press figures are the same as the first edition except for having P.F. 3 on p. 316. Copies: *Bodleian (2 copies: Vet. A5e.2571 and Vet. A5e.3715); *Yale (Im L998 760).

Note: The nine copies listed above are all Todd's Edition A or variants thereof; see William B. Todd, "Patterns in Press Figures: A Study of Lyttelton's *Dialogues of the Dead*," *SB*, VIII (1956), 230–235.

II. Todd, Edition B. First edition title-page, but otherwise composed primarily of mixed sheets from the first and second editions. Copies: *Bodleian (Godw. 8°.518); *British Museum (244.b.7); *Cornell; *Folger Library (PR 3542 L78 D5 1760). These are made-up copies in which certain sheets have been reimpressed. For example, in the British Museum, Cornell, and Folger copies the press figures in the last half of the book are those of the first edition; in the first half they are usually those of the second edition, but also have P.F. 155-7 which is not found in any other edition (see Todd, p. 235). The British Museum and Cornell copies also have P.F. 133-3.

Notes:

1. Dialogue XXIII, between Pericles and "Cosmo de Medicis, the First of that Name," is found on pages 241–259. The political arguments in this dialogue are refuted by John Brown in his *Additional Dialogue of the Dead*, 1760 (see above, no. 61).

2. Lyttelton's *Dialogues of the Dead* became very popular and went through numerous editions and translations, especially in the 1760's but also later—e.g., the first American edition was published in 1797. However, since Brown replied to Lyttelton's arguments in 1760, I list below only those editions and translations of Lyttelton's work published in that year.

134. *The Second Edition (1760)*

DIALOGUES / OF THE / DEAD. / [rule] / The SECOND EDITION. / [rule] / [ornament] / [double rule] / *LONDON:* / Printed for W. SANDBY, in Fleet-street. / [rule] / M.DCC.LX.

Collation: 8°: A^4 a^2 $\chi 1$ B–I^8($\pm$I2) K–X^8

Contents: Page *i* title, *ii* blank, iii–vii Preface, *viii* blank, ix–xii Contents, *xiii* Errata, *xiv* blank, 1–320 text. (Some copies lack the errata leaf, $\chi 1$. In the Cornell, New York Public Library and Harvard copies, the errata leaf is bound following X8.)

Press figures: vi-7, xi-5 or none, 10-2 or none, 21-1, 26-7, 36-7, 46-8, 54-3, 56-1, 77-7, 78-8, 93-4, 94-2, 98-3, 108-7, 124-9, 126-8, 140-3, 142-7, 155-4.

Size of an uncut copy: $8\frac{13}{16}''$ × $5\frac{3}{4}''$ (D. D. Eddy copy, in original blue paper wrapper).

Date of publication: May 22, 1760 (*Daily Advertiser*; *London Chronicle*). Advertisements: "Next Thursday will be publish'd . . ." (*Daily Advertiser*; *London Chronicle*, Tues., May 20, 1760); "Tomorrow will be publish'd . . ." (*Daily Advertiser*, Wed., May 21, 1760); "This Day is publish'd . . ." (*Daily Advertiser*; *London Chronicle*, Thurs., May 22, 1760).

Copies: *Bodleian; *British Museum (8406.ccc.9); *Cornell; *Harvard; *New York Public Library; *Yale; *D. D. Eddy (2 copies).

Note:

Both the first and second editions have press figure 4 on page 93 (outer forme of the G gathering). This is a coincidence, for the two formes are of different settings of type in the two editions.

All eight copies listed above are Todd's Edition C.

135. *The Third Edition (1760)*

DIALOGUES / OF THE / DEAD. / [rule] / The THIRD EDITION. / [rule] / [ornament] / [double rule] / *LONDON:* / Printed for W. SANDBY, in Fleet-street. / [rule] / M. DCC. LX.

Collation: 8°: A^4 a^2 B–X^8

Contents: Page *i* title, *ii* blank, iii–vii Preface, *viii* blank, ix–xii Contents, 1–320 text.

Press figures: vi-4, xi-5, 25-3, 36-4, 46-5, 54-8, 79-7, 84-6, 98-5, 105-3 or none, 137-3, 143-7, 186-2.

Copies: *Bodleian; *British Museum (8405.ccc.14); *Library of Congress (Thomas Jefferson's copy); *Cornell; *Folger Library (imperfect copy); *Harvard; *D. D. Eddy.

Note:

In this edition the a gathering appears to be printed from the same setting of type as the second edition; both have press figure 5 in identical positions on page xi.

All seven copies listed above are Todd's Edition D.

136. *Dublin Edition (1760)*

DIALOGUES / OF THE / DEAD. / [rule] / [ornament] / [double rule] / *DUBLIN*: / Printed by OLI. NELSON, in *Skinner-Row.* / M, DCC, LX.

Collation: 12° (in 6's): A–2D^6 2E^4

Contents: Page *i* title, *ii* blank, iii–viii Preface, ix–xii Contents, 1–320 text. Pages 280–288 misnumbered 300–308.

Press figures: none.

Size of an uncut copy: $7\frac{3}{8}'' \times 4\frac{1}{2}''$ (British Museum copy 1485.i.7, in original boards).

Copies: *Bodleian; *British Museum 1485.i.7; *D. D. Eddy.

136A. *French Translation (1760)*

DIALOGUES / DES / MORTS: / COMPOSÉS / Par Mylord LYTTELTON; / ET / Traduits de l'Anglois / Par JEAN DES CHAMPS, / Prêtre de l'Eglise Anglicane, Ministre de la Chapelle / Roïale de la Savoye, & Recteur de Pillesdon / dans la Comté de Dorset. / NOUVELLE EDITION, / faite sous les yeux de l'Auteur. / [double rule] / LONDRES, / Chez G. SEYFFERT, 1760.

Collation: 12°: A^6 χ1 (=P6?) B–O^{12} P^6(−P6 = χ1?)

Contents: Page *i* title, *ii* blank, *iii* iv–viii Préface de l'Auteur, *ix* x–xii Table des Dialogues, *xiii–xiv* Errata, 1–322 Contents.

Press figures: none.

Copies: *Bibliothèque Nationale (2 copies). I have examined a Xerox print of one of the copies.

137. *French Translation (1760)*

DIALOGUES / DES / MORTS, / *TRADUITS DE L'ANGLOIS* / PAR MONSIEUR LE / PROFESSEUR DE JONCOURT. / [ornament] / *A LA HAYE,* / Chez PIERRE DE HONDT, / *M. DCC. LX.*

Collation: 8°: *6 A–X^8 Y^2

Contents: *1r title, *1v blank, *2, 3 Author's Preface, *4 Translator's Preface, *5, 6 Table of Contents, pages *1* 2–339 text, *340* blank.

Press figures: none.

Copies: Bibliothèque Nationale; *Library of Congress.

Notes:

1. Another French translation was published seven years later, "faite sur la quatrieme edition." Its imprint reads: "A Amsterdam. Chez J. H. Schneider, MDCCLXVII." Copies: Bibliothèque Nationale (2 copies); British Museum; *Yale.

2. A German translation, "Herausgegeben von Johann George Henrich Oelrichs," was published in 1761. Its imprint reads: "Berlin, Stettin und Leipzig, in Verlag Johann Heinrich Rüdigers. 1761." Copies: *Princeton University Library copy (3836.7.33.8) in original pink boards.

138. *Maddison, Robert*

AN / EXAMINATION / OF THE / ORATORIOS / WHICH HAVE BEEN / PERFORMED THIS SEASON, / AT / COVENT-GARDEN THEATRE. / [rule] / [quotation] / [rule] / [ornament] / [double rule] / LONDON: / Printed for G. KEARSLY, in *Ludgate-Street;* / R. DAVIS, in *Piccadilly;* and / J. WALTER, at *Charing-Cross.* / MDCCLXIII. / [Price One Shilling.]

Collation: 8° (in 4's): *A*² B–I⁴

Contents: Page *i* title, *ii* blank, *iii*–iv Dedication "TO THE Reverend DR. BROWN." *1* 2–63 text, *64* blank.

Press figures: none.

Date of publication: April 25, 1763 (*Daily Advertiser*; *The St. James's Chronicle*, April 23–25).

Copies: *Boston Public Library; *British Museum T. 933.(13.).

Notes:

1. The title-page described above is that of the Boston Public Library copy; in the British Museum copy there is nothing following the date—i.e., the price is not listed.
2. The title-page of the Boston Public Library copy is inscribed "By Robert Maddison, B.A. Fellow of Sidney College Cambridge."
3. This anti-Handelian piece praises the *Cure of Saul* highly, especially on pages 46–63.

139.

SOME / OBSERVATIONS / ON / DR. BROWN's DISSERTATION / On the RISE, UNION, &c. &c. &c. of / POETRY AND MUSICK. / In a LETTER to Dr. B*****. / [rule] / [quotation] / [double rule] / LONDON: / Printed for W. JOHNSTON, in Ludgate-Street. / M DCC LXIV.

Collation: 4° (in 2's): *A*² B–Q²

Contents: $A1^r$ half-title, $A1^v$ blank, $A2^r$ title, $A2^v$ blank, pages 1–59 text, *60* blank.

Press figures: 3-3, 8-2, 12-1, 16-3, 20-6, 23-5, 27-2, 32-4, 35-4, 40-1, 42-4, 48-3, 50-2, 54-2.

Size of an uncut copy: $11\frac{1}{4}'' \times 8\frac{5}{8}''$ (D. D. Eddy copy).

Date of publication: February, 1764 or earlier (see note 2, below). I have not found any advertisements for the date of publication.

Copies: *Bodleian; *British Museum (2 copies); *Library of Congress; *Harvard; *D. D. Eddy.

Notes:

1. In one British Museum copy (T.1164.[6.]) and in the D. D. Eddy copy, page 42 is correctly numbered; in the other British Museum copy (557*.e.25.[8.]) and in the Bodleian and Harvard copies, it is numbered 4.

2. John Langhorne reviewed this work in the *Monthly Review*, XXX (February, 1764), 123–130. The review ends by saying that "Upon the whole, we apprehend that the adventrous Doctor never met with a more formidable Opponent . . ." (p. 130).

3. John Brown replied to this work in his *Remarks on some Observations on Dr. Brown's Dissertation on Poetry and Musick* . . . London, 1764—see above.

140.

POLITICAL LOGIC / DISPLAYED: / Or, a KEY to the / THOUGHTS / ON / CIVIL LIBERTY, / Licentiousness and Faction. / [rule] / [quotation] / [double rule] / *LONDON:* / Printed for F. NEWBERY, at the *Crown*, in *Pater-* / *Noster Row*. 1765. / (Price One Shilling and Six-pence.)

Collation: 8° (in 4's): A^4 B–I^4

Contents: Page *i* title, *ii* Errata, *iii* Advertisement, *iv* blank, *v* vi–viii [A Poem] "To The Reverend Dr. B****" *1* 2–64 text. Pages 25–32 (the E gathering) misnumbered 49–56 (but this is corrected in the list of errata).

Press figures: none.

Date of publication: July 18, 1765 (*London Chronicle*, July 16–18).

Copies: *Harvard; *Princeton; *Yale.

Note:

This pamphlet is reviewed in the *Gentleman's Magazine*, XXXV (July, 1765), 337–338, but a much better review is in the *Monthly Review*, XXXIII (August, 1765), 163–164.

141. *Priestley, Joseph. 1733–1804*

AN / ESSAY / ON A COURSE OF / LIBERAL EDUCATION / FOR / CIVIL AND ACTIVE LIFE. / WITH PLANS OF LECTURES ON / I. The Study of History and general Policy. / II. The History of England. / III. The Constitution and Laws of England. / TO WHICH ARE ADDED, / REMARKS / ON A / CODE OF EDUCATION, / Proposed by Dr. BROWN, in a late TREATISE, intitled, / THOUGHTS ON CIVIL LIBERTY, &c. / [rule] / By JOSEPH PRIESTLEY, LL.D. / TUTOR in the LANGUAGES and BELLES LETTRES / in the ACADEMY at WARRINGTON. / [rule] / Printed for C. HENDERSON under the *Royal Exchange*; / T. BECKET and DE HONDT in the *Strand;* and by / J. JOHNSON and DAVENPORT, in *Pater-Noster-Row*, / MDCCLXV. / Price, in Boards, 3 s. 6 d.

Collation: 8°: $A^4(\pm A2)$ B–I^4 K–S^8 T–U^4

Contents: $A1^r$ title, $A1^v$ blank, $A2^r$ Dedication to John Lees, $A2^v$ blank, pages *i* ii–iii Preface, *iv* Errata, *1* 2–37 An Essay on a Course of Liberal Education, 38–68 A Syllabus of . . . Lectures on History, *69* 70–75 *76* 77–83 . . . on the History of England, *84* 85–98 *99* 100–134 . . . on the Laws of England, *135* special title for Remarks on a proposed Code of Education, *136* blank, *137* 138–213 Remarks on a proposed Code of

Education, *214* blank, *215–221* Contents, *222–224* Account of a Chart of Biography.

Following page *224* is inserted a plate, A Specimen of a Chart of Biography.

Press figures: none.

Size of an uncut copy: 8¾″ × 5⅜″ (American Philosophical Society).

Date of publication: Probably late in September, 1765. It is listed as published in the September, 1765 issue of the *Gentleman's Magazine*, and it is reviewed in the *London Chronicle* of October 3–5, 1765.

Copies: *American Philosophical Society; *British Museum; University of Chicago; *Cornell; Huntington Library; Pennsylvania State University (2 copies); *Yale; *D. D. Eddy. (Also, see Crook H/387.)

Subsequent printings:

1. London, 1765. Not in Crook; a ghost? However, see page 8 of J. F. Fulton's *Works of Joseph Priestley* (New Haven, 1937).
2. London, 1768. Copies: Bodleian (and see Crook H/388).
3. London, 1778. (Crook H/389.)
4. London, 1793. (Crook H/390.)

References are to Ronald E. Crook, *A Bibliography of Joseph Priestley 1733–1804*. London: The Library Association, 1966.

142. *Priestley, Joseph. 1733–1804*

AN / ESSAY / ON THE / FIRST PRINCIPLES / OF / GOVERNMENT; / AND ON THE NATURE OF / Political, Civil, and Religious / LIBERTY. / By JOSEPH PRIESTLEY, LL.D. F.R.S. / [cut] / LONDON: / Printed for J. DODSLEY, in Pall-Mall; T. CADELL (suc- / cessor to Mr. Millar) in the Strand; and J. JOHNSON, / N°. 8, Paster-noster Row. / MDCCLXVIII.

Collation: 8°: π1(=A4?) A^4(−A4[=π1?]) B–N^8

Contents: Page *i* title, *ii* blank, *iii* iv–vii Preface, *viii* Contents, *1* 2–14 *15* 16–48 *49* 50–126 *127* 128–191 text, *192* Advertisement. Page 92 misnumbered 62.

Press figures: none.

Copies: Australian National University, Acton; *Bodleian; *British Museum (2 copies); *Cornell; *Harvard (2 copies); Huntington Library; New York Public Library; Yale; *D. D. Eddy. (Also, see Crook PS/290.)

Note:

The first sentence of the preface reads: "This publication owes its rise to the *remarks* I formerly wrote *on Dr. Brown's proposal for a code of education*" (p. iii).

143. *The Second Edition (1771)*

AN / ESSAY / ON THE / FIRST PRINCIPLES / OF / GOVERNMENT, / AND ON THE NATURE OF / Political, Civil, and Religious / LIBERTY, / INCLUDING / Remarks on Dr. BROWN'S *Code of Education,* / AND ON / Dr. BALGUY'S Sermon on CHURCH AUTHORITY. / [rule] / The SECOND EDITION, corrected and enlarged, / [rule] / BY JOSEPH PRIESTLEY, LL.D. F.R.S. / [rule] / *LONDON:* / Printed for J. JOHNSON, No. 72, in St. Paul's Church-Yard. / M DCC LXXI.

Collation: 8°: π^2 A^6 B–U^8

Contents: Page *i* title, *ii* blank, *iii* Dedication, *iv* blank, *v* vi–xvi The Preface, *1* 2–300 text, *301* Contents, *302* blank, *303–304* Advertisement.

Press figures: none.

Copies: *American Philosophical Society; *Bodleian; *British Museum; *Cornell; Library of Congress; *Harvard (2 copies: Andover-Harvard Theological Library); *Newberry Library;

New York Public Library; Pennsylvania State University; Princeton; University of Toronto; *Yale. (Also, see Crook PS/292).

Subsequent printings:

1. Dublin, 1768. Copies: Pennsylvania State University. (Also, see Crook PS/291.)

2. Dutch translation. Leyden, 1783. (Crook PS/319.)

References are to Ronald E. Crook, *A Bibliography of Joseph Priestley 1733–1804*. London: The Library Association, 1966.

144. *Lowth, Robert. 1710–1787*

A / LETTER / TO / The Right Reverend Author of / *The Divine Legation of Moses Demonstrated*; / In Answer to / THE APPENDIX / To the Fifth Volume of that Work. / WITH / AN APPENDIX, / Containing a former Literary Correspondence. / BY / *A Late Professor* / In THE UNIVERSITY of OXFORD. / [rule] / [quotation] / [double rule] / *OXFORD* / Printed, at the Clarendon Printing-House; and / Sold by A. Millar and J. Dodsley, in London. / M DCC LXV.

Collation: 8° (in 4's): A–R^4 S^2

Contents: Page *1* title, *2* Imprimatur (dated Sept. 24, 1765), *3* 4–102 text of the letter (dated August 31, 1765 on page 102), *103* special title to the Appendix, *104* blank, *105* 106–139 Appendix: text of the 5 letters between Warburton and Lowth (dated from Sept. 9 to Oct. 14, 1756), *140* blank.

Press figures: none.

Size of an uncut copy: $8\frac{7}{8}''$ × $5\frac{3}{4}''$ (D. D. Eddy copy, unbound, stitched).

Date of publication: Later than Sept. 24, 1765 (the date of the imprimatur), but I have found no advertisements for the date of publication.

Copies: National Library of Australia; *Bodleian; *British

Museum; *Cambridge University Library; *Harvard; Yale; *D. D. Eddy.

Notes:

1. John Brown replied to this *Letter* in his *Letter to the Rev. Dr. Lowth* . . . (1766)—see above.

2. It has been said that Lowth's *Letter* "has never been surpassed in literary warfare." See A. W. Evans, *Warburton and the Warburtonians* (London, 1932), especially pages 247–255.

145. *The Second Edition (1766)*

A / LETTER / TO / The Right Reverend Author of / *The Divine Legation of Moses Demonstrated*; / In Answer to / THE APPENDIX / To the Fifth Volume of that Work: / WITH / AN APPENDIX, / Containing a former Literary Correspondence: / BY / *A Late Professor* / In the UNIVERSITY of OXFORD. / [rule] / [quotation] / [rule] / The SECOND EDITION. / [rule] / LONDON, / Printed for A. MILLAR, and J. DODSLEY. / MDCCLXVI.

Collation: 8° (in 4's): A–R^4

Contents: Page *1* title, *2* blank, *3* 4–102 text of the letter, *103* 104–136 Appendix.

Press figures: 8-4, 12-1, 18-1, 30-4, 36-4, 42-1, 62-2, 66-2, 76-1, 87-2, 95-1, *103*-2, 106-1, 118-2, 125-1, 135-2.

Date of publication: November 23, 1765 (*Daily Advertiser*). "Price 1 s. 6 d."

Copies: Bodleian (3 copies); *British Museum; *Harvard; Illinois; Newberry Library; Wayne State University; *Yale (2 copies).

Note:

William Bowyer printed 1,500 copies of the "third edition," the first 1,050 of which were delivered to Millar November 23, 1765 (Bodleian MS. DON b.4, folio 120). However, that is the same date that copies of the second edition were first advertised in the newspapers; and since the third edition is nothing more than a reissue of second edition sheets with a new canceled title (see next entry), then apparently the figure of 1,500 copies in Bowyer's ledger refers to both the second and "third" editions.

146. *The Third Edition (1766)*

A / LETTER / TO / The Right Reverend Author of / *The Divine Legation of Moses Demonstrated;* / In Answer to / THE APPENDIX / To the Fifth Volume of that Work: / WITH / AN APPENDIX, / Containing a former Literary Correspondence: / BY / *A Late Professor* / In the UNIVERSITY of OXFORD. / [rule] / [quotation] / [rule] / The THIRD EDITION. / [rule] / LONDON, / Printed for A. MILLAR, and J. DODSLEY. / MDCCLXVI.

Collation: 8° (in 4's): $A^4(\pm A1)$ $B\text{–}R^4$

Contents and Press figures: same as the second edition.

Copies: Bodleian; *Harvard; *Sion College Library; *Yale; *D. D. Eddy.

Note:

Except for a new title-page (a cancel), this "edition" is a reissue of second edition sheets. See the note to the second edition, above.

147. *The Fourth Edition, First Issue (1766)*

A / LETTER / TO / The Right Reverend Author of / *The Divine Legation of Moses Demonstrated*; / In Answer to / THE APPENDIX / To the Fifth Volume of that Work: / WITH / AN APPENDIX, / Containing a former Literary Correspondence: / BY / *A Late Professor* / In the UNIVERSITY of OXFORD. / [rule] / [quotation] / [rule] / The FOURTH

EDITION. / [rule] / LONDON, / Printed for A. MILLAR, and J. DODSLEY. / MDCCLXVI.

Collation and Contents: the same as the second edition.

Press figures: 7-4, 10-1, 26-4, 38-4, 47-1, 54-1, 64-4, 71-1, 78-4, 86-1, 93-4, 101-1, 106-4, 116-4, 127-4, 133-2.

Date of publication: Presumably January 10, 1766 (see note, below).

Copies: *Bodleian (2 copies).

Note:

William Bowyer printed 750 copies of the fourth edition, the first 100 of which were delivered to Millar January 10, 1766 (Bodleian MS. DON b.4, folio 120).

The first edition of John Brown's *Letter to . . . Lowth* was published January 7, 1766. Lowth replied "the day after Dr. Brown's letter came to hand," and the text of his reply is dated January 13 (see next entry). Lowth decided to reissue the fourth edition of his *Letter* to Warburton, substituting a new title which would mention his letter to Brown, and printing the text of that letter in an additional half-sheet, the new S gathering.

William Bowyer then reprinted "750 single Titles" plus "1,250 [copies] of an additional half sht containing a Reply to Dr. Brown" (Bodleian MS. DON b.4, folio 120). Since 750 titles were printed—enough for the entire fourth edition—presumably very few copies with the first issue title-page were ever sold. Also, note that 1,250 copies of Lowth's "Letter to Dr. Brown" were printed—enough for issuing with all copies of the fourth edition plus another 500 which, according to contemporary custom, probably were offered gratis to purchasers of earlier editions (see next entry).

148. *The Fourth Edition, Second Issue (1766)*

A / LETTER / TO / The Right Reverend Author of / *The Divine Legation of Moses Demonstrated;* / In Answer to / THE

APPENDIX / To the Fifth Volume of that Work: / WITH / AN APPENDIX, / Containing a former Literary Correspondence: / BY / *A Late Professor* / In the UNIVERSITY of OXFORD. / [rule] / [quotation] / [rule] / The FOURTH EDITION. / To which is added, / A Letter to the Reverend Doctor BROWN. / [rule] / LONDON, / Printed for A. MILLAR, and J. DODSLEY, / MDCCLXVI.

Collation: 8° (in 4's): A4($\pm$A1) B–S⁴

Contents: Page *1* title, *2* blank, *3* 4–102 text of the letter, *103* 104–136 Appendix, *137* special title: A / LETTER / TO THE / Reverend Dr. BROWN. *138* Note: "This letter was written the day after Dr. Brown's letter came to hand: And tho' it was sent, as a private letter, by the post; yet, as Dr. Brown's letter came from the press, it has been thought proper to communicate a copy of the Answer likewise to the Public." 139–143 text of the letter to Dr. Brown, dated Jan. 13, 1766 (p. 143), *144* blank.

Press figures: Same as first issue of the fourth edition, except adding P.F. 140-1 in the new S gathering.

Date of publication: January 18, 1766 (*The St. James's Chronicle*, Jan. 16–18). "Price 1 s. 6 d."

Copies: *Harvard; *Union Theological Seminary, New York; *Yale.

Notes:

1. The second issue differs from the first only in having a new title-page and the addition of Lowth's "Letter to the Reverend Dr. Brown" (the new S gathering).

2. Lowth's letter to Brown (the S gathering) is properly a part only of the second issue of the fourth edition. However, 500 additional copies were printed for separate issue (see the note for the preceding entry). Not unexpectedly, therefore, in addition to the three copies listed above we find that the S gathering is bound with the Bodleian copy of the first edition and with one Bodleian copy of the fourth edition,

first issue; also, the Beinecke Library at Yale has a separate copy of the S gathering which it has catalogued as a monograph, *A Letter to the Reverend Dr. Brown.*

149.

A / FREE ADDRESS / To the AUTHOR of the / ESSAYS on the CHARACTERISTICS. / IN / ANSWER to his LETTER / TO THE / Rev. Dr. LOWTH. / [rule] / [two quotations] / [double rule] / LONDON, / Printed for Messrs. RICHARDSON and URQUHART, at the / Royal-Exchange.

Collation: 8° (in 4's): *A*^{2} B–D^4 E^2

Contents: *A*1^r half-title, *A*1^v blank, *A*2^r title, *A*2^v blank, pages *1* 2–28 text. At the end of the text is the signature, "Publicus."

Press figures: 14-2, 21-3.

Date of publication: January 16, 1766 (*Public Advertiser*, Jan. 16; *The Gazetteer and New Daily Advertiser*, Jan. 16; *The St. James's Chronicle*, Jan. 14–16). Price 1 s.

Copies: *Bodleian; *British Museum; *Cornell; *Folger Library.

Note:

Both the British Museum and Cornell copies lack the half-title.

150.

AN / Expostulatory Letter, / TO THE / AUTHOR of ESSAYS / ON THE / Characteristics; / Occasioned by his / LETTER / TO THE / Reverend Dr. LOWTH. / [rule] / [quotation] / [double rule] / *LONDON:* / Printed for *J. Ridley*, St. *James's-street.* / M.DCC.LXVI.

Collation: 8° (in 4's): *A*^{4} B–D^4

Contents: Page *1* half-title, *2* blank, *3* title, *4* blank, *5* 6–22 text, *23–24* blank.

Press figures: none.

Date of publication: January 20, 1766 (*The Gazetteer and New Daily Advertiser*). "Price 6 d."

Copies: *Cambridge University Library (lacks half-title).

Note:

The half-title is listed in a copy offered by George W. Walford, 186 Upper Street, London, N.1, List No. HB/264 Division I (1968), item no. 40.

151. *Mason, William. 1725–1797*

ODE / TO THE / LEGISLATOR ELECT / OF / RUSSIA, / On his being prevented from entering on his high / *Office of* CIVILIZATION, / BY A / FIT *of the* GOUT. / [double rule] / *LONDON:* / Printed for W. NICOLL, in St. *Paul's Church Yard.* 1766.

Half-title: [rule] / ODE / TO THE / LEGISLATOR ELECT / OF / RUSSIA. / [Price One Shilling.]

Collation: 4° (in 2's): *A*² B–C²

Contents: Page *1* half-title, *2* blank, *3* title, *4* blank, *5* 6–11 text, *12* blank.

Press figures: none.

Date of publication: Presumably late in August, 1766; extracts from the poem were printed in the *St. James's Chronicle* of Aug. 26–28, 1766, and in the *London Chronicle* of Aug. 30–Sept. 2, 1766.

Copies: *Harvard (2 copies: one was given to Harvard by Thomas Hollis; the other belonged to Horace Walpole and was dated by him August [1766] on the title-page); *Yale.

Note:

That William Mason is the author of this poem is confirmed by Thomas Gray's letters to Mason; see letters 424 and 427 in the *Correspondence of Thomas Gray*, ed. Paget Toynbee and Leonard Whibley (Oxford, 1935), but especially see Appendix R (III, 1247–52). Also, see Philip Gaskell, *The First Editions of William Mason* (Cambridge, 1951), no. 42, item iii. Gaskell agrees that Mason wrote the poem, but he assumes incorrectly that it was first published in the *St. James's Chronicle.*

This *Ode* is not reprinted in the *Satirical Poems published anonymously by William Mason*, ed. Paget Toynbee (Oxford, 1926).

Appendix I

Chronological List

This list gives in chronological order according to date of publication all 155 items of the bibliography—the 104 by Brown and the 51 pieces of Browniana. Whenever possible I list the day and month of publication, especially of all first editions of works by Brown. Many items—such as American and Irish editions as well as French, German, and Italian translations—are listed only by year. For each year all items dated by day and month are listed chronologically first, followed, in no particular order, by those items dated only by the year.

In many instances the precise dating of items is very useful. For example, eight works listed in this bibliography—all closely related pieces forming part of a heated controversy—were published during the month of January, 1766. The day of publication of each of these works has been carefully established to show their respective relationships. On the other hand, merely the year is given for the date of publication of many items issued, as it were, in isolation—i.e., not showing any close relationship with other items published during the same year.

Short Title; number in bibliography in parentheses	*Date of publication*
Honour (1)	December 20, 1743
An Essay on Satire. 1st ed. (2)	April 24, 1745
"The Puppet Show" (4)	April 26, 1746
"Scating" (5)	July 5, 1746
The Mutual Connexion . . . (6)	January 8, 1747
An Essay on Satire. 2d ed. (3)	March 16 or 17, 1749
On Liberty: A Poem (7)	April 26, 1749

Short Title; number in bibliography in parentheses	*Date of publication*
On the Pursuit of False Pleasure . . . 1st ed. (8)	May 11, 1750
Essays on the Characteristics. 1st ed. (10)	April 18, 1751
Bulkley's *Vindication of Shaftesbury on Ridicule* (103)	August, 1751
Essays on the Characteristics. 2d ed. (11)	September 16, 1751
Animadversions on Brown's Three Essays . . . (104)	January 1, 1752
On the Pursuit of False Pleasure . . . 2d ed. (9)	[April 30, 1752?]
Bulkley's *Vindication of Shaftesbury on Morality and Religion* (105)	May 12, 1752
Essays on the Characteristics. 3d ed. (12)	[June 27, 1752?]
Essays on the Characteristics. 1st Dublin ed. (15)	1752
Essays on the Characteristics. 2d Dublin ed. (16)	1752
Ramsay's *Essay on Ridicule* (106)	June 1, 1753
On the Use and Abuse of Externals in Religion . . . (17)	1753
An Account of Barbarossa . . . (18)	December 9, 1754
Barbarossa. 1st ed. (19)	December 23, 1754
Essays on the Characteristics. 4th ed. (13)	January 31, 1755
Barbarossa. 2d ed. (20)	February 17, 1755
Barbarossa. 1st Dublin ed. (29)	1755
Athelstan. 1st ed. (38)	March 9, 1756
Critical Remarks on the Tragedy of Athelstan (107)	March 26, 1756
Turncoat, a Parody of Athelstan (108)	June 29, 1756
Athelstan. London: Ch. Robinson (39)	[1756?]

Short Title; number in bibliography in parentheses	*Date of publication*
Athelstan. 1st Dublin ed. (40)	1756
Barbarossa. 2d Dublin ed. (30)	1756
An Estimate . . . 1st ed. (42)	March 31, 1757
An Estimate . . . 2d ed. (43)	April 14, 1757
An Estimate . . . 3d ed. (44)	May 5, 1757
An Estimate . . . 4th ed. (45)	May 31, 1757
The Real Character of the Age. 1st ed. (109)	June 3, 1757
The Real Character of the Age. 2d ed. (110)	[after June 3, 1757]
An Estimate . . . 5th ed. (46)	July 4, 1757
An Estimate . . . 6th ed. (47)	September 1, 1757
The Prosperity of Britain . . . (112)	October 11, 1757
An Estimate . . . 1st Dublin ed. (49)	1757
An Estimate . . . 2d Dublin ed. (50)	1757
Barbarossa. 3d Dublin ed. (31)	1757
The Real Character of the Age. Dublin edition (111)	1757
Friendly Admonitions . . . (113)	January 10, 1758
Ralph's *The Case of Authors* . . . 1st ed. (114)	February 15, 1758
Wallace's *Characteristics* . . . 1st ed. (116)	March 11, 1758
Temple's *Vindication of Commerce* . . . (119)	April 4, 1758
An Estimate . . . Vol. II (55)	April 8, 1758
An Estimate . . . 7th ed. (48)	April 20, 1758
Letters to the Estimator . . . 1st ed. (120)	May 2, 1758
Power of Protestant Religious Principle. . . (59)	May 4, 1758
Letters to the Estimator . . . 2d ed. (121)	May 10, 1758
Some Doubts occasioned by the Second Volume . . . 1st ed. (123)	May 11, 1758

Short Title; number in bibliography in parentheses	*Date of publication*
Explanatory Defence . . . (60)	June 19, 1758
Letters to the Estimator . . . 3d ed. (122)	June 27, 1758
Wallace's *Characteristics . . .* 2d ed. (117)	July 13, 1758
A Letter to the Author of the Estimate . . . (125)	July 18, 1758
Some Doubts occasioned by the Second Volume . . . 2d ed. (124)	July 20, 1758
An Estimate . . . 3d Dublin ed. (50A)	1758
An Estimate . . . 1st Belfast ed. (51)	1758
An Estimate . . . 1st American ed. (52)	1758
An Estimate . . . French translation, 1st ed. (53)	1758
An Estimate . . . French translation, 2d ed. (54)	1758
An Estimate . . . Vol. II. 1st Dublin ed. (56)	1758
Wallace's *Characteristics . . .* Dublin edition (118)	1758
An Essay to prove the Superiority . . . (126)	January 10, 1759
A Letter to the Reverend Dr. Br—n (127)	January 15, 1759
Wallace's *Characteristics . . .* French translation (118A)	1759
Gordon's *New Estimate . . .* Parts I and II (128)	April 10, 1760
Lyttelton's *Dialogues of the Dead.* 1st ed. (133)	May 17, 1760
Lyttelton's *Dialogues of the Dead.* 2d ed. (134)	May 22, 1760
Additional Dialogue of the Dead. 1st ed. (61)	June 3, 1760
Additional Dialogue of the Dead. 2d ed. (62)	June 14, 1760

Short Title; number in bibliography in parentheses	*Date of publication*
Lyttelton's *Dialogues of the Dead.* 3d ed. (135)	1760
Lyttelton's *Dialogues of the Dead.* Dublin edition (136)	1760
Lyttelton's *Dialogues of the Dead.* French translation (136A)	1760
Lyttelton's *Dialogues of the Dead.* French translation (137)	1760
Natural Duty of a Personal Service . . . 1st ed. (63)	March 21, 1761
Natural Duty of a Personal Service . . . 2d ed. (64)	March 21–28, 1761
Natural Duty of a Personal Service . . . 3d ed. (65)	March 21–28, 1761
Natural Duty of a Personal Service . . . 4th ed. (66)	March 21–28, 1761
Natural Duty of a Personal Service . . . 5th ed. (67)	March 28, 1761
Natural Duty of a Personal Service . . . 1st London ed. (68)	March 31, 1761
Gordon's *New Estimate . . .* Part III (129)	April 23, 1761
Barbarossa. 3d ed. (21)	1762
Ralph's *The Case of Authors . . .* 2d ed. (115)	1762
The Cure of Saul. A Sacred Ode (69)	February 25, 1763
The Cure of Saul. 1st Oratorio version (70)	March 4, 1763
A Dissertation . . . 1st ed. (76)	March 17, 1763
The Cure of Saul. 2d Oratorio version (71)	April 25, 1763
Maddison's *Examination of the Oratorios . . .* (138)	April 25, 1763
On Religious Liberty . . . 1st ed. (82)	April 26, 1763
A Dissertation . . . 1st Dublin ed. (78)	1763

Short Title; number in bibliography in parentheses	*Date of publication*
On Religious Liberty . . . 1st American ed. (83)	1763
Some Observations on Dr. Brown's Dissertation . . . (139)	[February, 1764?]
Sermons on various Subjects (84)	March 29, 1764
History of the Rise and Progress of Poetry (85)	April 14, 1764
Essays on the Characteristics. 5th ed. (14)	[April 25, 1764?]
Remarks on Some Observations . . . (87)	May 12, 1764
Thoughts on Civil Liberty . . . 1st ed. (88)	February 1, 1765
Thoughts on Civil Liberty . . . 2d ed. (89)	February 19, 1765
Female Character and Education . . . (93)	May 23, 1765
Political Logic Displayed (140)	July 18, 1765
Priestley's *Essay on Liberal Education*. . . (141)	September, 1765
Lowth's *Letter* . . . 1st ed. (144)	[September (?), 1765]
Lowth's *Letter* . . . 2d ed. (145)	November 23, 1765
Lowth's *Letter* . . . 3d ed. (146)	[November, 1765?]
Thoughts on Civil Liberty . . . Dublin edition (90)	1765
Letter to Dr. Lowth . . . 1st ed. (94)	January 7, 1766
Letter to Dr. Lowth . . . 2d ed. (95)	January 10, 1766
Lowth's *Letter* . . . 4th ed., 1st issue (147)	[January 10, 1766]
A Free Address to the Author . . . (149)	January 16, 1766
Letter to Dr. Lowth . . . 3d ed. (96)	January 18, 1766
Lowth's *Letter* . . . 4th ed., 2d issue (148)	January 18, 1766
An Expostulatory Letter to the Author . . . (150)	January 20, 1766
Letter to Dr. Lowth . . . 4th ed. (97)	January 27, 1766

Short Title; number in bibliography in parentheses	*Date of publication*
Mason's *Ode to the Legislator Elect of Russia . . .* (151)	[August, 1766]
An Estimate of the Manners . . . of the Modern French (130)	February 11, 1767
The Cure of Saul. 3d Oratorio version, 1st ed. (72)	1767
The Cure of Saul. 3d Oratorio version, 2d ed. (73)	1767
The Cure of Saul. Octavo edition (74)	[1767?]
Barbarossa. French translation (37)	1767
Description of the Lake at Keswick . . . (97A)	[1767?]
History of the Rise and Progress of Poetry. French translation (86)	1768
Priestley's *Essay on Government . . .* 1st ed. (142)	1768
A Dissertation . . . Selections (79)	1768
A Dissertation . . . German translation (80)	1769
Another Estimate of the Manners and Principles . . . (131)	1769
Barbarossa. 4th ed. (22)	1770
Barbarossa. 5th ed. (23)	1770
Barbarossa. London: R. Butters (24)	[1770?]
Barbarossa. Dublin: J. Exshaw, *et al.* (32)	1770
Barbarossa. Dublin: Thomas Wilkinson (33)	[1770's?]
Description of the Lake at Keswick . . . 1st ed. (98)	1770
Description of the Lake at Keswick . . . 2d ed. (99)	1771
Thoughts on Civil Liberty . . . German translation (91)	1771

Short Title; number in bibliography in parentheses	*Date of publication*
Barbarossa. London, MCCCLXXI (sic) (25)	1771
The Cure of Saul. Octavo edition (75)	1771
Priestley's *Essay on Government* . . . 2d ed. (143)	1771
A Dissertation . . . Italian translation (81)	1772
Description of the Lake at Keswick . . . 3d ed. (100)	1772
A Dissertation . . . 2d ed. (77)	1773
Barbarossa. 1st Edinburgh ed. (34)	1774
Cumberland's *Odes*. 1st ed. (101)	1776
Cumberland's *Odes*. Dublin edition (102)	1776
Barbarossa. London: J. Wenman (26)	1777
Barbarossa. London: T. Caslon, *et al.* (27)	1777
Barbarossa. London: for the Proprietors . . . (28)	1778
Athelstan. German translation (41)	1778
An Estimate of the Manners of the Present Times (132)	1782
An Estimate . . . Vol. II. French translation (57)	[1789?]
An Estimate . . . Vol. II. French translation (58)	1789
Thoughts on Civil Liberty . . . French translation (92)	1789
Barbarossa. 1st American ed. (35)	1794
Barbarossa. 2d American ed. (36)	1809

Appendix II

Index of Printers, Publishers, and Booksellers

The names listed below are alphabetically arranged in each of four sections: I. English and Scottish imprints; II. Irish imprints; III. American imprints; and IV. European imprints. Each entry lists the name, the place (with its specific address, when listed on the title-page or in the advertisement), the year of publication, and in parentheses the number of the item in the bibliography. If the name is printed on the title-page of the book, then only the number in the bibliography is listed; if the name is given elsewhere, the reader is directed to the notes under the appropriate number in the bibliography.

I. *English and Scottish imprints*

Hughs, John
London. (#3 n.).
Johnson, Joseph
London, "No. 8, Paster-noster Row." 1768 (#142).
"No. 72, in St. Paul's Church-Yard." 1771 (#143); 1774 (#6 n.).
Johnson, Joseph, and Davenport
London, "in Pater-Noster Row." 1765 (#141).
Johnston, W.
London, "in Ludgate Street." 1764 (#139).
Kearsly, George
London, "at the Golden Lion in Ludgate Street." 1760 (#61 n.).
"No. 1, Ludgate Street." 1763 (#138); 1769 (#131).
Leake, James
Bath. 1750 (#8).
Lowndes, Thomas
London. 1770 (#22, 23); 1777 (#27).
Millar, Andrew
London, "in the Strand." 1753 (#106); 1758 (#116, 117); 1760 (#128); 1761 (#129); 1765 (#144); 1766 (#145, 146, 147, 148).
Murray, John
London, "No. 32, opposite St. Dunstan's Church, Fleet Street." 1773 (#77).
Newbery, Francis
London, "at the Crown, in Pater-Noster Row." 1765 (#140).
"No. 15, in Pater-noster Row." 1767 (#130 and n.).
Nicoll, W.
London, "in St. Paul's Church Yard." 1766 (#151).
London. 1770 (#22, 23); 1777 (#27).
Noon, John
London, "at the White Hart, in Cheapside, near the Poultry." 1751 (#103); 1752 (#104, 105).
Nourse, John
London, "at the Lamb opposite Katherine Street in the Strand." 1758 (#119).

II. *Irish imprints*

Armitage, J.
Dublin. 1776 (#102).
Burnet, G.
Dublin. 1776 (#102).
Colles, W.
Dublin. 1776 (#102).
Davis, William
Dublin, "at Newton's Head, on Temple Bar." 1756 (#30).
Dyton, T.
Dublin, "in Dame Street." 1770 (#32).
Edmond, B.
See Whitestone, W., and Edmond, B.
Ewing, George and Alexander
Dublin. 1756 (#40).
Exshaw, John
Dublin. 1755 (#29); 1756 (#40); 1757 (#31, 49, 50); 1758 (#50A, 56); 1765 (#90); 1770 (#32).
Faulkner, George
Dublin, "in Essex Street." 1752 (#15, 16); 1756 (#40); 1757 (#49, 50); 1758 (#50A, 56).
"on the Blind Quay." 1763 (#78).
Flin, Laurence
Dublin, "at the Bible in Castle Street." 1758 (#118).
Higly, P.
Dublin. 1776 (#102).
Hoey, James
Dublin. 1757 (#49, 50).
Hoey, James (senior and junior)
Dublin. 1758 (#50A, 56).
"at the Mercury in Skinner Row." 1757 (#111).
James, Alice
Dublin. 1757 (#31).
James, Richard
Dublin. 1755 (#29); 1756 (#40).
Jenkin, Caleb
Dublin. 1776 (#102).

Joy, Henry and Robert
Belfast. 1758 (#51).
Leathley, Anne
Dublin. 1765 (#90).
Main, Robert
Dublin. 1755 (#29).
Moncrieff, Richard
Dublin. 1776 (#102).
Nelson, Oliver
Dublin, "in Skinner Row." 1760 (#136).
Potts, J.
Dublin. 1776 (#102).
Price, Samuel
Dublin, "in Dame Street." 1757 (#31).
"in Henry Street." 1770 (#32).
Dublin. 1776 (#102).
Sheppard, Josiah
Dublin. 1776 (#102).
Smith, R.
Dublin. 1758 (#56).
Walker, T.
Dublin. 1776 (#102).
Watson, Samuel
Dublin. 1765 (#90); 1776 (#102).
Watson, William
Dublin. 1765 (#90); 1776 (#102).
Whitestone, William
Dublin. 1776 (#102).
Whitestone, W., and Edmond, B.
Dublin, "in Dame Street." 1755 (#29).
Wilkinson, Thomas
Dublin, "in Winetavern Street, the Corner of Cook Street." [177-] (#33).
Williams, J.
Dublin. 1776 (#102).
Wilson, William
Dublin. 1776 (#102).

III. *American imprints*

IV. *European imprints*

Reich
  See Weidmann (heirs of) and Reich.
Rüdiger, Johann Heinrich
  Berlin, Stettin and Leipzig. 1761 (#137 n.).
Schneider, J. H.
  Amsterdam. 1767 (#137 n.).
Valleyre, Jean-Baptiste Paul
  [Paris] "De l'Imprimerie de Valleyre, rue de la Bouclerie."
    [1789?] (#57).
Weidmann (heirs of) and Reich
  Leipzig. 1769 (#80).

Index

Many passing references to people or to literary works—for example, casual references made by John Brown in letters, quoted in this bibliography—are fully identified in this index; the more obscure the reference, the more detailed the entry. Information concerning printers, publishers, and booksellers is presented in Appendix II, but references contained in the notes are also indexed here.